Politics and the Press
in Indonesia

Politics and the Press in Indonesia explores the evolving political culture in Indonesia, by discussing the country's dominant political philosophies, then showing how those philosophies affect the working lives of ordinary Indonesian citizens. It focuses in particular on the working lives of news journalists, a group that occupies a strategic social and political position.

Angela Romano discusses the philosophies of 'Pancasila', the official national ideology, as well as paternalism, integrationism and corporatism. Romano also explores the 32-year period of New Order government and the rapid changes that followed President Suharto's resignation in 1998, concentrating on how the day-to-day workings of the news media are affected by paternalism, corporatism, corruption, and the evolution of the prevailing political culture.

Angela Romano lectures in journalism at the Queensland University of Technology.

Politics and the Press in Indonesia

Understanding an evolving political culture

Angela Romano

Routledge
Taylor & Francis Group

LONDON AND NEW YORK

First published 2003
by Routledge
2 Park Square, Milton Park, Abingdon, Oxon, OX14 4RN

Simultaneously published in the USA and Canada
by Routledge
270 Madison Ave, New York NY 10016

Routledge is an imprint of the Taylor & Francis Group

Transferred to Digital Printing 2009

Editorial matter © 2003 Angela Romano

Typeset in Times by LaserScript Ltd, Mitcham, Surrey

British Library Cataloguing in Publication Data
A catalogue record for this book is available from the British Library

Library of Congress Cataloging in Publication Data
Romano, Angela.
    Politics and the press in Indonesia : understanding an evolving political culture / Angela Romano.
        p. cm.
    Includes bibliographical references and index.
    1. Press and politics–Indonesia. I. Title.

PN5449.I5 R66 2002
070.4'493249'0958–dc21   2002072675

ISBN10: 0–700–71745–5 (hbk)
ISBN10: 0–415–54636–2 (pbk)

ISBN13: 978–0–700–71745–3 (hbk)
ISBN13: 978–0–415–54636–2 (pbk)

Publisher's Note
The publisher has gone to great lengths to ensure the quality of this reprint
but points out that some imperfections in the original may be apparent.

Contents

List of figures and tables

Figure

Tables

A note on spelling

Most Indonesian words and names in this thesis are spelt according to the current system of spelling that was introduced in 1972. Exceptions have been made for names of individuals and places that have maintained the old spelling, for organisations that existed only before 1972 and for direct quotations or titles of textual references. There is often variation in the spelling of names of individuals, with Soeharto/Suharto the best-known example. The spelling of such names conforms, where applicable, to that in *Apa dan Siapa: Sejumlah Orang Indonesia 1985–1986* (Tempo & Grafitipers 1986), the Indonesian equivalent of *Who's Who*, and *Wajah Dewan Perwakilan Raykat Republik Indonesia: Pemilihan Umun 1999* (Kompas 2000), a formal profile of members of Indonesia's parliament.

Introduction

I was intrigued when I joined about 40 Indonesian reporters at a Jakarta restaurant one rainy November day for a luncheon organised by the Department of Home Affairs. Although several Department officials sat with the reporters, drinking and dining at the same tables, none appeared to have any particular news or intelligence to impart to the journalists. The journalists were particularly keen to interview one very senior official in their company, but he acted as if he was content purely to satisfy their stomachs and not their news-making machines. After more than 90 minutes of waiting, two journalists convinced the senior official to answer a few questions. The remaining journalists swooped in a feeding frenzy with microphones and notebooks at the ready to capture his words. Capturing his words was a challenging task, since the logistics were poor. Only the few journalists who fitted into the small space next to him could have clearly heard his words; the remainder leaning over the far sides of the tables were unlikely to have understood much. None of the bureaucrats made any effort to ensure that all the journalists present could hear what the official said so that his comments could be reported by the many media organisations represented at the luncheon. After several minutes, the official stopped answering the journalists' many questions and walked out. The journalists pursued, dauntlessly continuing their questions in the few minutes' walk between the restaurant and his car, gathering crumbs of information as best they could.

I was perplexed by the event. For a Western political figure, it would have seemed a wasted opportunity. If Western bureaucrats or political leaders were to invite so many journalists to spend so much time with them, it would generally be with the aim of promoting their viewpoints or shaping the news agenda in some way. The Indonesian journalists chuckled at my mystification, but would or could not explain in any concrete fashion why a senior official would volunteer to sit with so many journalists for so long without hoping that the pleasure of their company might be matched by the pleasure of some publicity. Not only had the Department financed the journalists' lunch without reciprocal expectations of being covered in the news, the senior official was indifferent or even resistant to being covered. He clearly suffered no sense of loss at missing the chance to influence the day's news at his leisure. It was symptomatic of so many examples I have seen of Indonesian journalists performing their duties, working with the same equipment that I used when I had been a journalist in Australia, meeting the same deadlines, pursuing the same news issues and yet dancing to a tune that was somehow different from the ones I was familiar with. Many socio-cultural factors may have contributed to the difference, but it was the influence of the patriarchal political culture that emerged most distinctly to me.

The Department of Home Affairs luncheon had occurred towards the end of the 32-year period (1966–98) in which the dominant political culture of the 'New Order' government was often described as being guided by a 'family-oriented' or 'integralistic' philosophy. The term integralistic was coined by Supomo, one of Indonesia's founding fathers. Supomo was inspired by the mathematical concept of 'integral' numbers (Sirait 1997: 86), which are whole numbers without any fractions. In a system or object that is integral, every portion that goes into it is essential to the whole. No individual element is complete without the other parts that make up the whole. New Order government leaders often depicted the integralistic nation as being like 'the "traditional village" where social harmony reigns, neighbours pitch in for the common good and where decisions are reached by consensus under the guidance of a wise leader' (Bourchier 1993: 2). It was argued that every Indonesian citizen was linked by the kind of direct and intimate bonds that might be seen in a family, or the traditional village described above. Ideally, all would work together as one, and there would no 'divisive' distinctions between the heavens and the earth, humankind and nature, state and society, or the rulers and the ruled. In deciding the appropriate relationship between government officials and the general public, the New Order also quite consciously drew on traditional Javanese imagery, in which the moral state was built upon Javanese traditions in which the king (or president) was seen as God's viceregent and 'Father of the Nation'.

In short, political leaders claimed that rulers were spiritually at one with the ruled and that all the individuals and organisations that made up the family-like nation should cooperate, rather than compete for vested interests. Using this philosophy, they also argued that good government and popular sovereignty did not require the system of checks and balances inherent in *trias politica* (the three estates) model of Western political systems (Wahyono 1988: 61). In this model, derived from Montesquieu, the executive, legislative and judicial branches (or 'estates') of government are ideally free from each other's influence. The New Order, however, decreed that the three estates should engage in cooperation rather than mutual correction of each other's functions.

Many New Order ideologies thus automatically considered it inappropriate for the press to behave as the so-called 'fourth estate of politics', as it does in many Western countries, scrutinising the affairs of the first three estates. The philosophy that the press is the partner, not a watchdog of government, had multitudinous implications for the professional identity and practices of journalists. It also impacted on the attitude of the military and political élite who, like the bureaucrat mentioned above, did not feel the obligation to open themselves to public or media scrutiny or to seek publicity in order to win consent from the masses for their policies and programs. Working with news sources who do not feel any compulsion to provide information had an intense and obvious impact on the way that journalists organised their working days.

This is just one example of the way in which the prevailing political culture of the New Order had marked, visible effects on the general framework in which journalists operated and on the minutiae of workplace routines. *Politics and the Press in Indonesia* critiques the evolving political culture in Indonesia by discussing the country's dominant political philosophies and then exploring how these philosophies affect the working lives of Indonesian citizens. It does this by focussing on the professional identity and working practices of one politically strategic sector of Indonesian business and society – the news media.

This book details how the day-to-day working conditions and professional routines of journalists (who represent a micro-culture) are shaped by the wider system of Indonesian politics (the macro-culture). The book describes how the New Order government had the power to define 'culturally appropriate' relations between society and the state, influencing political and civil society not just at an ideological level but also at a practical level. For example, the patriarchal, militaristic, corporatist New Order system constrained journalistic culture by:

- legally defining an officially sanctioned role for journalists within politics and society,
- limiting the ability of reporters to deal with news sources,
- restricting journalists' ability to share information through direct and indirect forms of censorship,
- controlling the capacity of journalists to organise as professionals and workers,
- defining who was permitted to enter the profession and influencing which journalists might be promoted to senior editorial positions, and
- circumscribing the potential for gender equity in the profession.

Although this book concentrates primarily on journalism, it compares changes within the news industry with those seen in other areas of socio-economic activity. It demonstrates that the patterns that can be observed in the news media have historically been indicative of the trends that have occurred in political parties, business, industrial relations and other economic and political sectors. Changes in journalistic culture might therefore be considered a harbinger of change for political and civil society in a broader sense.

It is difficult to talk of one Indonesian political culture, as there such diversity of cultures between and within regions, social and ethnic groups, organisations and factions. The aim of this book is explore the *dominant* political cultures and political philosophies in Indonesia, and readers are advised to remember that there is much contestation of and deviation from these cultures.

How to use this book

Culture, like politics, is neither monolithic nor static. This book details how the evolution of political culture in Indonesia affects journalistic and broader socio-economic culture. Chapter 1 briefly explores how the formative years of anti-colonial struggle in the early twentieth century and the early era of Indonesia's independence established the philosophies that enabled the emergence and consolidation of Soeharto's governance in the 1960s to 1980s. Chapter 2 describes the practical systems for implementing New Order philosophy. Chapter 3 explores the deepening cracks that incrementally emerged in the political framework in the late 1990s as the economy floundered, ultimately fracturing the myth that the New Orders' patriarchal, corporatist structure was essential for economic development and prosperity. As relations between Soeharto and competing military factions became increasingly fractious, many previously quiescent sections of society began increasingly lively participation in political life. Chapter 3 also depicts the impact on civil society of Soeharto's resignation from the presidency and the establishment of the more reformist, or at least revisionist, governments of B.J. Habibie (1998–99), Abdurrahman Wahid (1999–2001) and Megawati Soekarnoputri (2001+).

The swift post-New Order dismantling of corporatist culture led to rapid and radical alterations in journalism and in newsrooms. Within the news media, struggles over journalists' rights to freedom of expression, organisation and affiliation were among the high-profile symbols of the national push towards democratisation. Despite the initial exuberance of journalists and the general populace at increased political freedom, attempts to democratise the nation have been uneven and inconsistent. In this unstable environment, journalists have allied themselves with politically disparate figures in industry, non-government organisations and other sectors of civil society in the push for stronger, long-lasting reform in the post-Soeharto, post-Habibie regulatory framework. While political change has been accompanied by a perceivable transformation of journalistic practice and professional self perception, steps towards positive change in one area of professional life have often been matched by regressive developments in another. Such patterns have been typical of Indonesia's wider socio-political environment.

At the time this book was written, Megawati's government was just a few days old, and it was too early to tell what changes her leadership would bring. This book demonstrate how readers might deduce what impact these changes may have on journalism, by showing how the macro-political culture affects the practices and culture of the news media – or any other social sector for that matter – at a daily level. Chapter 4 outlines how the developmental, *Pancasila*-oriented integralistic philosophy shaped state definitions as to the appropriate form and functions of the Indonesian press, and how these definitions have changed following the demise of the New Order. The next four chapters consider the journalists' self-perception of their identity, needs and aspirations and how these are accommodated within the political culture. Chapter 5 contrasts the views of journalists with those of the state as to their roles and goals. Chapters 6 and 7 study the impact of corporatist doctrines on the journalists' ability to independently organise and represent their interests as workers and as professionals. Chapter 8 explores the impact of the patriarchal culture on the gender balance and workplace relations within journalism. Chapters 9, 10 and 11 contain analyses on how the New Order's perspectives on journalism have impacted on news sources' understandings of their relationship with journalists. Chapters 9 and 10 focus on the ambivalent attitude many sources display towards journalists and the challenges this creates for news-gathering processes. Chapter 11 follows with a study of the ways in which the culture of source ambivalence and client–patron relations have perpetuated bribery, gift giving and graft in journalism. Chapter 12 concludes by summing the integralistic influences on these different elements of journalistic culture and the shift that has occurred with the transition to a new political regime.

The 'professional' community of journalists

This book differs from most writing to date about the role and practices of journalists, which usually focus on the opinions of politicians, bureaucrats, academics and a limited list of prominent journalists such as Mochtar Lubis, Aristides Katoppo or Goenawan Mohamad. Zelizer notes, by contrast, the value of also studying journalists as 'interpretive communities' (Zelizer 1992: 1–10; 1993: 223–7). This involves examining journalists' informal networks, the ways in which they interpret and describe their practices, their definitions of the community's history, and their techniques for negotiating what Claude Lévi-Strauss calls 'hot moments'. These 'hot moments' do not exist as an objective reality, but instead result from the individuals and groups whose discourses assign meanings and social significance to events regarded as benchmark moments or historically notable occasions. Such discourses proliferate when there are unresolved dimensions in everyday news work (Zelizer 1993: 222).

The move towards studying journalists as interpretive communities progresses from the findings of sociologists – such as Gans (1979), Fishman (1980) and Tuchman (1978) – that journalists' work is imbued with a distinct sense of journalistic collectivity. Journalists have a strong social identity, so that there is commonly a uniformity of opinion among them about their role in society, their rights and responsibilities, and the 'correct' way that they should operate. Such self identity is based on their horizontal relationship with colleagues who work at the same level, rather than from vertical management or pressure from editors, managers or other figures more senior to them within the newsrooms' hierarchical chain of power. Reporters, in particular, absorb 'rules, boundaries and a sense of appropriateness about their actions without ever actually being informed of them by their superiors' (Zelizer 1993: 221).

Although Indonesian journalists generally consider themselves to belong to a 'profession', rather than a craft, trade or mere occupation (as is discussed in Chapter 6), this book does not examine the formal trappings of journalistic professionalism and authority – such as training, licensing and professional ideology – in isolation of lived experiences, community discourses and culturally significant 'hot moments'. Most existing research on Indonesian journalism concentrates on these formal trappings, usually involving a study of the official links between government and the press, mechanisms of censorship, professional organisation and the top end of news-industry management. It is important to move beyond such an approach, because journalists function informally as a community, even when, as discussed in Chapter 7, the formal mechanisms of professional affiliation are moribund. The interpretive-communities approach prioritises analysis of not just the formal, standardised patterns of professional association and interaction but also 'cultural discussion'. This includes what topics journalists talk about in their own work spaces, how they accomplish work by discussion, mediation and challenge of colleagues, how they check the suitability of their activities with other journalists, the nature of their social interaction and similar issues.

This book details the results of ethnographic research, involving both ideational and materialistic perspectives. Observation and participant observation studies were conducted at four daily newspapers in Jakarta and Central Java. Additionally, a small survey was conducted with a snowballing sample of 65 journalists, and interviews were conducted with more than 100 sources. The research methodology is detailed in greater depth in the Appendix. The book presents a comparison of insights obtained from observation and interviews about the lived experience of journalists against the dominant government and academic theories as to their ideal role and function.

Ethical issues of source identification

At the time in which the survey and ethnographic research was conducted, informants had reason to fear sanctions, including dismissal or prosecution, if details of their behaviours and statements were publicised. Those who admitted receiving envelopes of money, as is discussed in Chapter 11, were in breach of the Code of Ethics. Those working without PWI (*Persatuan Wartawan Indonesia*, Indonesian Journalists' Association) membership, as is discussed in Chapter 7, were in breach of the law. Some respondents' statements could also have been considered to breach sections of the Criminal Code that prohibit public insult or expression of hatred of the government or of disrespect towards the president and vice president. Curiously, respondents expressed more fear of retribution for their derogatory comments about the PWI than they did for their critiques of the government.

Issues relating to maintaining the privacy of informants and the possibility of exploiting or harming informants often create ethical problems in ethnographic and observation studies (Diener & Crandall 1978; Kvale 1996: 114–15; Spradley 1980: 23–5). Vidich and Bensman (1968: 397–401) admit that participants in their classic 1958 study of small-town American life were subsequently easily identified by other local people, demonstrating that merely giving fictitious names to informants may be insufficient to conceal their identities. Issues of confidentiality are also important in interview research, because interviewees need to feel confident that they will not be penalised for full and frank responses. As several theorists have noted (e.g. Philliber 1980: 89; Robson 1993: 167–8), surveys are only appropriate where participants are willing to report accurately. For such reasons, it remains a convention of ethnographic and survey technique that the identities of informants and survey respondents are generally not revealed.

This work follows conventional standards regarding confidentiality. Although the book includes quotes from journalists in the ethnographic or survey studies, the informants have not been identified except through broad categorisers of the informant's workplace and status (e.g. a *Kompas* subeditor or a *Suara Merdeka* reporter). In the rare cases where it appeared that journalists could be identified even through such broad details as name of organisation and journalistic position, such problems were overcome by using the revealing information as 'deep background'. The names of other interviewees who expressed concern about the revelation of their identities have also been concealed. Only those who agreed to speak on the record have been named. All other information sources, such as industry representatives, journalism educators, media analysts and other strategic actors, who provided on-the-record interviews in circumstances not connected to the survey, have been fully identified by name and occupation.

1 The 'authentic' Indonesian character

For many decades, the agenda and space permitted for public debate and media activity in Indonesia was influenced by the ideology that the national character had given birth to a *negara integralistik* (an integralistic nation). The integralistic nation is a system of institutions, practices and ways of living that encompasses, protects and yet also transcends the interests of all individuals and groups (Hariyati 1995: 1). Integralistic philosophy is derived from a selective study of the ideas of Supomo, a leading scholar of *adat* (traditional laws, customs and cultures), who was also a key contributor to the national Constitution written in 1945 (Bourchier 1993; Simanjuntak 1994). Supomo drew inspiration from organic political theorists such as Georg Hegel, Baruch de Spinoza, Adam Müller and pre-WWII Japanese 'family-oriented' ideologues. He envisaged the model integralistic nation as an organic whole, with rulers and the ruled linked in harmony and all groups joined in unity by 'the spirit of mutual cooperation, [and] the spirit of familial solidarity' (Supomo 1945: 113).

Bourchier (1996: 31–41) and Reeve (1985: 4–6, 212) trace the impact of Dutch organic scholars – particularly the 'Master', Cornelis van Vollenhoven – on Supomo, other colonial-era legal experts and the wider nationalism movement. A major channel for this Dutch influence was the law faculty of Leiden University, a centre for *adat* study, where many nationalists, including Supomo, studied during the late colonial period. The Leiden law faculty followed an organic philosophical tradition, which in turn stemmed from the German romantic, anti-liberal, anti-individualistic scholarship of the early 19th century. This tradition rejected French Enlightenment theories and concepts of social contract in favour of monist, collectivist, corporatist approaches to law and governance (Bourchier 1996: 22–6). Van Vollenhoven, a legal anthropologist, concluded from his cataloguing of Indonesian traditional customs that a consistent characteristic of ethnic groups across the archipelago was a coherent and consistent familial culture that prioritised (i) communal over individual interests, (ii) strong links between man and nature and (iii) dispute resolution through conciliation and consensus (Bourchier 1996: 26–30; Reeve 1985: 5). This glorification of communitarian 'Indonesian' culture as being different to that of Western, liberal culture suited the Javanese *priyayi* (petty aristocracy) background from which many of Indonesia's leading nationalists hailed (Reeve 1985: 8). It should be noted that the culture that the Javanese *priyayi* came to define as 'Western' culture was in fact French Enlightenment culture, in contrast to German and Dutch organic culture, and that the *priyayi* were a politically influential but a numerically small class. The distinction between Indonesian and Western culture was thus not so simple as many *priyayi* legal experts claimed.

Contact with the Japanese in the earlier decades of the twentieth century reinforced these organic, collectivist philosophies, particularly among the generation who would subsequently form the Indonesian armed forces. In the 1930s, the Japanese provided role models and some tactical support for Indonesian nationalists (Bourchier 1996: 54–9). Following the 1942 Japanese invasion of Indonesia, which led to the Dutch promptly fleeing the archipelago, the occupying Japanese military administrators established a system of governance suited to organic principles. This included closing the legislature, imposing censorship, banning independent political activity and enlisting the support of prominent political and religious leaders as heads of new Japanese-created organisations. Prominent Indonesian proponents of familial, communitarian philosophies were appointed to significant positions within the Japanese bureaucracy, including a key advisory council, *Panitia Pemeriksa Adat dan Tata Negara* (Committee for the Examination of Adat and State Administration) (Reeve 1985: 61–5).

Almost every social grouping on Java was organised into corporatist organisations representing industries, youth, women and sports (Kanahele in Reeve 1985: 78). The council was headed by Supomo, who worked closely with the Japanese administration. More than one and a half million men were inducted into programs providing military exercises and anti-Allied propaganda, with 25,000 trained to fight in the *Heiho* auxiliary service alongside Japanese military personnel (Ricklefs 1981: 192). This instilled a vast number of men with a respect for obedience, uniformity and force (Kahin 1952: 107), and Japanese militarism still flavours many modern Indonesian institutions and policies. It was especially evident during the New Order in the military-style discipline of the Indonesian education system, the language and command of obedience, taboos on asking questions, anti-individualistic philosophy, neighbourhood associations, corporatist social organisations and government regulation on intellectual activities (Mangunwijaya 1994: 84–5).

As Japanese prospects of victory waned, the military occupation organised two important committees in May and June 1945 to prepare for the transfer of power and to draft a constitution. The Japanese appointed 70 Indonesians to the *Badan Penyelidik Usaha Persiapan Kemerdekaan Indonesia* (BPUPKI, the Investigating Committee for the Preparation of Indonesian Independence), which wrote the 1945 Constitution. Some theorists have characterised the proceedings and the resulting Constitution as being Japanese made, being conducted at the point of Japanese bayonets (e.g. Nasution 1992: 90–1; Simajantak 1994: 76–80). Others more moderately suggest that the Japanese administration did not interfere greatly in the proceedings, but helped to determine the outcome through judicious selection of BPUPKI members (Bourchier 1996: 75).

Supomo's vision

The debates of the BPUPKI plenary session had far-reaching consequences on the ideological foundations of the Indonesian state.[1] The debate on organic political philosophy in the session typified the historic struggle between paternalism and pluralism in Indonesia (Mahfud 1993: 41). However, in the New Order years, state ideologues often quoted the organic-style speech of Supomo as if he were the sole contributor to the constitution (e.g. Hariyati 1995; Sudharmono 1986; Wahyono 1988) or as if the opposing or competing perspectives were non-existent or of marginal importance.

Supomo (1945: 110–111) described the three main typologies of political systems as:

- liberal systems based on social contract, following the theories of Thomas Hobbes, John Locke, Jean Jacques Rousseau and Herbert Spencer,
- class-oriented systems based on a dictatorship of the proletariat, following the theories of Karl Marx, Friedrich Engels and V.I. Lenin, and
- organic or integralistic systems in which the whole community forms an organic unity, based on the theories of Spinoza, Hegel and Müller.

Supomo dismissed the liberal system as imperialistic and exploitative (Supomo 1945: 112). He rejected parliamentarianism as being based on a false philosophy of individualism, which assumed that all community sectors had the same value and that society could be based on numbers (Supomo 1945: 119). He said that class-oriented systems made 'the state an instrument through which one group (one class) might oppress other classes' (Supomo 1945: 111). He found the organic system appropriate to 'authentic' Indonesian consciousness, community spirit and social institutions (Supomo 1945: 113).[2]

Supomo argued that Indonesia was characterised by a 'unity of life, unity of servant and master,[3] that is between the external and the internal, spiritual world, between the microcosmos and the macrocosmos, [and] between the people and their leaders' (Supomo 1945: 113). This organic conceptualisation specifically rejects individualism and the idea of 'social contract' as the basis of protecting individuals. Supomo went so far as to argue – admittedly with limited success (Mahfud 1993: 41; Nasution 1993: 67) – that the Constitution should not contain safeguards of human rights and civil liberties. He believed that such provisions would create a dualism between state and individual and between rulers and the ruled that would violate social solidarity (Supomo 1945: 114; Yamin 1959: 315). The incarnation of popular sovereignty was described as not the parliament, but the president, who should have the quality of the *Ratu Adil* (Just King) (Supomo 1945: 120). Supomo believed that the head of the nation should not be elected, because elections are based on individualism, but should be like a *raja* (king), president, Burmese *adipati* (governor) or German *führer*, who were 'one in spirit with all the people' (Supomo 1945: 119).

The overall shape of the 1945 Constitution was guided by Supomo's logic, although other BPUPKI members[4] proposed different models of governance and asserted the need for rights to express opinion, to organise, to associate and to vote. It allowed elections and expressed commitment to the principle of popular sovereignty, but vested most power in the president and a super-parliamentary congress, the *Majelis Permusyawaratan Rakyat* (MPR, People's Consultative Assembly). A final compromise on the differing viewpoints regarding rights was reached through Article 28 of the Constitution which provided not 'rights' but 'freedoms' by stipulating that: 'The freedom to associate and to assemble, to express thoughts orally, in writing or the like will be prescribed through statute'. Although the inclusion of such a passage should have ultimately subverted Supomo's underlying logic, a critical reading of Article 28 shows that the freedom it provides is illusory, because 'it empowers the government, or those who create the laws, to neuter those basic rights' (Nasution 1993: 67; also Mulya Lubis 1993: 158–9).

The world view of organic philosophers

Since this book considers journalism's positioning within the wider political system, it is useful to examine the world view of the theorists and systems that Supomo perceived as harmonising with Indonesia's own national character. Supomo's rejection of socio-political dualism follows Spinoza's monist philosophy that all elements of the universe originate from one substance and are thus unified with no possibility of dualism between body and mind or God and nature (Simanjuntak 1994: 133–4). Also influential was Spinoza's argument that societal security depends upon reaching consensus so that community life does not depend upon human strength and passions, but rather the will of all; consequently all individuals must submissively surrender their rights to the sole authority of the state's sovereign power (Simanjuntak 1994: 134–8). Such influences are reinforced by the theories of Müller, who similarly found that all private life was part of the state and that the state represented the dynamic and enduring kingdom of community aspirations (Simanjuntak 1994: 141–2). Müller was also significant to Supomo because of his perspective that liberalism reduces human relations with the God-willed universe, and fails to develop autonomous individuals (Hariyati 1995: 4).

Simanjuntak (1994: 11–13) argues that specific emphasis should be placed on the contribution of Hegel to Supomo's thought. The Hegelian ideal of 'ethical life' requires individuals to transcend self-interested activities that serve themselves or their loved ones so that they instead serve 'the universal', or in other words, the community interest. In Hegel's tripartite division of society, the family and civil society encompass elements of the universal but are less rationally developed than the state because they serve self-interest and physical need, while the state is supposed to be totally dedicated to serving the community. Family life represents unconscious ethical life, with family members' unification and work activities motivated by nature, love and passion, which are associated with divine law, rather than reason, rights or 'ethical' human law (Hegel 1977: § 451). Agricultural life was similarly described as a mode of subsistence 'which owes comparatively little to reflection and independence of will' and its success rests on the basis of the particularity and immediacy of family relationships and trust (Hegel 1941: § 203).

Above the family and subsistence agriculture, civil society revolves around economic relations between individuals, who act in social cooperation because of mutual need. Hegel classified the relations of production and exchange as involving a higher level of public service than family relations. Marketplace relations represent higher consciousness and selfhood through human creativity, freedom, individualism and law and order, because they require reflection, intelligence and the social mediation of needs, resources and labour (Hegel 1942: §§ 199, 204, addition 129). Hegel envisaged that labour would be organised into 'corporations', which, under the surveillance of public authorities, would protect the interests of their members while also ensuring that members' efforts were directed towards the universal, common good (Hegel 1942: § 252).

While the business sector provides the material base for a universal subjectivity, the automatic mechanisms of the market are deemed insufficient to serve the totality of human relations. Individuals involved in pursuing private gain are unlikely to have the time, inclination or dedication to devote themselves totally to the larger life of the universal community. Hegel proposed that the state balances, unites and regulates the familial agricultural and civil estates, binding all subjectivities together, not on the basis of immediate feeling, economic needs or the relations of production, but on the interests of the community as a whole (Hegel 1942: §§ 257–8, addition 152). In this formulation, the bureaucracy is the 'universal class'. The rational, fully ethical civil servants should be supported by an adequate salary from the state that claims their industry, so that they may act without reference to private emotional or economic interests (Hegel 1942: §§ 205, 303). Hegel allocated the landed gentry a special role in political life, because although civil service posts should be based on merit (Hegel 1942: § 291), their inherited wealth made them more independent and therefore more able to dedicate themselves entirely to the affairs of state (Hegel 1942: §§ 305–7, addition 181). This formulation attributed social inequalities – inequities in class positions and access to resources – to the inherent inequality of human beings in nature (Hegel 1942: § 200).

Supomo's final inspiration was early 20th century, right-wing, military-feudal Japanese nationalism. The army rather than political parties directed Japanese political life of the time (Radek 1934: 33–4; Tanin & Yohan 1934: 184). The bureaucracy established corporatist, mass organisations as umbrella bodies for military, cultural and sporting organisations as well as organisations to mobilise women, youth, journalists and other social sectors. Citizens were expected to show filial piety and loyalty to the emperor, relinquishing all rights and authority to the national leader (Japan Ministry of Education 1937: 47–8). Japanese theorists argued that the 'inherent character' of Asian culture rejected the 'unwholesome self-interest' of liberal societies, emphasising self-sacrifice, patriotism and harmony of the individual with national goals (Japan Ministry of Education 1937: 49). Such a system saw a restriction on political freedoms, contempt for elections and parliamentary democracy (Ikki 1958: 21) and a perception that citizens were 'fundamentally one body' with the state (Japan Ministry of Education 1937: 47).

A clear pattern arises in the familial, organic, corporatist doctrines described above. Although Supomo was inspired by right-wing sources, political ideologues who revived the integralistic concept during the New Order denied that the philosophy was connected to totalitarianism. Supomo himself lauded the *negara totaliter* (translating literally as 'totalitarian nation') throughout his BPUPKI speech. New Order theorists attempted to suggest that Supomo did not intend to refer to totalitarianism but in fact meant *totalitas,* the totality – a national unanimity that avoids dualism (e.g. Hariyati 1995: 2; Silalahi 1993: 66; Sirait 1997: 14, 128). Several critics argue otherwise (Anto 1995: 19; Rahmanto et al. 1998), with some finding that significant sections of Supomo's BPUPKI speech reproduce the wording, rhetoric and discourses of texts by key Nazi German and totalitarian Japanese ideologues on law, society and the state (Bourchier 1996: 57–8; Nasution 1992: 103, fn 85; Simanjuntak 1994: 117–22).

The 'experiment' with liberal democracy

The use of the term 'integralistic' ceased after the BPUPKI completed its activities, and the word did not re-enter political discourses until the birth of the New Order (Simanjuntak 1994: 5, 232). During the revolutionary struggle that followed when the Dutch colonisers refused to recognise Indonesia's 1945 declaration of independence, practical politics deviated from the Constitution because 'theories of government tended to be overshadowed by the facts of war with the Dutch and the internal troubles of the Republic' (Reeve 1985: 87). After the Dutch finally ceded power in 1949, the new Indonesian constitutions of 1949 and 1950 strengthened parliamentary democracy and added new rights to strike and demonstrate. Myriads of groups and political parties emerged over the country representing a multiplicity of political perspectives, and the collectivist, integralistic perspective was 'pushed rather rudely to the political sidelines' (Reeve 1985: 95).

During the turbulent period of liberal democracy in the 1950s, the multiparty political system proliferated to such a degree that at one stage as many as 43 parties existed. The failure of any one party to produce a majority led to a series of short-lived governments based on weak coalitions between the parties. The 17 cabinets that operated between 1945 and 1959 – with an average lifespan of eight months – lacked the direction and continuity required to develop the economically debilitated nation. Socio-political conflicts and tensions also arose from cleavages between and within groupings of the predominantly *abangan* nationalists, the *santri* Muslims and the *priyayi* class as well as other socio-religious and ethnic conflicts.

Even the army was similarly divided into blocs and factions along ethnic, religious and other ideological lines (Ricklefs 1981: 225–41).

The state of journalism reflected the wider state of political life, with newspapers notably partisan along sectorial lines. Although publications did not necessarily describe themselves as party mouthpieces, almost all newspapers of the period could be classified as party related (Dhakidae 1991: 43; Hasibuan 1957: 38–9). Vice-president Hatta was among the many to complain that lack of journalistic neutrality and impartiality had made newspapers the 'voice of particular political parties', so that they were no longer channels of public opinion or platforms for public speaking and debate (Said 1988: 98). Suardi Tasrif (1955: 20), for example, warned at the 1955 PWI Congress that the post-independence era might become known as 'the dark age of Indonesian journalism' due to lack of objectivity and honesty, publication of baseless gossip and gratuitous assertions, and the preponderance of 'news flavoured with the interests of certain groups'. It was clear that neither political nor media systems followed Supomo's concept of familial, cooperative political representation unified under the leadership of the universally accepted presidential father figure.

Despite this, integralistic philosophies remained attractive to two influential groups. These were the upper ranks of the *pamong praja* (a term for the bureaucratic class, that literally means 'guardians of the realm')[5] and army elements associated with Army Chief of Staff Major General Abdul Haris Nasution. The *pamong praja* were largely descended from the petty aristocracy and had previously enjoyed quasi-hereditary access to bureaucratic positions. This pro-*adat* group had seen their status, control over appointments and powers over law, policing and other socio-political jurisdictions eroded by the burgeoning of popular democracy (Feith 1962: 567; Reeve 1985: 111). Nasution and his colleagues were close to the *pamong praja* and were strongly influenced by both the strategy of the Japanese army and the philosophies of Professor Djokosutono, a Dutch-educated *adat* and constitutional expert (Bourchier 1996: 119–26; Reeve 1985: 96–7). Djokosutono – trainer and mentor to a generation of military lawyers and administrators through his Military Law Academy – fostered a belief in strong government, constitutionalism and army participation in decision making. His philosophies provided the framework for Nasution's political thinking as well as the thinking for much of President Sukarno's Guided Democracy (Jenkins 1984: 229).[6] Army groups also promoted the concept of *karyawan*, functionaries or workers, and established corporatist associations, the Golkar (*golongan karya*, functional groups). The Golkar were rivals to left-oriented labour unions and agents for the organic vision (Boileau 1983: 39–43; Notosusanto et al. 1985: 106–13; Reeve 1985: 208–46).

Revival of integralistic ideology

In 1956, Sukarno, frustrated at the limitation of his powers under the 1950 Constitution, began dismantling what he deemed a failed experiment with alien, liberal democracy by announcing his *konsepsi* (concept) of Guided Democracy.

The concept initially lacked widespread support, but following a series of political crises, the multi-party liberal system was replaced with Guided Democracy in 1959 and 1960, increasing the powers of the army and *pamong praja* (Feith 1962: 517–20, 538–55; Feith 1963: 395–400; Reeve 1985: 163–74). Declaring a need to rediscover the revolution, Sukarno abolished the 1950 Provisional Constitution; dissolved the elected Constitutent Assembly, which had almost finished drafting a new constitution; and banned all but ten of the political parties. In place of these structures he established a Nasakom[7] presidential cabinet, appointed a handpicked *Gotong Royong* parliament and returned the nation to the 1945 Constitution, which provided for a strong executive. Despite representation of the masses through political parties and functional groups, political decision-making power was vested in the president and bureaucratic officials (Reeve 1978: 94).

The new culture immediately permeated media life, as journalists were expected to play a key role in Sukarno's *Manipol* (Political Manifesto) of 1959. The press was supposed to act under state guidance to oppose counter-revolutionary influences and to increase mass consciousness of 'Indonesian socialism' and the *Pancasila* ideology. Various regulations (such as the Peraturan Penguasa Perang Tertinggi No. 10/1960, Peraturan Penguasa Perang Tertinggi No. 2/1961) and presidential decisions (including the Keputusan Presiden No. 307/1962, Keputusan Presiden No. 376/1962, Penetapan Presiden No. 6/1963) were directed at cleansing the press of enemies of the revolution. They aimed at encouraging journalists to spread the *Manipol* and ensuring that the media helped battle the perceived counter-revolutionary evils of imperialism, liberalism, colonialism, federalism and separatism.

The Sukarnoist and PKI (*Partai Komunis Indonesia*, Indonesian Communist Party) 'revolutionary offensive' was hardly universally palatable and was vigorously countered by various social and state groups. The opposition forces included large sectors of the army which, as Pabotinggi (1995: 244) notes, had little tolerance following the crushing of various regional rebellions for political parties and ideologies that were not primarily oriented towards national unification and defence. A continuing tension existed in the uneasy balance of power between the triumvirate of Sukarno, the army and the PKI (*Partai Komunis Indonesia*, Communist Party of Indonesia), which, with two million members, was the third largest communist party in the world.

The media was an important playing field for the games of political brinkmanship. One important centre of anticommunist resistance was the BPS (*Badan Pendukung Sukarnoism*, Body for Support of Sukarnoism). This sardonically titled organisation was established by journalistic luminaries Burhanuddin Mohamad Diah and Adam Malik to form a nucleus of conservative opposition to the PKI's revolutionary offensive. BPS founders ostensibly aimed to use the mass media to popularise Sukarno's independence-era philosophies, as opposed to his later policies and ideologies, which they perceived as tainted by communism (Said & Moeljanto 1983: 33–9). Most of ABRI and more than half the political parties supported the BPS. Its strongest detractors were the PKI and the Indonesian National Party. Just as Indonesian political and social groups were broadly divided between those that opposed and those that supported communism, the media industry was strongly divided between those publications that sided with the BPS and those that were sympathetic to the PKI. The respective newspapers acted as forums for heated debate between communists and anticommunists.

Two additions to the Sukarno-era organic system, SOKSI and Sekber Golkar, came from conservative forces. In 1960, the army established SOKSI (*Sentral Organisasi Karyawan Sosialis Indonesia*, Central Organisation of Indonesian Socialist Employees), a mass labour organisation for *karyawan* employed in nationalised enterprises and members of existing mass organisations. SOKSI was meant to compete with SOBSI (*Sentral Organisasi Buruh Seluruh Indonesia*, Central Federation of Indonesian Labour Organisations), which was the PKI's labour division and also the nation's largest labour movement (Boileau 1983: 40–2; Hawkins 1963: 269; Indoc 1981: 79; Leclerc 1972: 78–9; Reeve 1985: 218–25).

A late addition to the Sukarno-era organic system came from the conservative forces through the corporatist Sekber Golkar (*Sekretariat Bersama Golongan Karya*, the Joint Secretariat of Golkar Organisations), a corporatist organisation for *karyawan*. Former students of Djokusutono with strong military connections established the Sekber Golkar in 1964 in order to coordinate the military-sponsored functional groups that, as was discussed above, had operated since 1957 in opposition to leftist mass organisations (Boileau 1983: 45; Reeve 1985: 243). The formation of the Golkar and later the Sekber Golkar was tied to the military's suspicion of organised labour. For many army leaders, all left-wing politics and organisations were permanently discredited following the 1948 involvement of communist leaders in an attempt to establish a People's Republic in Madiun. This event, which was described for decades as 'the stab in the back', temporarily diverted army efforts from Indonesia's struggle for independence. When nationalistic Indonesian unions seized Dutch assets in 1957, the problem was exacerbated further. The military assumed management of those assets, and in their capacity as an employer across a range of key industries, army leaders were wary of the militant, strike-oriented unionism of the era (Hadiz 1997: 29; Hadiz 1993: 189). The attitudes of conservative military-political leaders, more accustomed to military discipline than industrial bargaining, were also shaped by their increasingly bitter relations with the PKI and the leftist parties that most unions were affiliated with (Hawkins 1963: 267).

The establishment of the Golkar, SOKSI and Sekber Golkar were not just organisational means of creating organic structures for workers and other functionaries in socio-political groups. SOBSI, as its name implied, labelled workers as *buruh*. In an important semantic shift, SOKSI and the Sekber Golkar labelled them as *karyawan*. In most circles, workers were commonly known as *buruh*. *Buruh* originates from the Javanese term for agricultural peasant labourers and is suggestive of an uncultured proletariat. *Karyawan* is derived from the word, *karya* (to work), by using ritualised Sanskrit rules. *Karyawan* embodies performance of a function, duty or mission. Some argue that it has strong elitist and intellectual connotations, in common with most words adopted from Sanskrit (Leclerk 1972: 81–7). Anti-communist forces also promoted the use of the word, *pekerja*, as an alternative to *buruh*. *Pekerja* comes from the root word *kerja* (to work), which refers to the minutiae of minute-by-minute work. *Pekerja* does not differentiate between the factory hands who may earn less than $100 per month or their bosses who may earn more than $1,000,000. Various critics have observed that the change from *buruh* to *karyawan* and *pekerja* blurs the distinction between workers and management, devalues the claims of workers, and transforms the conceptualisation of workers from active subjects to passive objects. It has been argued that these integralistic terminologies stripped the workers' language of its agitative and adversarial potential (Indoc 1981: 78; Indoc 1984: 15; Leclerc 1972: 90; Setiadi 1997: 123).

Sekber Golkar and the functional groups had little popular or institutional support outside the military. Despite this, the key political decision-making powers had been transferred to the president and his bureaucratic officials, and corporatist bodies to represent community interests were widespread. Thus the main mechanisms for integralistic representation were established, even though they were not always thriving or cooperating with each other, during the period of Sukarno's Guided Democracy.

The organic woman

Organic culture is intensely partriarchal, and so the adoption of integralistic philosophies had particularly profound implications for Indonesian women. Both Hegelian and *priyayi* philosophies see women as unsuited to public life, because their ties to family life mean they are unable to serve the universal. In Hegelian philosophy, only the state is solely dedicated to serving the community. As was discussed on page 4, family and civil society are seen as less rationally developed than the state because they serve self-interest and physical need. Family life represents unconscious ethical life, because family members are driven by primal passions associated with divine law rather than reason, rights or 'ethical' human law.

Hegel acknowledges that women's general relationships with husbands or children serve the universal, public interest rather than mere personal passion. However, a woman's relationships with a particular child or a particular husband is not purely 'ethical' (Hegel 1977: § 451), because her service to her family is not contingent upon, and may sometimes even be contrary to, the public good. Hegel found women to be unsuited to civil service and political life, arguing that a government controlled by women would threaten the state as they are driven by a 'vague unity of feeling' rather than a comprehension of universality (Hegel 1942: §166 addition 107; Hegel 1977: § 475). He argued that women only become rational, fully ethical beings through their relationships with men (Hegel 1977: § 463). Men, by contrast, are judged as capable of separating the private, particular world of family from the universal, maintaining freedom and distance from emotion and desire (Hegel 1977: § 457).

In common with Hegelian ideas, *priyayi* notions similarly position women as unlikely to possess power because of their supposedly self-interested nature. Anderson's (1990) and, to a lesser degree, Koentjaraningrat's (1980) frequently quoted theses on Javanese conceptualisations of power describe conditions for power that are unattainable in most Indonesian women's lives. While the theses are dated and have limited utility for those seeking to analyse the practical expression of power in modern contexts, they remain indicative of traditional Javanese aristocratic ideologies of authority and rulership in an idealised world. Despite the differences between the theses, both identify power as tied to conceptions of refinement, mental strength, self-composition and serenity. In common with the Hegelian vision, the surrender to the animalistic condition of emotion, attachment to particularity and the striving for influence or material possessions are seen as threats to power (Anderson 1990: 50–4; Koentjarangin-grat 1980: 135).

Indonesian women are often considered to be *pamrih* (self-interested or acting in a fashion motivated by perceived profit), a condition that reduces power (Cooley 1992: 233; Djajadiningrat-Nieuwenhuis 1992: 46). The definition of *pamrih* is, on the surface, paradoxical, considering that the Indonesian ideal of motherhood involves women serving their families without consideration of personal power and prestige. Despite this, women are also seen as materialistic and consumeristic because of that duty to attend to household needs (Noerhadi 1982: 34; Suryakusuma 1982: 9). While the Javanese desire money in a general sense, the pursuit of profit and handling of money is also perceived as a vulgar activity that sullies the spirit and reduces power (Anderson 1990: 53). The matters of marketing and money handling that are left to wives allow those women considerable autonomy at one level, but at another level the activity is ignoble and crude and below the sphere of the Javanese male (Sullivan 1994: 9). Wives and mothers may not act for personal interest, but they constantly seek profit and advantage for their families. Javanese men, by contrast, whether in the court or the village, have traditionally remained distant from their children and have avoided involvement in household and business affairs (Carey & Houben 1992: 23; Geertz 1961: 45, 107). Women thus have considerable control over their homes and lives, but they are less likely to possess the types of power that are desirable to *priyayi* sensibilities or conducive to political power.

In practice, despite the claims that integralistic theory was drawn from Indonesia's culture and history, there has been traditionally little gender-based division of public and private spheres. Because Indonesia was predominantly an agrarian society until recent decades, both men and women have generally had equal access to resources and worked together to share domestic and farming duties (Robinson 1983: 112–13, 125). In Java, for example, women were dominant in domestic matters relating to the kitchen and preparation of socially and economically significant ceremonial meals, but they also governed the harvesting, distribution and sale of produce (Geertz 1963: 87; Geertz 1961: 46, 122–6; Stoler 1976: 126–9; Willner 1976: 117–18; Raffles 1978: 353). The need for women's labour increased under the Dutch colonial system, which forced the mobilisation of all labour potential in peasant households to meet the requirements of subsistence production as well as new taxes (Wertheim 1956: 94). Indonesian women are integral to the peasant economy (Manderson 1983: 4–7), and observers have long commented on their economic independence, freedom of movement and self-reliance (Hull 1996: 79).

Compared to the freedoms of peasant women, the concepts of womanhood and motherhood were comparatively limited for the Javanese *priyayi* (upper class or petty aristocracy). *Priyayi* women of the late nineteenth and early twentieth century were generally confined to their home compounds, and their lives were devoted to the successive roles of daughter, sister, wife and mother (Tiwon 1996: 52; Vreede-de Stuers 1960: 51–2). *Priyayi* women who engaged in economic activities tended to operate from their homes as sponsors or brokers for local artisans, as did the turn-of-the-century feminist and national hero, Kartini (Gelman Taylor 1989: 157). Although there are marked differences in the position and status of women across the archipelago, with traditions ranging from matrilineal to patrilineal to bilineal, it is important to consider the Javanese *priyayi* positioning on women, because Javanese culture has dominated Indonesian politics since the achievement of national independence in 1945. This is merely in order to identify key streams of thinking within the political hegemony and should not be seen as a denial of the richness and importance of other ethnic identities or the influence of religious, class, economic status and other social referents.

Change of order

The long-running tensions between the communist party and conservative army forces erupted with the so-called Gestapu coup of 1965, which gave the conservative forces the rationale they needed to eradicate communist supporters and ideologies. With communist and leftist figures murdered, jailed or 're-educated' in 1965 and 1966, integralistic principles dominated the ideological void. The leaders of the New Order government, which effectively gained power in March 1966 under the authority of then General Soeharto, fine-tuned and expanded the integralistic political apparatus of the Sukarno era, initially under the name of *kekeluargaan* but later in the name of integralistic nation. During the 1980s, the terms *kekeluargaan* and *integralistik* were often used interchangeably. The New Order realised its family-oriented, integralistic vision through programs of *depolitisasi* (depoliticisation) involving *deparpolisasi* (departy-politicisation) and *golkarisasi* (golkarisation) in the name of economic development, *Pancasila* democracy, stability, order and the spirit of the 1945 Constitution (Heryanto 1990: 290–1).

This chapter has looked at the family-oriented semantic and philosophical foundations of the integralistic concept. The next chapter describes how the New Order executive, which represented itself as the guardian of the nation, used integralistic theory to develop a practical system to sustain its authority and to absorb or manage competitors to its power.

2 The organic New Order state

From its earliest phases, the New Order sought to validate its leadership by emphasising the rhetoric of law, especially its 'pure' intepretation and realisation of the 1945 Constitution (Simanjuntak 1994: 6; Van Langenberg 1990: 130–1). In particular, the New Order claimed that the Constitution embodied the people's sovereignty and was impregnated with integralistic philosphy (Besar 1984: 126; Sudharmono 1986: 5; Wahyono 1988: 61). In theory, this integralistic sovereignty was realised through the activities of the MPR and the formulation of the five-yearly *Garis-garis Besar Haluan Negara* (Broad Outlines of State Policy, GBHN) (Besar 1984: 128–9).

The New Order described *Pancasila*, 'the five principles' that were written into the Constitution's preamble, as the basis for democratic life (Department of Information 1996–7: 34). '*Pancasila* democracy' is mentioned in the 1945 Constitution, but the term was only popularised during the New Order (Mahfud 1993: 42). While *Pancasila* was initially formulated to unite peoples of numerous ethnicities, religions and ideologies in the struggle for independence, the New Order stripped *Pancasila* of its revolutionary connotations and prioritised integralistic interpretations. A 1968 decree passed by the MPRS (*Majelis Permoesjawaratan Rakyat Sementara*, Provisional People's Consultative Council) defines *Pancasila* democracy as deliberation for consensus. New Order ideologues similarly described the fourth tenet of *Pancasila* – democracy, led by the wisdom of consensus from representatives – as an identifying characteristic of Indonesian democracy (Wahyono 1988: 61). After 1973, all students, from kindergarten to university, were obliged to undertake annual *Pancasila* courses. Bourchier's (1996: 239–41) study of texts used in *Pancasila* courses finds that the key discourses revolve around order, harmony, *kekeluargaan*, the leader's role in directing *musyawarah* and consensus-forming and the God-willed inevitability of social inequality.[1]

The New Order rapidly saturated socio-political life with the language of harmonious, family-like, organic relations. The New Order based and sustained its supremacy in imposing these definitions as consonant with authentic Indonesian culture by continuously promoting itself as the 'bringer of "development"' (Robison 1982: 135; also Liddle 1985: 23–4). With a scarcity of goods and services and spiralling inflation peaking at 650 per cent in 1966

(Sadli 1967: 50; Santoso 1997: 22), popular slogans at the beginning of the New Order were 'Politics, No; Development, Yes' and 'Economic development is commander'. After Sukarno signed the order in March 1966 that effectively passed control to Soeharto, the latter relied on a pool of technocrats, most notably many U.S.-educated economists, to formulate economic policy. These technocrats also served the ideological function of legitimising the state's claim to be the centre of scientific wisdom about national development and policies for protecting the common good. This helped to validate the exclusion of alternative social forces from political participation (Robison 1981: 12).

Soeharto's technocrats were not necessarily interested in integralistic ideology, but many elements of integralistic philosophy matched the influential modernisation and political order paradigms of the time, as promoted by Daniel Bell, Seymour Martin Lipset and Samuel P. Huntington. These theorists posited that social and economic change in developing countries leads to a precarious adjustment period; this creates the need for a strong, authoritarian leadership to oversee socio-economic reintegration. Order and stability were seen as essential for growth. Subordination of civil rights and freedoms were considered necessary in cases when they conflicted with the greater interests of social integrity and development. It was implicit in New Order philosophy that economic and socio-political development could not occur at the same time (Mulya Lubis 1993: 38–40; Mahfud 1993: 99). The state reinforced the credibility of such theories by continually reminding citizens of the ideological divisiveness and political chaos that accompanied the economic stagnation of Sukarno's Old Order government (Van Langenberg 1990: 126–7). The state thus developed an extensive rational for its patrimonial rule by blending theories about the need for political 'order' and 'modernisation' to build an industrial base and provide the economic stability that might eventually enable future democratic growth (Higgott and Robison 1985: 20–1; Van Langenberg 1986: 14, 19–20).

Paternalistic concepts of the protective powers of father figures were enshrined in the New Order's integralistic theorems of state and development. New Order ideologues interpreted the 1945 Constitution as reflecting integralistic human rights that in turn reflected 'the character and functions of guardianship' (Wahyono 1988: 60). In the integralistic vision, sovereignty of the masses results through their delegation of power to the guardianship of government infratructure. The president was compared to a good father who protects the rights of his children (Silalahi 1993: 66).

ABRI developed its self-declared *dwi fungsi* (dual function), a doctrine that had evolved from since the 1950s from Djokosutono's *jalan tengah* (middle way). The *jalan tengah* described the army as following a path between domination of the government and complete removal from politics. *Dwi fungsi* was formulated as a rationale for the military to act not just as an institution that safeguarded the nation from military threat; ABRI was to also serve a second function of protecting society from harm by taking a leading role in social and economic activity, political life and policy making. This philosophy was powered by ABRI's opposition to the multiparty system and its sense that it had a 'civic mission' to aid development (Crouch 1988: 24–42; Penders & Sundhaussen 1985: 133–4; Reeve 1985: 189; Soeharto 1989: 427–33).

Notosusanto and colleagues trace the correlations between the philosophies of Hegel, Müller and Spinoza and the organic ideology surrounding the *dwi fungsi* (1985: 191–3). ABRI's *dwi fungsi* is consonant with integralistic principles, such as 'paternalism, the legitimacy of non-elected rulers and the idea that it is possible for an élite to represent the whole society's interests rather than simply its own' (Bourchier 1993: 13; also Jenkins 1984: 113–17; Ramage 1995: 125–30; Ramage 1994: 166). The New Order developed the themes of bureaucratic and military guardianship, discussed in Chapter 1, to rationalise state and military interference in all major socio-political institutions. All theorists who have studied the New Order, regardless of their ideological positioning, describe the key element of New Order governance as an autonomous strong state, supported by the military as the primary actor in coalition with technocrats (Mahfud 1993: 138; Mas'oed 1994: 62–9). As 'upholders of the tradition', government, community and, by implication, military leaders were able to enact justice and materialise community aspirations because they were supposedly 'one soul with the people', united to the community through deliberation and the spirit of *gotong royong* and *kekeluargaan* (Supomo 1945: 113–14).

Managing the three estates of government

The New Order's military leaders began entrenching their authority from the time of the Gestapu coup in 1965. General Soeharto, credited with having quashed the coup, augmented military power by establishing Kopkamtib (*Komando Operasi Keamanan dan Ketertiban*, Operational Command for Restoration of Security and Order), a security organisation that initially had unlimited powers to investigate, arrest, detain and summarily execute those connected with the coup. This was later extended to investigate any activity deemed to threaten national security (Asia Watch 1986: 56–62; Crouch 1988: 222–3). Although it was formally stripped of extra-judicial powers to arrest and detain suspects, Kopkamtib's successor, Bakorstansas (*Badan Koordinasi Bantuan Pemantapan Stabilitas Nasional*, Coordinating Agency for Assisting the Consolidation of National Stability), was in practice similarly empowered to interfere in any activity at any time or place under its brief of restoring and consolidating security and order (LCHR & ELSAM 1995: 373–38; Mulya Lubis 1993: 106; Tanter 1990: 220–1). These organisations were among a network of military intelligence instruments engaged in systematic surveillance and intervention aimed at creating terror among 'deviant' groups (Tanter 1990: 241–71). The next step was to manage the systems of administration, political representation and popular control of the government.

ABRI affirmed its self-declared *dwi fungsi*, as both a military and socio-political force, through a series of seminars between 1965 and 1967 which established the foundations for military involvement in all aspects of civilian life (Crouch 1988: 344–345; Mulya Lubis 1993: 196). The dual-function philosophy was used as the grounds to guarantee ABRI permanent participation in cabinet, the DPR (*Dewan Perwakilan Rakyat*, the parliament) and other decision-making bodies. Soldiers could not vote, but ABRI was automatically allocated a block of seats, making the military the second-largest political group in parliament after the state's political representative, Golkar. Thousands of officers were appointed to replace civilian ministers, department heads, ambassadors, university rectors, governors, managers of state enterprises and other administrative positions so that within a decade of the New Order, active and retired military *karyawan* occupied more than half Indonesia's ministerial and higher bureaucratic postings (Jenkins 1984: 195–6; Emmerson 1978: 103; MacDougall 1982: 89–90; Notosusanto et al. 1985: 378–9). Regional Leadership Councils (Muspida, *Musyawarah Pimpinan Daerah*), introduced in 1967, increased army influence on civilian administration by bringing the heads of the regional military, bureaucracy, police and prosecutor's office together to discuss security and coordinate strategies (Jenkins 1984: 49). All these military leaders were ultimately subject to the direct or indirect influence of Soeharto, the Supreme Commander of ABRI who controlled all top-eschelon appointments (Santoso 1997: 33).

Golkar provided the bureaucratic vehicle through which *dwi fungsi* could be realised and surrounded the military's political role with signs of popular participation (Boileau 1983: 95–7; Mas'oed 1994: 58–61; Reeve 1985: 346). During the New Order, Golkar evolved from the army-sponsored Sekber Golkar into a political-party format and achieved landslide victories for the Soeharto government at each of the five-yearly national elections. Although Golkar operated as any other political party, New Order leaders insisted that it was a 'functional group' representing all societal interests rather than a party organisation. Golkar comprised a range of state-sanctioned corporatist organisations that acted as the sole legitimate groups entitled to represent, negotiate with government and integrate disparate societal sectors such as youth, labour, peasants, fishermen and women. Many of these functional organisations joined Golkar due to New Order pressure and patronage (Reeve 1985: 331). The Indonesian Civil Servants' Corps was one such group, and government bureaucrats were barred by law from affiliating with any political group other than Golkar.

Golkar was not a source of independent power or leadership renewal. Despite attempts at independence from ABRI (see Vatikiotis 1994: 238–9), Golkar has historically been entwined with the military apparatus (Hasjim 1979: 650–66; Hidayat 1979: 73; Reeve 1990: 163–70). Golkar chairmanship and other leadership positions were commonly held by retired ABRI officers (Reeve 1990: 168–9; Vatikiotis 1988: 28–9). Selection of Golkar candidates and office bearers was in the hands of Soeharto, then general chairman of Golkar's *Dewan Pembina* (Supervisory Council) (Jenkins 1984: 127).

The growth of Golkar accompanied the demise of party politics, with the New Order passing a series of decrees and laws from 1966 that strengthened the state and weakened political parties. Drawing from Huntington's theories, the New Order evaluated that developing countries with multiparty systems were less stable and thus less able to develop systems than those dominated by one party (Gaffar 1992: 63–75; Reeve 1985: 264; Sirait 1997: 73). The 1969 election law (Law No. 15/1969) permitted only officially vetted candidates from nine political parties and Sekber Golkar to contest the first election of the New Order in 1971. Following that election, the nine parties that rivalled Golkar were amalgamated into two parties. The new titles and mergers were devised without consideration of the histories, purposes and orientations of the individual constituents. The resulting parties were weak and vulnerable, broken by internal conflicts about programs and ideologies.

The power of political parties was diminished in various other ways. The 1975 law on the 'floating mass' (Law No. 3/1975) prevented parties from conducting political activities outside the cities except in the weeks prior to five-yearly elections, because the masses were deemed vulnerable to political manipulation, prone to ideological conflict and easily distracted from the development task (Boileau 1983: 69–70; Sundhaussen 1978: 50; Suryadinata 1989: 79–83). Golkar, however, maintained a permanent presence and consequent electoral advantage in the villages because of the local activites of the public service and military (Boileau 1983: 107; Suryadinata 1989: 131–2). The parties' public identity was undermined further when the government introduced a decree in 1983 (Decree No. II/MPR/1983) requiring all political parties to adopt *Pancasila* as their *asas tunggal* (sole ideological foundation). New Order officials said the simplification was necessary to prevent the fractious party politicking and ideological conflict that disrupted political life during the Old Order (Department of Information 1996–7: 34; Soeharto 1989: 409). Political analysts, however, found that it eroded the parties' ideological clarity and political purpose in the eyes of their constituents (Ramage 1995: 35–9). There were also widespread claims that the parties were disadvantaged during elections by fraud, intimidation and legal violations perpetrated by the state (*White Book* 1994: 12–39, 53–60; Loveard 1997: 24).

The balance of the parties in parliament was not as significant as one might assume, since the parliament's main role was to act as a rubber stamp to the executive. The integralistic state concept blurred the distinction between branches of power, leaving the executive extraordinarily dominant and all other branches impotent (Mulya Lubis 1993: 179). Draft bills always came from Soeharto's handpicked Cabinet and were usually endorsed with little change. DPR members' independence was limited because deliberation and consensus was emphasised over critical dissent, no concept of 'opposition' parties or politics was tolerated and members could be recalled by their parties if they acted autonomously (Mulya Lubis 1993: 180; Mas'oed 1994: 62; Sulasmono 1991: 71–82).

The executive also dominated other branches of political life, even though the president was technically lower in stature than the MPR and equal to the DPR, Supreme Court and other branches of government (Department of Information

1982: 81). The MPR was described as a 40 per cent democracy because it consisted of the 500 DPR members, comprising 400 elected representatives and 100 military appointees, plus another 500 appointed representatives from political organisations, the regions and provinces and professional groups. Although the MPR was authorised to endorse or reject the president, in reality only one presidential candidate was ever nominated for MPR members to choose from and they were unlikely to refuse a mandate to the president who had just appointed them. The president's title as the MPR's *Mandataris* (proxy) was indicative of his unlimited authority (Nasution 1992: 429).

The judicial system was also subject to executive interference. Such a system supposedly suited the integralistic Constitution, which emphasised the distribution of powers rather than the separation of powers (Sundhaussen 1978: 49). The impact was that judges were reluctant to act independently in cases that were unpopular with the government, because the Minister of Justice controlled their appointment, promotion, transfer, dismissal and salary (ICJ 1987: 61–2). The true legal and administrative decision-making centre was the unelected, unaccountable State Secretariat, whose staff included many organic-oriented graduates of Djokosutono's Military Law Academy (Jenkins 1984: 21; Sundhaussen 1978: 77). Notable among these was Soeharto's ally, Sudharmono.

Incivility in the civil society

There was little opportunity for political activities outside the formal institutions of politics, since the government suppressed the expression of protest or dissent outside the family-oriented institutions of representation, i.e. the MPR, DPR or courts (Mulya Lubis 1993: 190; Sudharmono 1986: 5). The government regulated significant community groups with direct links to the masses through a 1985 law (Law No. 8/1985) that obliged all non-government organisations (NGOs), religious groups, professional associations and other mass associations to make *Pancasila* their *asas tunggal* and to register with the government. The legal stipulation that the government would supervise these organisations was again connected with New Order state's fatherhood role. In the New Order's integralistic theory, there was no perceived a conflict between the notion of supervision and the autonomy of the community organisations being supervised (Mulya Lubis 1993: 222). Student activism was similarly limited by the New Order's Normalisation of Campus Life policy, which culminated with a 1980 presidential decree restricting active politics on campus grounds. Groups representing professions and other societal sectors were also circumscribed, forced to amalgamate into compulsory, non-competitve, corporatist organisations that were granted monopoly status in exchange for observing controls on leadership selection and articulation of demands and supports (Robison 1993: 45).

Even activism by individuals was limited. In the well-known example of the 1980 *Petisi 50* (Petition of 50), 50 prominent citizens who wrote to Soeharto complaining that he had portrayed himself as the embodiment of *Pancasila* in order to destroy his political opponents were themselves politically isolated and economically crushed (Bresnan 1993: 207; Jenkins 1984: 164–71). The kidnapping, torture and, in several cases, murder of political activists in early 1998 by ABRI's Special Forces was another indication of the vulnerability of individuals who spoke out during times of political tension. The military subsequently admitted to involvement in the 1998 'disappearances' (Polglaze 1998).

The leaders of the embryonic New Order government rapidly controlled Indonesia's radical media immediately after the Gestapu coup, banning 46 newspapers with leftist leanings and issuing new publication permits to the survivors of the crackdown (Swantoro & Atmakusumah 1980: 206). The government continued to supervise media activities through laws that required prospective publishers to obtain a publishing licence – initially called a SIT, but from 1982 called a SIUPP – for each and every newspaper or magazine they printed. These licences could be suspended or withdrawn, effectively banning the publication from printing. Licensing controls over television and radio were similarly strict.[2]

Business and labour in the New Order

The fledgling business sector never rivalled executive power, because state-owned enterprises controlled large portions of the economy and even private enterprise was fused with the state and reliant on government patronage and protection. In the practical application of order and modernisation theories, Indonesia's élite argued that socio-economic policy was best devised and implemented by the bureaucracy and ABRI (Higgott & Robison 1985: 21). Cooperatives were also a priority in economic development plans since such Hegelian-style organisations are based on cooperation, family principles and Article 33 of the 1945 Constitution (Antara 22 Mar. 1988b: C12–C13; Antara 10 Dec. 1987: H11; Suyono et al. 1995: 2).

Despite the consistent growth of the private sector throughout most of the New Order, the bureaucratic–military machine dominated economic activity, holding major stakes in numerous primary-industry operations, factories, trading companies, banks, and other business organisations. State industrial planning involved a wide range of mercantilist state interventions, ranging from direct ownership to state authority over trade and investment activities, providing bureaucrats and the military with opportunities to collaborate with and control corporate capitalist clients (Case 1998: 13–14; Crouch 1988: 283–5, 355; Robison 1993: 44–5; Robison 1986: 134). Many military and bureaucratic officials built big businesses, generally with Chinese partners, assisted by access to public credit and privileges (Crouch 1988: 285–99; Crouch 1994: 116–17; Liddle 1985: 24–5; Robison 1993: 46; Robison 1987: 28; Robison 1985: 316). The interests of the non-government business sector were also embedded within the New Order regime, because they depended on licences, tariffs, monopolies, concessions, state-funded projects and patrimonial appropriation of other state resources (Crouch 1988: 299–303; Robison 1993: 55–60; Robison 1987: 17–18).

Although unions often form an alternative centre of power to that of political and economic leaders in many countries, the position of unions was downgraded during the New Order. Chapter 1 outlines how the military's antipathy to unions long predated the formation of the New Order. SOKSI, for example, competed with the union movement. ABRI leaders envisaged that SOKSI would connect the conception of *karyawan* with economic development, the family principle and the elimination of class struggle (Reeve 1985: 196–7, 225).

Following the 1965 Gestapu incident, the army wiped out the PKI, SOBSI and its 62 union affiliates, leaving behind only a small number of anticommunist unions with weak support bases. A primary concern of the victorious New Order forces was to prevent radical mass-based movements from resurfacing (Cahyono 1997: 109; Hadiz 1997: 25). In military thinking, independent unionism and other dynamic labour organisations that questioned the differential between labour and capital would heighten the risk of economically and socially disruptive 'communistic' labour movements that encouraged class conflict (Hadiz 1997: 32–3; Lambert 1997: 79; Manning 1998: 203–4). The political-military leadership's continuing control of major sectors of the economy through a system of patron-client relations also meant a direct economic as well as political interest for the New Order in controlling the working class (Lambert 1997: 58). The New Order labour culture became dominated by developmentalist rhetoric, and full workers' rights were described as an unaffordable luxury for a developing nation (Indoc 1981: 65; Hadiz 1997: 47–8).

In the labour market, the New New Order progressively marginalised the word *buruh* as vulgar, leftist and deviant, replacing it *karyawan* and *pekerja* (Eldridge 1995: 110; Leclerc 1972: 88–9; Setiadi 1997: 141). As early as 1966, the Minister for Labour (*Perburuhan*) was replaced by the Minister for Manpower (*Tenaga Kerja*). During Sudomo's 1983 offensive against the very notion of *buruh*, the guiding principle of *Pancasila* Labour Relations (*Hubungan Perburuhan Pancasila*) was changed to *Pancasila* Industrial Relations (HIP, *Hubungan Industri Pancasila*). Union organisations dropped the word *buruh* from their names. The changes were indicative of the dilution of the discourses of labour relations.

In the HIP, all labour associations were fused into a single entity, the FBSI (which later became the SBSI). The military were directed to intervene in labour disputes, on the grounds that the use of strikes to make demands from employers opposed HIP principles and threatened national security (Indoc 1982: 3; Indoc 1983: 8). Retired military personnel, Golkar party members and management were appointed as union heads (Indoc 1981: 89; Indoc 1986: 16; Lambert 1997: 73, 75). The combination of the 1985 Social Organisations Law, requiring all organisations to adopt *Pancasila* as their sole ideology, and the restructuring of the FBSI into the more centralised SPSI reinforced the capacity of the state 'to intimidate and pacify' the labour forces within the *Pancasila* Industrial Relations system (Lambert 1997: 62; also Fehring and Lindsey 1995: 3). In the 1990s, the government liberalised some aspects of industrial relations policy following increasing labour unrest and domestic and international criticism of labour rights (Levine 1997: 197–214; Manning 1998: 212–16). However, the state continued to oppose new, independent unions on the grounds that they would threaten economic stability (Manning 1998: 223).

Nepotism in the family

In the 'New Order pyramid' (Liddle 1985: 18), it was clear that the exercise of authority and the distribution of state assets was controlled by a small élite. Power flowed downwards from the presidency, to the armed forces, to an enormous bureaucracy that formed the hub of policy implementation, to Indonesian society. There were relatively few mechanisms to ensure an appearance of bureaucratic and institutional accountability of the top layers of the pyramid, and little emphasis on informed participation of the bottom-layer polity in decision-making. With no substantive structure ensuring the public responsibility of socio-political guardians, nepotism and corruption became institutionalised.

The potential to use bureaucratic or military leadership positions to aid clients reinforced a wider cultural tendency towards *bapakisme* (patron-client relations or, literally, paternalism), in which senior political figures were patrons of a range of semi-dependent clients in their employment, the business sector or other fields (Boileau 1983: 17–19; Brown 1994: 117–18; Jackson 1979b: 374–5). Whole sectors of the bureaucracy were maintained by 'a system of parallel financing of favored sectors of the bureaucracy through the invisible flow of corruption running alongside the formal salary structure', with the effect that bureaucratic orientation shifted increasingly towards immediate patrons or rulers at the centre (Anderson 1990: 60; also Young 1990: 156–7). Soeharto had substantial resources of patronage that he used to attract support from a range of societal interests, from powerful bureaucratic and military figures through to local community leaders (Robison 1993: 48). His family became the most prominent beneficiaries of corruption, collusion and nepotism,[3] although similar patterns of political patronage continued down the levels of governance (Antlöv 1994: 90–2). In business, bureaucracy and politics, hard work and ability were seen as less important for a good career than being clever at developing and using personal connections (Boileau 1983: 89; *Kompas* 1990: 170–1; Muhaimin 1980: 23).

A combination of patrimonial and modernisation theories provided ideological rationalisation for social injustice and corruption, at least to some degree. Both monist philosophy and *Pancasila* programs describe physical, social and financial disparities between individuals as humankind's God-determined and natural fate. Modernisation theorists, especially those who followed Huntington's doctrines, similarly argued that Indonesian culture was characterised by dependence and passivity. This supposedly promoted the hierarchical patron-client structure and validated differences in social and material conditions and opportunities. Weberian theories were also used to support arguments that gift giving was historically entrenched behaviour in socio-politicial life. For example, Karl Jackson (1978a: 37) said:

> [O]n meeting a village headman for the first time it is not improper to bring a gift, and the presentation is not perceived as bribery. But in accepting the gift the official is obliged to reciprocate in some manner. To give a gift is to initiate a potential dependency relationship; if the recipient does not give some token, and preferably more valuable, gift in return, it is an implicit admission of the recipient's subordinate position. What is important is not the nature and magnitude of the gift, but the act of giving.

Such theorists claimed that Indonesians perceive social justice as 'carrying out the responsibilities of justly unequal roles' in which the patron's 'God-given high status and wealth' was directed towards assisting a large group of clients (Jackson 1978a: 34–5). Within this framework, it was argued that the community only felt that the advantages gained by the patron were improper, unjust or corrupt if the patron failed to redistribute his bounty among his clients (Jackson 1978a: 36; Shiraishi 1997: 98–100).

Indonesian complaints of systemic corruption in the New Order emerged in the first years of Soeharto's rule.[4] Even early supporters of the government were often disillusioned that corruption was not attacked but merely insitutionalised (Schwarz 1994: 33). The New Order's lack of commitment about cleansing the politico-economic environment from corruption contrasted starkly with the fervent intensity of campaigns to create an ideologically 'clean environment' (*bersih lingkungan*) free from communist and radical Islamic influences.

The New Order femme

Although organic philosophies suggest that the proper place for women was in the home, Chapter 1 discusses how there was no particular division between male-public sphere and female-private sphere domains before independence. In the late colonial period, the struggle for women's emancipation was identified with aspirations for national sovereignty. Women were often the sole or major breadwinners during WWII, but the valuation of women's participation in the public sphere diminished following the achievement of independence (Blackburn 2001: 6–8; Hafidz 1992: 95; Kartowijono 1976; Noerhadi 1982: 31; Suryochondro 1984: 75–114; Vreede-de Stuers 1960: 154, 162–4; Wieringa 1993: 28). 'Women were pressured to feel that men needed jobs more than they did in order to support their families, and for the sake of "harmony" and "stability" in general, women gave in' (Suryakusuma 1982: 13; also Locher-Scholten & Niehof 1992, pp.43–4; Sjahrir 1985: 14–15; Wieringa 1993: 28).

The New Order steadfastly connected its development ideologies and policies with very limited notions of women's feminine *kodrat* (intrinsic character or God-given nature). Saskia Wieringa notes that the New Order definition of female *kodrat* demanded that women be obedient, self-sacrificing and submissive. 'This *kodrat* entails that women are *lemah lembut* (soft and weak), don't speak loudly and certainly not in their own interests, don't push their own interests against those of husbands and fathers, but are instead docile wives and mothers and dutiful daughters' (Wieringa 1993: 26). In his autobiography, Soeharto (1989a: 299) says that 'improving the role of women without disavowing their *kodrat* is the key to future development success'. In describing a woman's contribution to development, he allows that: 'She may have a career, but she may not sacrifice her duties as mother of the household.' This description of women's function does not engage with the possibility that women may be childless or unmarried or that they might have positions and powers independent of their wife and mother roles.

The *Repelita* (Five Year Development Plans) passed between 1974 to 1998 also defined women as contributing to national development in their roles as wives, mothers and homemakers. Although early New Order policies failed to recognise women as workers (Sen 1998: 39), the Ministry of Women's Affairs' 'women and development' program began encouraging the concept of the *peran ganda wanita* (dual roles of women) in the late 1970s. This allowed women to participate directly in economic development through paid labour as long as this work did not interfere with their wife-mother duties. From 1983, the development plans and the Broad Outlines of State Policy (GBHN) increasingly focused on the *peran ganda*, but tightly circumscribed women's participation in the public sphere through continual reference to women's *kodrat*.

The legal framework was also driven by a 'different but equal' ideology in which men were meant to protect, provide for and represent the family in the political and economic sphere while women fulfilled the family's physical and emotional needs at home (Sullivan 1991: 80; Sullivan 1994: 111–14). One of many examples is the 1974 Marriage Law (Law No. 1/1974), which explicitly defines the husband as head of and provider for the household while the wife is mother and homemaker. The New Order philosophy and legal framework thus appeared to follow the Hegelian definition of husband and wife as the 'active middle term' of the whole, with the man drawing his wife into 'the light of day and to conscious [universal] existence' of public life and the woman grounding her husband in the particular and the emotional of a healthy family life (Hegel 1977: § 463).

Wives, mothers and patriarchal politics

The impact of integralistic philosophies was seen at a practical level in the organisations that represented women in society and politics. The New Order coopted women into its corporatist structure by establishing 'non-political' women's groups that heavily emphasised wife-mother roles. The wives of all male civil servants, for example, were obliged to join *Dharma Wanita* (Women's Duty), while the wives of military and police personnel had to join *Dharma Pertiwi* (Earth Mother's Duty). Other women were recruited into the New Order's development mission through the PKK (*Pembinaan Kesejahteraan Keluarga*, Family Welfare Movement). When the government announced in 1973 that all citizens and not just the state would be responsible for national development, it outlined a crucial role for married women. The PKK became a central institution for encouraging women to better fulfil a combined wife–mother–development agent role (Rustam 1986: 77; Sullivan 1994: 129). The PKK placed women's roles as wife and mother over their citizenship, by defining the *Panca Dharma Wanita* (Five Duties of Women) as being:

- the loyal supporter of her husband,
- the caretaker of the household,
- the producer of future generations,
- the family's prime socialiser, and
- an Indonesian citizen (Hull 1996: 95; Sullivan 1991: 64)

Although the PKK's millions of 'volunteers' were women, its programs were 'designed by men to support an authoritarian, in its own words "paternalist", state structure and to uphold male authority in the family' (Wieringa 1993: 25).

The position that women held in these groups directly mirrored the position that their husbands held in the political or bureaucratic hierarchy. The PKK, which ran under the auspices of the Department of Home Affairs, was headed at the national level by the wife of the Home Affairs minister. The wife of the *bupati* (rural district or regency) led the PKK at the rural level, the wife of the mayor (*walaikota*) led the city level, and the wife of the RW (local level administrative unit) chief led the local level (Cooley 1992: 239; Rustam 1986: 79–80; Sullivan 1994: 60–1). *Dharma Wanita* and *Dharma Pertiwi* followed similar organisational structures, where a woman's organisational role was determined by her husband's administrative position rather than her personal talents, application or ambition. The structure thus attempted to bind husband and wife into one neat package, with the identity of the husband representing the social, economic and political standing of the total entity. Although more than one-third of civil servants are women, there are no corresponding husbands' organisations to help men support female public servants.

Julia Suryakusuma (1996) finds that these wives' organisations created what she calls State Ibuism (State Motherism), an overlaying of gender and bureaucratic power hierarchies in a formula in which the state controlled civil servants, who controlled their wives, who reciprocally controlled their husbands and the wives of junior officials (Suryakusuma 1996: 96; also Suryochondro 1984: 175–7). The *Panca Krida* (Five Creeds) of New Order's Fifth Development Cabinet, describes national development as being pioneered by honourable civil servants, who are 'supported by a harmonious family life' that enables them to perform state duties 'without being disturbed by family problems' (Surayakusuma 1996: 97). These wives provided the supportive daily functions necessary for the operation of a strong military and government apparatus (Suryakusuma 1996: 95, 114) and to implement its developmental philosophies across society. Gender policy thus underpinned the integralistic, developmentalist system that the New Order had infused into all sectors of social, political and economic institutions.

3   The era of 'reform'

The New Order's legitimacy finally disintegrated following the collapse of the economy from late 1997. The value of the Rupiah plummeted, inflation spiralled and, due to the high number of companies with debts in foreign dollars, 60 to 80 per cent of listed businesses were considered technically bankrupt. Millions lost their jobs. It was estimated that 56 per cent of the population was living below the poverty line (*Kompas* 18 June 1998: 8). Although the figures regarding the numbers of people living in poverty were later revised downwards (see Booth 2000), they were given credence at the time, and reinforced the sense of economic and socio-political stagnation. The New Order's main performance legitimisers of order, stability and development had clearly fallen apart by mid 1998. The period was characterised by escalating protests, riots, outbreaks of violence and several arson attacks in which thousands lost their lives. Demonstrations were held almost daily about KKN (*Korupsi, Kolusi dan Nepotisme*, Corruption, Collusion and Nepotism). Heated calls for Soeharto's retirement were made by students and intellectuals, and as time progressed, by bureaucrats and military figures. After losing the support of his main allies, Soeharto's relinquished the presidency on 21 May 1998 to his deputy, B.J. Habibie.

Habibie had little popular support outside his home region of Sulawesi. Although he had a tentative alliance with ABRI Chief Wiranto, he was disliked by many important ABRI figures, who resented his increasing control over the procurement of arms and defence equipment since the 1980s. This had robbed ABRI of profitable commissions and much of its independence during the late New Order period. The new president shored up his fragile position by supporting the *reformasi* (reform) movement and abandoning classic integralistic policies and discourses. He promised to change the government's authoritarian ways, calling for reform of the military, expressing regret for the state's past human-rights' abuses and pledging action against the 'disease' of corruption (Spencer 1998). Reversing previous philosophies of the wise and powerful father-figure leader, Habibie's adviser, Dewi Fortuna Anwar, claimed it was good that her president was 'a weak leader with no major political force of his own'. She said this provided 'an opportunity to prevent the rise of another strongman and personal rule' (*Straits Times* 14 Aug. 1998). A series of international conventions on human rights, on the elimination of torture and protecting the right to organise were signed in 1998 to signal the leadership's commitment to altering the balance of power in society.

The major institutions of state and public life immediately began work on self reform – or at least publicising efforts that created a public image that reform was underway. Within weeks of Soeharto's departure, Golkar was planning progressive internal restructuring, including the abolition of its Supervisory Council and rescinding restrictions on bureaucrats' involvement in political parties (Reuters 7 Jul. 1998; *Jakarta Post* 5 Jan. 1999: 2). The renaming of the 'Golkar Party' acknowledges the organisation's party-political nature. The courts also sought to free themselves from the power of the executive through autonomous administration (*Kompas* 15 Jun. 1998: 7). A rapid boom occurred in the numbers of NGOs because of two factors. The first arose because the state simply stopped tightly regulating and monitoring their existence. The second sprung from a surge of international aid money to NGOs that had the ostensible aims of monitoring election processes, facilitating democratic growth and related targets. Many of these NGOs have indeed provided critical support to support the poor and engaged in other activities that aid political or economic development. However, with little scrutiny of such groups, many failed to fulfil their self-appointed social or humanitarian charters.

While it took decades during the New Order for workers to win restricted rights to affiliate and organise, it took Habibie just four days to announce that all unions would be permitted 'as long as they support *Pancasila* and aim to increase the welfare, safety and professionalism of workers' (*Kompas* 26 May 1998: 6). Despite the loaded proviso that unions had to 'support *Pancasila*' – with the potential that future governments might re-interpret the definition of what supporting *Pancasila* involved – the official position conceded that unions had a role in protecting worker welfare as well as raising professionalism. Within a fortnight, the new government ratified Convention No. 87 of the International Labour Organisation, which states that all workers have the right to establish and join organisations of their own choosing. Union bodies declared illegitimate during the New Order, such as the SBSI, were officially recognised (*Kompas Online* 3 Jun. 1998). This was subsequently reinforced by Law No. 21 of 2000, which enshrines the rights to form and join unions and other worker organisations. It furthermore forbids attempts to intimidate union organisers, union members or their campaigns or interfere with or halt the formation of unions.

In the reformist climate, ABRI expressed a commitment to trimming its political role (*Jakarta Post* 5 Aug. 1998a: 2). The exposure of past military violence and harassment of citizens eventually motivated several key ABRI leaders to acknowledge that wide-scale human-rights abuses had occurred. They blamed such conduct on the New Order paradigms and orders under which the military operated (Crouch 1999: 136–7). After extensive debate as to the appropriate representation of the military in parliament, the number of ABRI and police designates in the DPR was reduced to 38 in the 500-member house, while 10 per cent of seats were allocated to the ABRI/police faction in regional parliamentary bodies. However, Golkar leaders opposed ABRI's plans to sever connections from the organisation (*Jakarta Post* 6 Jan. 1999b: 1), and ABRI leaders made a conscious decision to interfere with the process of selecting Golkar's General Chairman at its July 1998 congress (Crouch 1999: 131–2).

Following an end to restrictions on forming political parties, 98 parties met the February 1999 deadline to register with an independent screening body to contest the June 1999 election. Forty-eight of these parties were deemed eligible to compete in the campaign, which focused on personalities and political identity rather than any substantive discussion of policies. Despite widespread fears both locally and internationally that the elections might be marred by widespread unrest or bloodshed, the administration was generally smooth and the atmosphere often party-like, with some exceptions, especially in hotspots like Aceh and Maluku. This led to optimism that Indonesia's democratisation process would progress successfully.

The PDI-P, led by Sukarno's daughter, Megawati, was the most successful party, yet it fell short of achieving an outright majority, with 153 seats. Support for Golkar dropped to about one-third of the levels it enjoyed during New Order elections, at 120 seats. However, the figure was still enough to make it the second-largest party in parliament. Golkar's strong electoral performance resulted from its well-entrenched networks and support mechanisms across the nation. The five largest parties – which, in order of size, were the PDI-P, Golkar, the PPP, PKB and PAN – won 416 seats in the national parliament, while 16 smaller parties won the remaining 46 contestable seats.

Under the Constitution, Habibie was entitled to remain president until 2003, serving out the remainder of the 1998–2003 term in office. However, with his credibility and integrity under question following the Bank Bali financial scandal and other problems, the MPR held presidential elections at the end of 1999. Although Megawati had the most support among the populace, she lacked the skill and political will to lead the PDI-P into the kinds of coalitions with Golkar and certain other parties that it needed to obtain a majority in the 700-member MPR. PKB leader Wahid – aided by his former rival, PAN's ambitious leader Amien Rais – engineered sufficient support among the factions to win him the presidency, but the process left him vulnerable to the disparate demands of his newly found assortment of political allies (see Mietzner 2000). Wahid's appointment was rationalised by claims that it would avoid bloodshed between the disappointed followers of the PDI-P and Golkar if a leader from either of those opposing parties became president. It also tapped into debates about the unsuitability of a woman as head of a predominantly Islamic nation.

Compromising politics

Wahid – a moderate Islamic scholar who had previously chaired Nahdlatul Ulama (NU), a traditionalist Islamic organisation with 35-million members – may have appeared a suitable compromise choice because he was one of the few

Indonesians with extensive leadership experience whose reputation had not been heavily tainted by connections to New Order corruption and repression. However, Wahid's administration was hampered from the start, because the makeup of his 'rainbow cabinet' was coloured by the favours he owed as a result of his political machinations in his run for the presidency. Several subsequent reshuffles failed to create a team that could cooperate while providing a balance of skills. Wahid's eccentric leadership was characterised by long absences on overseas trips, *ad hoc* and personalised decision-making, frequent changes in political direction with the aim of unbalancing his opponents, and undisciplined public comments that he often had to withdraw or clarify. His well-known foibles of inconsistency and disregard for regulations soon alienated many of his supporters in parliament and cabinet, erased his efforts to build partnerships with old political adversaries, and damaged his previously high social standing.

The economy, which had stabilised in 1999, initially remained relatively steady in 2000 despite a rise in inflation. As political infighting and community unrest continued in early 2001, the value of the Rupiah again dwindled, inflation crept inexorably upwards and official forecasts of economic growth for the year were revised downwards. The IMF questioned Indonesia's commitment to economic reform, suspending loans disbursements as a punishment on several occasions.

The suffering caused by a faltering economy was compounded by the ongoing regional ethnic, religious and separatist conflicts that had flared in the late Soeharto, Habibie and Wahid eras. In many cases, problems emerged as regional socio-political leaders took advantage of the change in the national political culture to pursue various political and economic interests by reviving long-standing ethnic and religious divides. The resultant violence left thousands dead and an estimated million displaced from their homes in pressure points such as Kalimantan, Ambon, Maluku, Aceh, Irian Jaya/West Papua, East Timor (both prior to and immediately following the 1999 referendum that led to Timorese independence), and the border between East and West Timor. Although the roots of these conflicts had developed long before Wahid's presidency, the continuing failure of the administration to resolve or in many cases to even ameliorate the situation reflected poorly on both his administration and his lack of power to command the military to take appropriate action.

Much governmental power moved from the executive to the DPR, but despite its acerbic debates, the parliament produced little tangible progress. The DPR was set an official target of finalising 64 laws in 2000–1 under the Wahid leadership. By May 2001, less than 10 had been ratified (astaga.com 3 May 2001). By comparison, 69 new laws were passed in the 17 months of Habibie's leadership.

The struggle for legitimacy

With the rules of engagement between the three estates and civil society subject to reconsideration, contestation and revision, this period was characterised by the efforts of different political sectors to establish their powers as decision-makers and to depreciate the legitimacy of competing centres of influence. Struggles emerged between the executive, legislature, judiciary, police and ABRI over acceptance of the authority of others to make decisions. Wahid's ability to realise policies and plans was poor, with the military sometimes ignoring instructions and administrative staff often failing to implement cabinet decisions. Wahid himself was accused of interfering with matters outside his jurisdiction. This included demanding the Central Bank governor resign and dismissing and appointing a replacement national police chief in 2000 without consulting parliament, as is required by decree. In 2001, when Wahid tried to suspend Suroyo Bimantoro, his replacement national police chief, Bimantoro turned the tables by refusing to hand over the trappings of office, arguing that the president did not have the authority to change the head of police without parliament's approval.

Corruption remained entrenched in the system, despite the investigation of government and business leaders and the successful prosecutions and jailing of a few kingpins such as Mohamad (Bob) Hasan. Public trust in the government's commitment towards combating the centres of corruption was lowered by the dismissal of investigations into the activities of several Golkar figures. Public disillusionment was also exacerbated when Soeharto's son, Tommy, disappeared just before he was due to commence an 18-month sentence over a corrupt land-swap deal and the South Jakarta District Court refused to hear corruption charges against Soeharto on the basis of his ill health.

Allegations that Wahid had been involved in two multi-million dollar corruption cases precipitated his political downfall. The so-called Bruneigate and Buloggate scandals, which involved irregularities in the use of Rp35 billion (US$3.6 million) fund belonging to Bulog (*Badan Urusan Logistik*, the National Logistics Agency) and a US$2 million donation made to Wahid by the Sultan of Brunei. Wahid was not perceived to have personally enriched himself in the way of Soeharto and his children had done. However, these cases became a weapon to discipline a president who was unable to deliver political openness, regulated and reliable systems of government, economic prosperity or social stability. Parliament called on Wahid to explain his involvement in Bruneigate and Buloggate, and it also demanded answers about various other controversial actions, such as the sackings of cabinet ministers for alleged corruption. Wahid's inconsistent and incomplete answers on these issues and his disregard for official procedures increased the weaponry of those wishing to remove him.

Wahid tried to stem the damage by removing problematic ministers through repeated cabinet reshuffles and disputing the legal validity of the procedures that the parliament used to interrogate him. As his grip on power weakened, he explored the possibility of imposing a state of civil emergency, suspending the parliament and arresting political opponents. His senior ministers, ABRI and the police rejected such options. The Attorney General cleared Wahid in 2001 of wrongdoing in the Bruneigate and Buloggate cases in May, but by that stage the list of complaints by those trying to topple him had changed from corruption to his overall performance and policies. He was accused of violating his presidential oath, which requires the president to faithfully implement the laws and other regulations.

As moves to impeach Wahid gained momentum in 2001, mobs numbering several thousand vandalised Golkar offices in Jakarta and East Java. In April 2001, thousands publicly pledged to defend Wahid if necessary, with some even vowing to fight to the death. This reflected the general pattern of relations between the state and civil society, in which politics centred on the mobilisation rather than the participation of the masses. It became commonplace for political parties, interest groups, the military and police to agitate or pay people to engage in mass demonstrations and even violence under the banner of 'religious', 'ethnic' or other 'community' interests (see Lindsey 2001: 4). Elite groups then pointed to these expressions of 'popular' support as proof of the legitimacy of their favoured causes.

The end of Wahid's presidency typified the nature of the power plays that occur key political institutions. In his final days in power, Wahid warned that he had mass public support and could not be responsible for the consequences if he was impeached. At 1 a.m. on 23 July 2001, he issued a decree that declared a state of emergency, suspended the parliament and the MPR from further meetings, dissolved the Golkar Party and prepared for new elections to be held in the next 12 months. Alternative sources of state power rallied against him. The Supreme Court ruled that Wahid lacked the constitutional power to dissolve the legislature. ABRI and the police, which had earlier refused to implement Wahid's state of emergency, protected the MPR session that day. MPR delegates voted, as had been expected, to end Wahid's 21-month rule and appoint Megawati in his place. The struggle over who had constitutional decision-making power over whom was prolonged when Wahid refused for several hours to acknowledge the MPR's decision or leave the presidential palace. He subsequently congratulated Megawati on her promotion and left the palace voluntarily a few days later. The feared backlash from NU and other Wahid supporters never emerged, with the exception of some small actions, including some small 'bomb' explosions that were described as being like firecracker blasts. The relative community calm was attributed to NU's entreaty for its supporters to respond to Wahid's dismissal with quiet prayer rather than violence.

Women and political brinkmanship

Wahid's removal brought Indonesia its first female president, but in general, women appear to have been the subject of brutal political manipulation in the transitional era between one government to another. The closing weeks of the New Order were marked by a period of violence that included the apparently systematic rape of ethnic Chinese women in Jakarta and four other cities. Despite wide-ranging perspectives on the scale and significance of the May 1998 rapes, many analysts argue that sexual violence was a mechanism used by elements of the patriarchal, militaristic state to attempt to assume political control (e.g. Ariva 1998; Sukidi 1998; Rahayu 1999). The newly appointed Habibie government responded by issuing a decree to form the National Commission on Violence Against Women, but the slow and inconclusive investigations into the attacks were much criticised (e.g. Leksono-Supelli 1998). Additionally, Soeharto's resignation meant little to the pattern of politically motivated sexual assaults against women in areas of national political tension, such as East Timor, Aceh and Irian Jaya.

In mainstream politics, the delegitimation of the patriarchal government did not necessarily translate into benefits for women. When Megawati became vice-president in 1999, she reached the highest public office ever held by a woman in the republic. However, her career path also stands as an example of the continuing politicisation of gender. Her failure to reach the number one position in 1999 was not surprising, given reservations about her policy-formulating skills and leadership abilities. Much debate about Megawati's suitability for the presidency, however, was couched in religious terms, with many of her opponents claiming that Islamic teachings forbade women from holding such high public office. Several, including Wahid, launched indirect attacks by suggesting that Indonesians were not ready for a woman president (*Republika* 27 Nov. 1998: 8; 2000: Platzdasch 2000: 343–7). The debates mimicked those that had occurred in 1997, when the prospect of Soeharto's daughter Tutut reaching the vice-presidency or presidency was the subject of public speculation. The view that women should not take leadership positions appears inconsistent with public opinion. An official survey, conducted to keep politicians in touch with popular concerns, found that 62 per cent of a stratified random sample of 3,000 Indonesians agreed with a woman becoming president (Konsorsium Lembaga Pengumpul Pendapat Umum 2000: L–5).

Paradoxically, Wahid – who had helped revived the gender debate in the lead-up to the 1999 presidential elections in an apparent attempt to boost support for his own bid for the presidency – had previously been involved in stimulating debate on gender equity during his period as NU chairman. He was among many leading Islamic figures to dismiss claims that the Koran prohibited women from the presidency and other leadership positions (Wahid 1999: 37–8). His wife Sinta Nuriyah, who holds a Masters degree in women's studies, also publicly and prominently promoted gender equity, and she continued to do so during her 21-month period as First Lady.

It became evident in 2000 and 2001 that many of those who claimed that the Koran bans women from such high postings were acting from political rather than religious motives. As efforts increased throughout 2000 and 2001 to remove Wahid from the presidency, many politicians and party figures who had objected to Megawati becoming president on the grounds of religion and gender reversed their position and began to support her elevation to the top job. In revising their stance, some adopted new arguments that a woman can be an acceptable president, as long as she is a practicing Muslim. Others invoked the Constitution, which states that if a president should be replaced by the vice-president if the former is incapacitated, resigns or is unable to complete a designated term of office. They claimed that the interpretations of religious law had to take these constitutional stipulations into account when deciding on Megawati's suitability for the presidency (*Media Indonesia* 4 Mar. 2001: 1; Nurdi 2001: 8). Megawati successfully played to the changing mood, by making efforts to be publicly seen wearing headscarves and attending religious activities, thus making it easier for those who had previously rejected her on the basis of her gender to reverse their position and support her on the basis of her religious affiliation.

Women's empowerment

Official policies relating to women no longer stress women's *kodrat*. Instead, they focus on women's *pemberdayaan* (empowerment) in education and in the legal, political, socio-cultural and economic spheres. The need to build the quality and independence of women's organisations is also recognised (Badan Perencanaan Pembangunan 1999: 210). The brief section in the 1999–2004 GBHN on women (Ch. IV, F3) talks of raising their position and status and of improving women's organisations with the aim of empowering women and raising family and community welfare. The Development Planning Board acknowledges that women's *peran ganda* is in fact a *beban ganda* (a double burden). The Board also finds that women's status and role in community life is yet to be equalised with that of men, as they are subordinated, marginalised and subjected to discrimination (Badan Perencanaan Pembangunan 1999: 209).

In the spirit of *reformasi*, wives' auxiliary associations have undergone major reconstruction. For example, *Dharma Wanita* ended its affiliations with Golkar and changed its name in December 1999 to *Dharma Wanita Persatuan*, to show a paradigm shift towards empowering women. Civil servants' wives are no longer obliged to join the association, and the leadership is decided through the democratic vote of members rather than women's marital links. The PKK has also examined its organisational structure and redirected its focus from *pembinaan* (guidance) towards *pemberdayaan* (empowerment).

The Wahid government attempted to signal its commitment to women's empowerment by adopting *perempuan* as its standard expression for 'woman' instead of *wanita*, which was favoured by the New Order. Although both words mean woman, some feminists argue that *perempuan* should be used because it is based on the word *empu*, which refers to someone honoured and respected because of his/her learning and knowledge, ability, spiritual depth or wisdom. *Wanita* is a derivative of the Javanese words *wani ditata* (willing to be guided). Within the government apparatus, the Ministry of State for the Administration of Women's Affairs changed its name twice to become the Ministry of State for Empowerment of Women (*Kementerian Negara Pemberdayaan Perempuan*). The name change reflected the Ministry's move away from being a conduit of programs managing women's contribution to national development towards a new role of redistributing power within a patriarchal system. The aim is to 'mainstream' gender policies into all aspects of government and to reform several laws that define wives as second to their husbands, such as the laws on marriage, citizenship, labour/the work force, health and taxation. However, during the Wahid era, then State Minister for Empowerment of Women Khofifah Indar Parawansa admitted that ministerial coordination and cabinet meetings were dominated by 'talking about the latest emergencies', and it was 'hard to get gender on the agenda' (Johanson 2001: 4).

Post-New Order governments have thus made some efforts to alter the dominant patriarchal political discourses. However, it may take years if not decades before the changes result in increased participation of women in formal politics or recognition of women's issues as politically significant. All political parties that contested the 1999 elections recognised imbalances in gender relations, but none pushed women's issues in their political agenda (Khamami 2000). Although 57 per cent of voters in 1999 were women, women only constituted 8.8 per cent of members in the DPR. The trend is negative compared to 1997, when 51 per cent of voters were women, but women constituted 11.2 per cent of DPR members (BPS 2000a: 59). Ironically, because the end of Soeharto's patriarchal government has also been accompanied by high-profile anti-KKN campaigns, senior male political figures are no longer bold enough to nominate their wives and children as candidates for political positions. This has reduced the pool of females in the DPR and MPR (BPS 2000a: 59). The decrease has prompted calls for quotas for women to comprise 25 and even 30 per cent of the legislature and executive (*Media Indonesia* 5 Jan. 2001; *Suara Pembaruan* 20 Oct. 2000).

The women who are politically active are often relegated to less prestigious positions. Khofifah argues that: 'If women are in the leadership, it is usually as treasurer. That is regarded as a housewife's job!' (Johanson 2001: 5). She furthermore warns that the numbers of women in politics may fall again if the proposed new general elections act changes the system from a proportional to a district system of voting (Johanson 2001: 4).

Moving on with Megawati

The recent instalment of Megawati to the presidency is seen as a positive step towards overcoming the political deadlocks that emerged during the Wahid era. However, she is reputed to have little ability to generate new policy. Many of her public statements as vice-president were prefaced with the words 'according to Brother Dur' (a reference to Wahid's popular nickname, Gus Dur). She is considered in many ways to be as conservative as politicians of the New Order period, with her strong attachment to the 1945 Constitution and traditional concepts of nationalism. Although Megawati and her supporters suffered at the hands of ABRI in 1996, military leaders are generally closer to her than they were to Wahid. She welcomes senior ABRI figures to her home, and they appear to believe that she shares their basic values.

Megawati's oratory style is also considered to resemble the 'old model' of both the Sukarno and Soeharto eras, relying heavily on emotions rather than rationality (Mashuri 1999: 3). She maintains the 'traditional Javanese' inscrutable political style that was a feature of the New Order. This involves subtle and indirect mechanisms for expressing difference, rather than straightforward communications of concern or conflict. Before she was appointed to the presidency, political analysts spent more time attempting to determine what her silence on key issues and absence from major political forums might mean, as she made relatively few explicit statements on matters of public importance.

This book refers to periods of history such as the New Order, the Habibie era, the Wahid era and the Megawati era. This is to indicate to the reader which period of time that various phenomena are related to. However, there is no tidy division between the political cultures of one era and another. Although the New Order refers, in a formal sense, to the period of Soeharto's rule, the New Order did not neatly end when Soeharto resigned. Most contemporary political figures were politically active during the New Order, and parliament is still predominated by figures from that era. Many of the old philosophies remain strong for leaders such as Megawati and her allies. Many of these figures claim to be reformist, but in fact owe their position and power to their active involvement in Soeharto's patriarchal system. Many individuals and social groups have taken advantage of the post-New Order state of political flux to agitate for 'reform'. Some are motivated by a genuine desire for social, economic and political equity, while others are merely cynically attempting to build popular support by associating themselves with the reform movement.

The reform process has been uneven and could be reversed by a future government with less need to establish credibility through the appearance of responsiveness to community pressure. In particular, the old *dwi fungsi* logic appears to dominate military thinking. Although the police were separated from the military through MPR Decree No. 7 in 2000, there remains a poor distinction between external defence and internal security. As internal security also involves politics, military figures believe that important political issues should involve ABRI (Purba 2001: 4). Thus the integralistic ideologies of guardianship still endure. The MPR has also guaranteed ABRI and the police a block of seats in parliament until 2009, opting for a very gradual rather than rapid phasing out of the *dwi fungsi*. This increases the possibility that the *dwi fungsi* could be revived or revised before the end of the decade.

Journalists and the political structure

The transitional period has heralded considerable change in the news media. At the end of the New Order, only 289 publications had licences to publish. Once Soeharto stood down, the government immediately began interpreting its strict SIUPP legislation very loosely, granting publication licences to anyone who requested one. It is estimated that between the time of Soeharto's resignation and the September 1999 passage of Law No. 40 on the Press, the Department of Information handed out 1,800 to 2,000 licenses (Wisudo 2000). The 1999 Law rescinded the requirement for publications to obtain SIUPP licences, meaning that new publications can be set up at will. In mid-2001, the parliament was still considering a new broadcast law, but a relaxation of regulation has again meant new radio and television stations have been permitted to set up and operate.

The remaining chapters of this book discuss how the revocation of strict, formal state controls on the press and other socio-political institutions has affected the workplace cultures and operations of the media. The following chapters describe how the New Order leadership culture – which, in the style of the old Javanese kingdoms, removed leaders from obligations to subject themselves to public scrutiny – had major implications for journalists at both the individual and occupational level. It also explores how the ongoing changes in the political culture – which has liberalised and yet maintained many entrenched trends from the New Order era – has led to a new range of challenges as a hitherto unexpected array of economic problems, community pressures and professional conundrums emerge. Similarly, the high-speed and erratic transition process has created observable changes at the most fundamental level in the activities and expectations of individuals, news organisations and occupational groups.

4   The enigma of the *Pancasila* journalist

Indonesian media theorist Ashadi Siregar notes that most discussion by academics, bureaucrats and journalists about his country's press has been of a normative nature (Siregar 1995a: 4). Normative theory identifies dominant social values and how the mass media should ideally operate if they are to encompass such values (McQuail 1987: 4). The guiding premise of such theorists has long been that 'the press always takes on the form and coloration of the social and political structures within which it operates. Especially, it reflects the system of social control whereby the relations of individuals and institutions are adjusted' (Siebert, Peterson & Schramm 1956: 1–2). Societies rarely explicitly outline their own media theories, so scholars usually examine the many, often conflicting social conventions, ideologies, rules, laws and constitutional provisions when attempting to derive normative theories of the press (McQuail 1987: 109–10).

Normative theories posit that the true relationship between social systems and the press can be understood by examining social beliefs regarding the nature of human beings, knowledge and truth, and relationships between individuals and the state. Normative theories expose the connections between social understandings of truth, the masses and the state on the one hand and press ownership, functions, controls and taboos on the other. Using such an approach, it would be possible for anyone to guess what the characteristics of a country's press would be like, by observing particular elements of the country's socio-political characteristics (as listed in Box 1 in Figure 4.1). Alternatively, it would be easy to guess what that country's dominant political culture was like, merely from studying the elements of that country's press characteristics (as listed in Box 2).

Raymond Williams (1966) stipulates, however, that merely listing a series of values, characteristics and roles for an idealised press model is unlikely to lead to the realisation of such a press system. In other words, governments, journalists or citizens can write down any set of characteristics that they would like to see in Box 2, but those characteristics will not emerge unless the social and political cultures support such a set of characteristics. Theorists who wish to devise a model to explain any country's media culture must first engage in systematic observation and analysis of the country's historic and present conditions and the processes through which media cultures may become consistent with democratic

Box 1: Characteristics of Society
- *Historical Context*
- *Dominant Understanding of the Nature of the 'Masses'*
- *Dominant Understanding of the Nature of Truth*
- *Dominant Understanding of the Nature of State Power*

Relationship mediated by the nature of
the legal system, especially
laws affecting the mass media

Box 2: Characteristics of the Press
- *Dominant Understanding of Appropriate Forms of Media Ownership*
- *Dominant Understanding of the Press's Social Role*
- *Level of State, Legal or Community Control of the Press*
- *Taboos on Reporting Particular Topics*

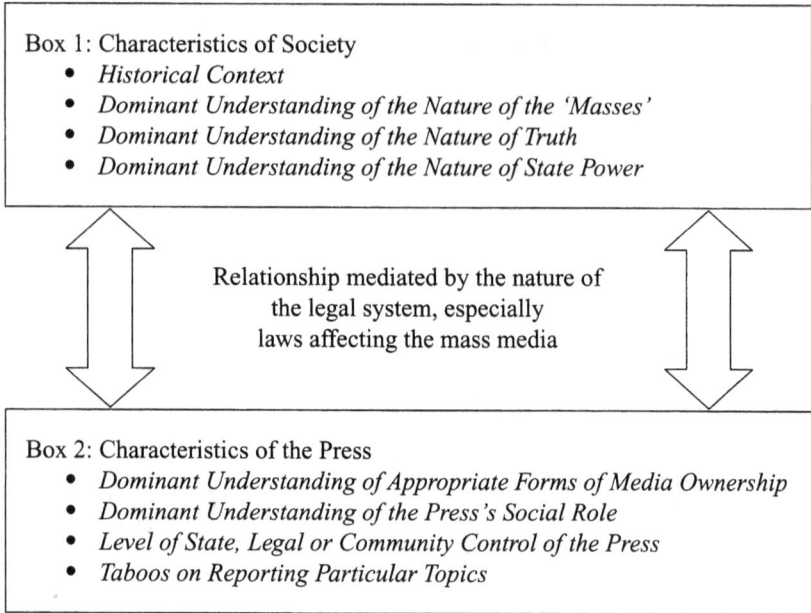

Figure 4.1 Interrelation of socio-political and media cultures

cultures, resources and institutions (Williams 1966: 120–3). Williams' comments, although made almost four decades ago, remain relevant in examining Indonesia's *Pancasila* and development press model.

Development, but what kind?

Development-journalism theories arose in the late twentieth century when many developing states, which had thrown off the yoke of colonialism in previous decades, attempted to formulate appropriate models of journalistic roles and practice in accordance with their desires to establish independent national identities. Dominant paradigms on development journalism have mirrored changes in wider discourses about the nature of development and the ways in which the mass media assists that development.

Study of development communications often grew out of post-WWII agricultural extension programs, with universities in the United States and the Philippines running training courses on how to effectively communicate about agricultural development policies (Quebral 1975: 197; Stevenson 1994: 232). In line with the post-war development philosophies, promulgated by economists such as Walter Rostow (1960) and Everett Hagen (1962), development was envisaged mainly in terms of economic growth. It was argued that such growth was hampered in developing countries by perceived internal deficiencies and lack of entrepreneurialism. Adopting Rostow's notions of economic take off, Lucian Pye (1963), Daniel Lerner (1958), Wilbur Schramm (1964), E. Lloyd

Sommerland (1966) and other theorists encouraged the use of the modern mass media to stimulate a sense of national cohesion and to displace the traditional values that they assumed hindered economic progress. They expected to mobilise human resources by substituting these traditional values with Western norms, attitudes, systems of rationality and behaviours that would supposedly enhance upward mobility, industrialisation and modernisation (e.g. Lerner 1958: 43–75; Pool 1963: 249). Journalism, in particular, was seen as a means of providing objective, impartial analysis of political and social processes (Pye 1963).

Many modernisation theorists revised their approach in the 1970s. They acknowledged that their programs had not produced the desired economic development, and that economic growth on its own was no guarantee of any improvement in living conditions (Chenery et al. 1974: xiii; Goulet 1996: 544). Communications theorists attributed the failures in their earlier hypotheses to their 'top-down' approach and advocated greater emphasis on interpersonal networks and interactions of media audiences in order to mobilise the people (e.g. Rogers & Shoemaker 1971; Rogers 1976). While the amended theories emphasised social context and elevated the position of media audiences, many were still based on the same assumptions as the earlier theories, merely shifting the focus from source to receiver and adding feedback loops (e.g. Rogers 1976: 233; Melkote 1991: 166).

Structuralist theorists attacked the basis of these development approaches. Realising in the 1960s that sovereignty had not brought economic emancipation or improvements in quality of life, many developing nations demanded reform of both international economic and communications systems. Cultural-dependency theorists and NWICO (New World Information and Communication Order) proponents built upon older critiques of colonialism and imperialism. They blamed Western monopolisation and manipulation of the media for perpetuating international and local inequalities and for imposing inappropriate Western values and cultural frames on developing societies (e.g. Mattelart 1979; Nordenstreng 1986; Schiller 1969; Tartarian 1978). Although the superiority and utility of Western modernity were contested, the mass media was still perceived as a tool that could aid education and engender national unity.

A third wave of theorists critiqued the basic constructs of both modernisation and structuralist approaches, foregrounding concepts such as quality of life and human dignity. Arguing that the economic development debate obscured the underlying systemic inequalities that prevented true 'human development', they attempted to develop new measures as an alternative to economic statistics to measure each nation's quality of life and success in meeting human needs (e.g. Gall 1996; Griffin & Knight 1996; Haq 1995; UNDP 1998a). Some preferred to speak of liberation rather than development because liberation denotes the control of a populace over change and oppressive elements, while development mainly stresses the material benefits that result from change without regard to problems in the process of change (e.g. Goulet 1996: 544–8; Hedebro 1982: 103–5).

Brazilian educator Paulo Freire inspired many such theorists with his contention that conventional communication and education – which aim to 'fill' the 'empty' spaces of the passive students' minds – maintain the domination, domestication and dehumanisation of the masses (Freire 1974: 2–3; Freire 1997: 52–3). His proposed 'pedagogy of the oppressed' aims at 'liberation' through 'conscientisation' – encouraging critical and enquiring thinking which empowers individuals to understand the causes of social injustices and to organise effective action to influence the socio-cultural reality that shapes their lives (Freire 1974: 2; Freire 1997: 60). Development communication was conceptualised as an aid to the emancipation of deprived groups, helping them to participate in political process and empowering them to fulfil their destinies (Quebral 1975).

Freirian concepts were primarily adopted and disseminated by various non-government organisations. By contrast, cross-national governmental institutions – such as the United Nations Development Program (UNDP), World Bank and International Monetary Fund (IMF) – reformulated development philosophies by combining concepts of sustainable human development and good governance. The UNDP (1998b), for example, describes good governance as the political sector, business and civil society working together to promote sustainable human development for all, including the poorest and most marginalised. The basic characteristics of good governance are defined as participation, rule of law, transparency, responsiveness, consensus orientation, equity, effectiveness and efficiency, accountability and strategic vision (UNDP 1997: ch. 1). During the 1990s, the World Bank and IMF began promoting free-market principles in concert with good governance. Support for this approach was strengthened by economic research, which associates good governance with economic growth, reduced poverty and other development outcomes (e.g. Kaufmann, Kraay & Zoido-Lobatón 1999; Mauro 1995; Knach & Keefer 1995).

Development journalism

Development journalism evolved along synchronous although not identical lines to general development theories. Alan Chalkley coined the term 'development journalism' in 1968 after chairing the first long-term training course for economic writers. Regional media theorists and leading journalists formulated new visions for Asian journalism. They initially devised a liberal conceptualisation of development journalism in this era, which involved teaching journalists the reporting and writing skills required to provide comprehensive coverage of complex development processes in language simple enough for poorly educated mass audiences (Lent 1979: 66–7).

The concept of development journalism was also adopted by those in developing nations who expressed resentment at receiving Western news products that, catering to First World needs and values, were viewed as irrelevant and distorted (Szende 1986: 30). A common, continuing refrain of Indonesia and other developing nations is that First World journalists highlight the negative aspects of the developing nations – the coups, corruption, crises, catastrophes and chaos (Marpaung 1983: 28; Milne 1989: 447; Tartarian 1978: 6) – consistently overlooking change and progress. Proponents of this perspective argued that development journalism involves the advancing of 'positive news' that will provide momentum for development and balance the conflict-laden 'negative news' favoured by Western journalists. Such positive news encompasses economic, social and cultural issues arising from the struggle for stability and progress, particularly emphasising attempts to improve society, successful initiatives and individuals or institutions who have contributed to their communities (Ali 1994: 90; Marpaung 1983: 29; Oetama 1989: 144; Szende 1986: 38).

Positive news was not initially formulated to consist solely of 'sunshine stories'. Positive development journalism can involve reporting of negative issues as long as it avoids 'scare headlines' and sensationalism that may lead to or exacerbate existing social turmoil (Idid & Pawanteh 1989: 84). *Jakarta Post* editor Susanto Pudjomartono (1998: 105) describes such stories as 'constructive and corrective, but not destructive', because they do not overstep the line that separates useful news from that which causes unrest. Journalists are further advised to include details of causes and possible solutions when they examine developmental problems and disasters so that audiences can contribute to rectifying crises rather than being overcome by despair (Galtung & Vincent 1992: 13; Oetama 1989: 145).

Development journalism thus encompasses a strong sense of responsibility for the consequences of news reports. Debates on development journalism repeatedly involve discussions of the need to match journalistic freedoms with responsibilities. During the New Order, Indonesia accordingly defined its *Pancasila* press as a 'free and responsible press' (discussed further below), while Malaysian Prime Minister Mahathir Mohamad (1985: 213–15) describes the social-responsibility press model as the paramount of all models. Development journalism often crosses similar ideological territory to the paradigm of a free and responsible press first proposed in post-WWII U.S. and Britain – most notably by the 1947 U.S. Commission into Freedom of the Press, better known as the Hutchins Commission. However, the inherent resemblance between the development and Western social-responsibility models are rarely acknowledged.

Some supporters of the development- or positive-journalism approach also posit that freedom of the press should be restricted according to the nation's economic priorities and development needs (e.g. Mahathir 1985: 215; Soeharto 1989b: 132). They generally argue that 'order and stability are preconditions for economic growth, and that growth is the necessary foundation of any political order that claims to advance human dignity' (Kausikan 1994: 49; also Milne 1989: 448). Supporters of such a view of development journalism argued that the media should not engage in continuous, caustic attacks on the institutions of state, because their countries' 'fragile political structures cannot withstand this endless scrutiny' of their faults (Ng'weno 1978: 128; also Birch 1993: 20; Lent

1977: 18; Sommerland 1966: 142–3). Indonesia's New Order government supported such a model, regularly warning journalists that Western-style press freedom was a 'luxury' that might have adverse effects on public safety (van Dijk 1978: 129).

In societies where this model of development journalism is upheld, media production is also often described as a cooperative endeavour, in which the press is the state's 'partner' (Lim 1985: 103, 107; Loo 1995: 5–6). The media are meant to support the government, which works as the driver of the development engine, rather than to challenge it (Hachten 1987: 31). Journalists who deviate from officially sanctioned discourses are regularly accused of stirring social divisions, agitating interracial tensions and endangering the stability of the nation (Romano 1996: 158–9). In such a framework, information is often considered state property, hoarded by the centre, with the flow of information working from the top down (Hachten 1987: 31; Birch 1993: 29). In the case of Indonesia's New Order, authorities accepted that the media had a feedback function as a 'conduit for the people's aspirations' (Sinaga 1989: 132), but it was widely acknowledged that bottom-up communications were weak (e.g. Oetama 1989: 143). The critics of this press-as-government-handmaiden philosophy claim that the development journalism ethic had been coopted by governments as a mere apologia for dictatorial leaderships attempting to push their own ideologies and muzzle the press (Lent 1979: 67; Righter 1978: 189, 192; Sussman 1978: 77).

A third branch of development journalism, drawing from liberation and human development perspectives, also rejected the assumption that the state was the supreme, benevolent dictator of development policies. Theorists of this school define development journalism as an interactive, advocative and educational medium, which builds self-reliance and participant democracy (Hedebro 1982: 103–17; Ponteñila 1990: 22–4). Rather than merely top-down communications, there are also bottom-up and horizontal flows in which citizens share information with fellow citizens (Hester 1987: 9). Emphasis is placed on accessing the voices of the masses, including the marginalised, the minorities and the underprivileged (Dixit 1994: 23–4; Galtung & Vincent 1992: 163–5; Loo 1996: 122). Loo suggests that such journalism should be ethnographic, involving participant observation of communities and personal interaction with sources (1995: 8). Shah proposes that this type of journalism should be described as 'emancipatory journalism' because of the journalists' role as 'participants in a process of progressive social change' and 'challenging and changing oppressive structures' (1996: 144–5).

Concepts of good governance and sustainable human development have influenced a fourth branch of development journalism. As was discussed above, an important characteristic of good governance is transparency or, in other words, the timely release of reliable information about government activities. The UNDP, World Bank and IMF regard the mass media as important institutions that help to ensure governments communicate openly with citizens. This, in turn, enables the public to evaluate government actions and to pressure officials to act responsibly and efficiently. Inverting the logic that human rights may sometimes need to be sacrificed for the sake of economic development, the World Bank and similar institutions argue that restrictions on free speech, free press and other civil liberties are inimical to good governance and economic development. Civil-society organisations, such as the media among others, are seen as playing a crucial role in keeping governments honest and accountable; monitoring, protecting and promoting human rights; and routing out corruption (e.g. UNDP 1998b; Isham, Kaufmann & Pritchett 1997: 234–5; Stapenhurst 2000: 2–9). In this model, the media not only serves as a watchdog, warning of faults and problems in the system, but also acts as a channel for public opinion, providing communities with a voice in public affairs. IMF and World Bank leaders have become inclined, especially following the 1997 Asian economic crisis, to paraphrase the words of economist Armatya Sen (1990), that 'in the terrible history of famines in the world, there is hardly any case in which a famine has occurred in a country that is independent and democratic with an uncensored press'. The World Bank and similar organisations have attempted to encourage this form of development journalism by sponsoring courses in investigative journalism and other forms of advanced reporting.

Pancasila and authentic Indonesian values

True normative theories must closely match press roles and objectives with the socio-political values and organisation structures. With so many different definitions of development (or liberation or human development or emancipation or good governance) and how it should be achieved, and so many different socio-political systems in the developing world, it would appear not merely difficult but in fact futile to attempt to devise a coherent, universal development press model. Shared desire to raise GDP and overcome problems related to economic underdevelopment do not, without consideration of other community or national values, provide sufficient basis for a normative model. In Asia, attempts to tie development philosophies to particular, localised cultural and political systems and concepts of development has engendered an emphasis on so-called 'Asian values' and, in Indonesia, the *Pancasila* press.

Southeast Asian leaders have long exhorted journalists to preserve the 'existing values system' as part of their development role (Lent 1979: 69). Supposedly essential 'Asian values' that have been identified as relevant to journalists are respect for elders and leaders, maintenance of harmony and concern for 'saving face' (Chu 1988: 126; Khaiyath 1996: 4; Lent 1979: 69–70, Snijders 1994). Islamic values furthermore encourage communicators to veil the deficiencies of others, and to speak to all people in a 'mild manner' and 'kindly way' (Hasnain 1988: 185). This cultural system, it is argued, 'rejects the notion of an uninhibited and robust press that undertakes vehement, caustic and unpleasant attacks on government and public officials' (Mehra 1989: 4).

During the New Order, Indonesian Information Department officials described the liberal watchdog, fourth-estate press system as culturally

inappropriate, maintaining that a consensus-oriented press was more philoso-
phically suitable (*Forum Keadilan* 23 Dec. 1993: 28; Sinaga 1989: 38). The New
Order Department of Information official in charge of Indonesia's journalists,
Sukarno, said: 'Ours is not a watchdog press in the Western fashion. A watchdog
must stand guard outside the house. We prefer to keep our press inside along
with the rest of the family' (Asia Watch 1988: 207). As a member of the national
family and a participant in the totality of national development processes, the
Pancasila press as defined by the New Order 'does not stay outside the system
monitoring and checking as well as criticizing the system; it is, rather
'responsible within the system to develop the nation as a whole in all fields'
(Sinaga 1987b: 33)

Soeharto described the news media as the government's 'partner in the
process of nation building' and urged journalists to 'be vigilant and attentive' in
efforts 'to discourage the growing elements of narrow individualism' and 'to
protect the spirit of unity' (Soeharto 1989b: 134). He constantly called for the
press to be 'free and responsible' in 'guarding a dynamic national stability,
maintaining the strength of national unity and speeding development' from 'a
base of *Pancasila* and the 1945 Constitution' (Soeharto 1995: 29). The rhetoric
on the *Pancasila* press thus encapsulated the key tenets of New Order
integralistic ideology.

Systematic attempts to define the roles, practices, freedoms and restrictions of
Pancasila journalism as a normative model are best expressed by the decisions
of Indonesia's Press Council and several media analysts, especially Wonohito,
whose book on journalistic techniques of the *Pancasila* press system was a key
text for journalism courses for decades. Wonohito argues that the Western
communities and media focuses on the *aku* (I), i.e. the individual; the (now
defunct) Soviet communist system focused on *kami* (an Indonesian term for
'we', which refers to a group involved with the speaker but does not include the
person spoken to), i.e. the self-governing community without need for the state.
He finds both to be inherently concerned with material welfare, in contrast with
the *kita* (an Indonesian term for 'we', which includes the speaker and those
addressed in one all-encompassing group) of the *Pancasila* press framework.
This framework supposedly attempts to balance individual and community
interests and to protect both material and spiritual welfare (Wonohito 1977:
71–4). The concept of the all-embracing we-*kita* is also manifested by the Press
Council's 1974 'Guidelines', which refer to the press's responsibility 'to hold
high the national consensus' and to cooperate with community and government
'in a *gotong royong* fashion inspired by the zeal of the family principle'.

This discussion of *Pancasila* fell within Wonohito's brief summary of
Indonesian history which, in standard New Order fashion, refers to the political
fractiousness and instability of the nation during the early Sukarno years and the
rise of communist influence during the later period of Sukarno's reign (Wonohito
1977: 53–4). Wonohito tells the reader that Soeharto, on assuming the
presidency in 1968, declared a return to 'the original, authentic *Pancasila*'.
This authentic *Pancasila* not only rejected the atheistic communist approach,

which had been totally demonised in the post-Gestapu communist purge, but also 'the excesses of liberalism' (Dewan Pers 1974). Other analyses also described *Pancasila* as the only ideology which had 'proven' that it could unite a nation with such diversity of ethnic groups, religions, races and geographic settings – 'objective elements conducive to disintegrative and separatist movements' (Sinaga 1987a: 16; Sinaga 1989: 33–4). Throughout the New Order, journalists who deviated from dominant definitions of appropriate *Pancasila*ist behaviour were regularly accused of wearing 'foreign glasses' or being influenced by foreign ideologies (e.g. Harmoko 1997; *Jakarta Post* 13 Feb. 1997: 1), a political caveat with the same kind of menace as being dubbed un-American during the McCarthy era.

Free to serve

Debates about the *Pancasila* press and Indonesian values were often discussed in opposition to the perceived freedoms of Western societies. New Order theorists were inclined to emphasise the potential for supposedly recklessly commercial and uncontrollable Western journalists to engage in a 'dictatorship of the press' (Sinaga 1987b: 18). The freedom of the *Pancasila* press was described as distinct from both the negative freedom of the libertarian press that is free *from* external control, as well as the positive freedom of the social-responsibility press that is free *to* serve societal needs and maintain ethical values. Effendi (1993: 122) argues that the *Pancasila* press, by contrast, is not free *from* or free *to* but free *and*, because it is free *and* responsible. Oetama (1989: 143) explains that the *Pancasila* press is granted 'functional freedom' to assist in programs for improving economic and social conditions, rather than freedom from government control. IIc says that in an environment in which the state determines the design and purpose of development, there is 'no other way' but to acquiesce to a strong government role.

Practical examples of such freedom are most commonly expressed as the freedom *not to* harm society. The Kopkamtib security organisation developed its famous MISS SARA acronym to guide the press on what topics to avoid. MISS SARA prohibits the press from covering subjects likely to stimulate sedition (*menghasut*), insinuation (*insinuasi*), sensation (*sensasi*) or speculation (*spekulasi*) or which might ignite ethnic (*sukuis*), religious (*agama*), racial (*rasialis*) or group (*aliran*) tensions. In the past application of MISS SARA, the media were regularly barred from reporting race riots on the grounds that publicising the violence could spread the riots further. Some journalists, however, questioned the effectiveness of the New Order's bans on stories about race riots and related issues, claiming that the gossip fuelled by information blackouts kindled greater problems (Rodgers 1982: 8–9; Awanohara 1984: 24–5). Others have noted that since it suited New Order figures to identify their survival with the national interest, it became easy for them to treat stories that questioned their performance or embarrassed them politically as 'security threats' (Jenkins 1986: 155).

Despite limitations on reporting topics deemed to be related to SARA, journalists' freedom and right to engage in *kontrol sosial* (social control) were supposedly protected by law. In the Indonesian language, *kontrol sosial* refers to the control of the state by society. In these laws, however, 'freedom' was always accompanied by the qualifier 'responsible', while '*kontrol sosial*' is always paired with the qualifier 'constructive'. The 1984 decree of the Indonesian Press Council's 25th Plenary Session describes the *Pancasila* press as serving as 'the disseminator of information that is true and objective, the channel of the aspirations of the people and of *constructive* social control' (emphasis added). The New Order amended the Press Law No. 11 of 1966, which stated that journalists had a duty 'to fight for truth and justice based on freedom of the press', with the Press Law No. 21 of 1982, which obliged journalists 'to fight for truth and justice based on *responsible* freedom of the press' (emphasis added).

Honour thy father

The *Pancasila* press is presumed to be organised around the family-oriented political structure which, Wonohito (1977: 79) says, is essentially feudalistic in nature. Wonohito (1977: 79–80) argues that the demands of liberals to eliminate feudalism are misguided and that the authority of traditional-style leaders should be upheld because 'citizens usually gather around a trusted leader due to his/her authority'. State officials and community leaders have a high position not just because of their occupations, but also because they 'are felt to be the father of people in their area. The President is not just Head of the Nation, but also Father of all citizens' (Wonohito 1977: 85; also Khaiyath 1996: 8–9). *Pancasila* and familial philosophies further entail that 'constructive' news does not 'offend the feelings' or 'disturb the authority' of honoured father-leadership figures (Wonohito 1977: 86).

Such tenets were indirectly expressed in the 1982 Press Law and the Press Council's often-quoted 1984 Decree. The latter stipulated that the press should nurture 'positive interaction' and develop an atmosphere of 'mutual trust between the people, the press and the government'. Several provisions of the penal code, remnants of colonial-era legislation, also encourage journalists to safeguard the authority of national leaders and refrain from slandering them. The *Haatzaai Artikelen* (hate sowing articles) prohibit public insult or expression of hatred of the government or any social groups. Several prominent Indonesian lawyers protested that the articles were too oppressive and that the New Order preserved the articles purely in order to intimidate political opponents, journalists and publishers (ICJ 1987: 201; *Kabar dari Pijar* 1995). The *Lese Majeste* Articles also criminalised 'deliberate disrespect' towards Indonesia's leaders, prohibiting the publication of literature or photographs that may insult or offend the president, vice-president or government authorities. Since colonial times these laws have been criticised for being *pasal karet* (rubber clauses) because they can be interpreted widely to suit government whims (Atmo & Vidarta 1995; Lubis 1992: 2; Siregar 1995a: 4). The International Commission of Jurists (1987: 86) deemed the laws to be inappropriate for a political system in which the president, as the elected head of government, should have been considered the target of popular scrutiny.

In determining the balance of freedom and responsibility, Department of Information official Edward Janner Sinaga suggested that journalists should rely on the 'conscience of the press and the conscience of the Society and the Government, in essence, all parties who have any sense of responsibility for the upbuilding of the nation as a whole' (1987a: 19). Within the framework of New Order politics, the conscience of the people was said to be embodied in the Main Guidelines of State Policy (GBHN), approved by the five-yearly MPR session that supposedly represented 'all contending political forces' (Sinaga 1987b: 13; also Malik 1974: 11). Despite many indications that the politically vetted MPR members reflected the will of Soeharto more than the will of the people, the Press Council decreed that the GBHN represented the 'national consensus' (Press Council Decision No. 79/XIV/1974). The New Order did not tolerate contestation of the GBHN's definition of national priorities, so journalistic responsibility and constructiveness accordingly assumed to involve assisting the implementation rather than the critiquing of government policy. In the mid-New Order years, former *Harian Kami* editor Nono Makarim (1978: 269) noted that:

> In this conceptual framework there is not much place for open dissent and criticism, let alone the denunciation of policies or public figures .... His [the newspaper editor's] critical appraisals are directed most of the time to marginal aspects of policy and rarely touch the tenets of the regime.

Breakdown of the New Order model

Attempts to define *Pancasila* journalism or development journalism theories were fraught with inconsistencies during the New Order period, because the government's development paradigm aimed for stability as both a means and an end, while the community and the development process itself are dynamic. The *Pancasila* press ideology replicated the contradictory drive of the New Order towards both modernity and feudalism. On the one hand it sought to help development by educating modern, rational citizens and supporting an environment conducive to economic 'takeoff'. On the other hand, it attempted to protect 'authentic' integralistic Indonesian traditions in the form of family values, organic wholeness, esteem for leaders and spiritual piety.

The invocation for journalists to be faithful to *Pancasila* was a mainstay of the New Order's relationship with the press, although the delineation of journalists as the *Pancasila* press came under increasing question in the final years of Soeharto's reign. Even Alwi Dahlan, then deputy head of the BP7, the body for inculcating *Pancasila* values nationwide, said that the press everywhere struggles for the community interest and that the term, *Pancasila* press, could only *mengungkung* (shackle or enslave) Indonesia's press (*Pedoman Rakyat* 15 May 1996: 2). Dahlan's comments were quickly 'corrected' by a number of figures, including the head of the Centre for the Research and Education of the *Pancasila* Press. Centre Director Anwar Arifin argued that *Pancasila* must be the base of all national activities, including journalism, and the *Pancasila* press was needed to defend and develop Indonesia's 'authentic national identity' in an era of globalisation (*Fajar* 15 May 1996: 2; Arifin 1996).

Attempts to reassess Asian values and *Pancasila* philosophies was accelerated following the so-called 'Asian flu' of mid-1997, in which most economies suffered varying degrees of economic downturn. Press philosophies were subject to re-evaluation after many, including the high-profile, Hong Kong-based Political and Economic Risk Consultancy (PERC), argued the economic crisis was exacerbated by the lack of transparency and poor-quality financial reporting in the region. 'This hid problems from public view and inhibited intelligent analysis of the risks. People did not have the information they needed to have an accurate understanding of how radically conditions could change.' While government censorship was blamed in part, PERC also argued that the quality of reportage was poor even in countries where the media was free (PERC 1998). Following such critique, there has been increased emphasis on improving press freedom and reporters' watchdog skills. The Confederation of ASEAN Journalists, for example, now replicates the IMF and World Bank terms of 'free market', albeit with a stronger focus on 'business ethics, and 'good governance'. The association identifies the media's role as alerting policy makers to potential problems and reporting on (and therefore supporting) good bureaucratic performance (e.g. Razak 1999).

Towards the end of the New Order, when much of the economic crisis was blamed on KKN and the 'opacity' of the Soeharto regime, the tenets of good governance had obvious appeal. From early 1998, when it was increasingly feared that both the Rupiah and the economy were heading into an uncontrollable downward spiral, intellectuals and some bureaucrats urged a new emphasis on transparency. The rhetoric used in speeches by key bureaucrats, such as Dailami, then the Information Department's Director General of Press and Graphics, echoed the incremental change in political paradigms. The discourses of development, NWICO, *Pancasila*, and positive press-government interaction, which were common in Dailami's speeches up until November 1997, were progressively replaced after the height of the economic crisis with the catchcries of *reformasi*, anti-KKN, human rights, freedom of expression, freedom of information and the rule of law (Dailami 1998). In the weeks prior to Soeharto's resignation, United Nations' Secretary General Kofi Annan described freedom of information as a prerequisite for democracy, development and peace. Annan's observation that freedom of the press was 'an investment against tyranny' was enthusiastically repeated by Indonesians eager to pursue change at home (e.g. Suroso 1998).

The changed economic circumstances disturbed the balance that had been established in the previously prevailing press-as-government-partner model. In 1998, the Soeharto government attempted to maintain the existing pattern of political relations by penalising journalists deemed too critical. One prominent example was the pressure placed on the editor of *D&R* magazine in March 1998, who was forced to resign over a cover illustration deemed discourteous to Soeharto. However, with its credibility low due to the Rupiah's freefall, the Soeharto government was unable to enforce the severe penalties it had commonly employed in the past. There was much speculation among journalists at the time that the government had wanted to impose harsher sanctions against *D&R* by delicensing the magazine, thus forcing it out of print, but was unable to take such action because the government would face public protests if it pushed *D&R*'s staff out of their jobs when unemployment levels were soaring. Ultimately, the dissent in the following months from the media and other sectors of civil society proved to have greater power than the government's will. The growing unrest forced Soeharto to withdraw from office, thus allowing a formal redefinition of the press's role and the appropriate relationship between the government, press and society.

Legal basis for a reformist press system

The resignation of Soeharto was followed by rapid change in political sectors, including the media. Many international conventions were passed during Habibie's term as president in an attempt to signify Indonesia's commitment towards reform and protection of human rights. Of specific consequence to journalists was the MPR's 1998 decision (No. XVII/MPR/1998), which ratified the Universal Declaration of Human Rights. Articles 19, 20 and 21 of the Declaration protect citizens' rights to freedom of expression without interference and to seek, receive and impart information and ideas through any media. These civil liberties were reinforced by Article 14 of the 1999 Law No. 39 on Human Rights, which protect the right to seek, own, store and disseminate information through any channel. The MPR's amendments to the 1945 Constitution further strengthened Article 28 that specified that the freedom to gather, associate and express opinions would be determined by law. The amendments, passed in 2000, split Article 28 into 10 sub-articles. These contain 26 passages that explicitly safeguard various rights, including the right to seek and circulate information. The amendments furthermore deleted contentious words of Article 28 of the 1945 Constitution, which had specified that the freedom of expression would be fixed, and therefore possibly diminished, by law.

From the first weeks of Habibie's presidency, the existing array of Soeharto-era laws governing the media were either loosely interpreted or totally ignored. Journalists enjoyed the freedom to set up new media organisations and report in a forthright style unseen for decades. Bureaucrats largely abandoned pretensions to being guardians of the press. For the most part, they ceased habits such as the 'telephone culture', in which officials called journalists to offer 'advice' on what stories should be run, what should be avoided and what angles to take on issues. However, there was intense concern that Habibie's 'Reformation Era' bureau-cracy was merely interpreting the legislation in a more liberal fashion, and that the interpretation could easily tighten if political imperatives changed in the future. In this climate, an assortment of politicians, bureaucrats, journalists and other industry representatives, activists and non-government organisations aligned into several (often fragile) coalitions that respectively wrote and presented to the parliament six differing proposals for legislation that would enshrine journalistic autonomy.

The parliamentary and social debate on the proposed press legislation reflected the residual power of the New Order culture and the organisational intensity of the parties that hoped to cement a legislative framework that would provide the foundation for a more liberal press culture. Various supporters of the status quo in the Armed Forces and other socio-political institutions argued that removal of the old restrictions on the press could lead to civil strife and even national disintegration (e.g. Jakarta Post 6 Feb. 1999; *Suara Karya* 17 May 1999; *Suara Pembaruan* 15 May 1999). Yunus Yosfiah, the Information Minister during the short-lived Habibie government, was a key figure in opposing such arguments. In a fashion that was to become typical of politicians of the era, Yunus reinvented himself as a prime mover towards *reformasi* and liberalisation of press laws, despite concerns that were expressed about his possible implication in the deaths of five Western newsmen in East Timor in 1975. Yunus and others promoted media-law reform by using the same precepts that were supported by the UNDP, World Bank and IMF, i.e. that a free press was the pillar of democracy, which could help to eliminate KKN, promote responsible government and reduce the social conflicts and riots that often resulted from rumours.

In September 1999, the DPR passed Law No. 40 on the Press, which amalgamated and modified the six proposals that had been presented to it, but largely maintained the liberal spirit of each. The Law's preamble states that freedom of expression and the right to obtain information are 'legitimate (*hakiki*) human rights that are needed to maintain justice and truth, advance general welfare and enlighten the life of the nation'. The law describes freedom of the press as 'one of the materialisations of community sovereignty' and prohibits censorship of the media. In Article 4.3, the Law uses the words *kemerdekaan pers* for press freedom, instead of the term *kebebasan pers*, which was conventionally used in New Order policy and legislation on journalism. The use of the word *kemerdekaan* was considered to represent a significant change in official consciousness, as it has powerful connotations of liberation, indepen-dence and emancipation, as in the sense of a person or nation becoming free of an oppressive power. *Kebebasan*, by contrast, is more commonly used to refer to freedom from smaller impediments or obstacles. The Press Law also forbids censorship and attempts to restrict media publications or broadcasts.

Although these legal changes indicated a transformation of the Indonesian government's press paradigm, media analysts have described the 1999 Press Law as being limited by the way in which it maintains a compromise mix of old and new political paradigms (Kristanto 2000: 12). At the time the legislation was drafted, even Department of Information staff critiqued the limitations in the philosophy underpinning the legislation. Dailami, for example, suggested that Indonesia should follow countries such as neighbouring Australia, which does not have specific laws protecting or limiting freedom of the press. Such countries instead allow the press to be governed by the general laws and regulations that apply to all citizens, including laws of defamation, contempt of court and so on. He argued that a Freedom of Information Act would be of more practical value to journalists than a Press Law (Dailami 1999: pers. comm.). Additionally, in common with the World Bank and IMF approaches, the 1999 legal changes try to enable journalists to engage in investigative journalism and to protect them when they probe the institutions of power. In no way do they encourage journalists to access the voices of community members outside élite circles.

Concerns have also been raised about the philosophies underlying proposed revisions to the criminal code. Legal analysts argue that the old criminal code contained 37 articles deemed to threaten press freedom, such as the *Haatzaai Artikelen* and others. They say the new criminal code has greater potential threat for press freedom, containing 42 articles that could be used to restrict the activities of journalists (Sapardjaja & Padmadinata 1999). At the time this book was written, the criminal code was one of many legislative reforms overdue for attention from a parliament that had been for months preoccupied with deliberations on Wahid's future.

Another changes of consequence to journalists was the demise of the Department of Information. Wahid's first action on obtaining the presidency was to effectively dissolve the Department by simply not appointing a minister of information to the new cabinet. A major function of the Department of Information had been to monitor and regulate the activities of journalists and media organisations on behalf of the New Order, thus becoming a department for controlling information. Media-industry concerns were raised in June 2001 by reports of a meeting involving the PDI-P and four other major political parties to discuss the possibility of reviving the Department. The rationale for resurrecting the Department was ostensibly to promote public awareness about the outcomes of the annual MPR session, but the reaction from many elements of the journalistic community was hostile (further details in Chapter 5).

Attitudes of the elite

Public statements by political and bureaucratic figures commonly reflect the cannons of the emerging post-Soeharto press model, which defines a free press as the scourge of corrupt and inefficient governance. However, lingering elements of the New Order are also evident. Typical are Habibie and Wahid. Both repeatedly argued that a free press was important for Indonesian society, but the longer they spent in office, the more they were inclined to be chary of the journalists who so bluntly criticised their performance and policies. Although both occasionally complained directly to the media about their harsh coverage, Habibie was more apt to veil his displeasure through warnings to journalists against 'misuse' of press freedom. For example, he cautioned journalists to 'take a hard line against agitation and propaganda', saying that press freedom did not give journalists a licence to publish rumours, lies or slander that could create community unrest (*Suara Karya* 10 Feb. 1999).

Wahid, on the other hand, regularly told Indonesian journalists directly that he thought they were unbalanced and inaccurate in their examination of his leadership. Wahid had been the media's golden child during the New Order but lost his lustre within months of assuming the presidency, as journalists tired of his changeable and confusing statements on public policy. In turn, Wahid's dissatisfaction with the media was so intense that he identified the media's deficiencies as a major factor prompting him to issue a special decree in May 2001, handing additional powers to Yudhoyono, then Coordinating Minister for Political, Social and Security Affairs. Wahid argued that his political enemies were attempting to use the parliament and the media to assassinate his character and withdraw his mandate, and that as a result of the tensions stirred, pro- and anti-Wahid forces would clash, leading to losses for all. The Minister's new powers to restore order and security proved less than significant when Yudhoyono was replaced in the next few days, effectively annulling the decree. The failure of the decree followed an unsuccessful attempt by presidential palace officials in the previous month to establish a media watchdog team, which was meant to monitor and take legal action against the supposedly misleading information in the media about the president and his administration. This information was blamed for disturbing the broader society and Indonesia's economic activity. Legal action would effectively allow the team to formulate and enforce guidelines for media reporting (Laksamana.net 21 June 2001).

There is considerable justification for Wahid's claim that the post-Soeharto media circulate inaccurate and ill-founded reports, with probable deleterious socio-economic consequences. However, his response to these problems was more flavoured by New Order style than the reformist qualities that he was once considered to embody. The next chapter highlights the attitudes of journalists to both the New Order's development-press model and the mixed reformist-traditionalist paradigms they encounter in the post-Soeharto era.

Megawati's statements on the press have been broadly supportive of press freedom but, like many of her public comments, are subject to various possible interpretations. In common with New Order rhetoric on the press, her opinions focus on journalists' nation-building role. Megawati says it is not enough to be professional. The press should 'participate in efforts to politically educate the public'. She defines a role for journalists in help to create a favourable political climate through constructive reporting 'to help bring the country out of the prolonged crisis'. She argues that reporters may worsen Indonesia's predicament if they adhere only to cannons of journalistic objectivity; they also need to distinguish which information should be shared with the public and which should not (*Jakarta Post* 10 Feb. 2001: 2). Given Megawati's conservative political perspectives, journalism activists fear that she would consider re-establishing the Information Department should she gain the presidency. That, they believe, might lead to a slow but measured return of the New Order press paradigm.

5 Professional image in the community of journalists

Although New Order politicians and bureaucrats invariably portrayed journalists as the *Pancasila* or development press, as was discussed in Chapter 4, this depiction was at odds with journalists' self-conception of their profession. When the journalists surveyed for this book in 1996 to 1998 were asked to describe their role in society, only 4.6 per cent volunteered the terms *Pancasila* press or development press to describe their function. When time permitted during interviews, respondents were prompted to give their opinions on the *Pancasila* and development press so that even though few broached the topic themselves, just over half the journalists (52.3 per cent) had discussed the philosophies by the end of the survey. Almost one-third of those who gave an opinion (29.4 per cent) expressed support for the *Pancasila* and/or development press philosophies, a few (8.8 per cent) were ambivalent and suggested that the term was not particularly relevant to journalists, while two-thirds (61.8 per cent) criticised the concepts as ideological tools to control journalists.

The supporters described the development- and *Pancasila*-press philosophies as the elements of responsible and ethical conduct that separated the Indonesian press from that of Western societies. The freedom of the Western liberal press was delineated as 'permissive', 'licentious' and 'uncontrolled', whereas the *Pancasila* and development press were described in the dominant political discourses of freedom matched with responsibility. One Antara news agency reporter, for example, said the press were obligated to create security and stability in the arenas of *ipolek sosbud hankam*, a term created by the New Order government to refer to ideology, politics, economy, society, culture, defence and security, or in other words, all imaginable realms of Indonesian life. Others spoke of the Indonesian journalists' observance of the Code of Ethics, their protection of SARA sensitivities or their status as a 'uniter' or 'stabiliser'.

Critics of the *Pancasila* and development press rhetoric were, by contrast, inclined to describe the terms *Pancasila* press, development press and even 'free and responsible' as ill defined or meaningless. More than half of the critical journalists discussed the concepts by rhetorically asking what they meant. Even a journalism lecturer at Gadjah Mada University confessed that he could not ascribe any particular meaning to the terms, apart from repeating a limited range of government rhetoric on the subject (Ngurah 1997: pers. comm.). Other respondents expressed a desire for a clearer designation of their duties and rights under the *Pancasila* and development systems. They expressed frustration at intangible and changing definitions of related terms such as stability, security and national interest. A few respondents suggested further that the terms were distractions or 'window dressings', devoid of meaning. One editor, normally noted for his refined and sophisticated mien, bluntly described the development and *Pancasila* press philosophies as 'bullshit'. He argued that journalists 'cannot escape from the role to educate and inform' regardless of what press system they work in.

Critics of the New Order commonly argue that the state defined both *Pancasila* and development in terms that served the government rather than the people. Journalists who opposed the *Pancasila*-development press philosophies similarly said that officials who described the New Order press system as culturally appropriate were cynically conflating what was appropriate for a perverted government culture to be the same for Indonesian culture in general. In speaking of *Pancasila* and development journalism, the respondents often spoke of being *terkekang* (bridled or curbed) by the instruments of power. One summarised this by saying: 'It is being always telephoned to be told to not write this or you must write that or you risk being banned. That is the *Pancasila* press for me.' The respondents who criticised *Pancasila* or development press ideologies, however, did not dispute the general premise that *Pancasila* and the aspiration to develop the nation's infrastructure and economy were good, but rather suggested that *Pancasila*/development philosophies were not being interpreted or applied in an appropriate fashion.

Given that few respondents used the terms *Pancasila* or development journalism to describe themselves, they were asked a number of broad, open-ended questions about their roles, ideals and aspirations to determine how they depicted themselves. This chapter uses those survey results to discuss how journalists described their aims, sense of professional identity and collective professional mission during the late New Order period. Due to the small size of the survey sample, the results in this chapter are not claimed to be statistically representative. Figures on numbers of journalists who supported the different perspectives have been included merely to indicate the strength of support for the five different viewpoints. The chapter concludes with an exploration of changes in journalistic identity that have followed the end of the Soeharto era.

The motivations of the non-Pancasila journalist

All respondents were asked how and why they had become journalists, an innocuous question that revealed what they thought the field of journalism could offer them and what they could offer to journalism and society. The most commonly nominated reasons for becoming a journalist was a sense of duty to help society by aiding the suffering, redressing social inequities and building democracy (see Table 5.1). One journalist said, for example, that he had hoped 'to create something to change this crazy world'. Several described journalism as a spiritual calling. One Islamic journalist described the media as *sarana dakwah* (a medium for proselytising or missionary endeavour) and his decision to enter journalism as 'an *amar* (command from God) to teach goodness and to guard against evil'. A Catholic journalist, one of a disproportionately large number of former seminarians to work in the news media, compared journalists to priests in the way that they spread knowledge. 'Good things are reported in the news. Inside there is a sense of mission.' These survey results resemble those from Anwar (1977: 197), who found that 38 per cent of 112 young journalists attending a 1977 PWI induction course had similarly been motivated by idealism to serve and teach the community.

The strength of mission expressed by Indonesian journalists contrasts with the results of David Weaver and Cleveland Wilhoit's U.S. survey, which found that only 11 per cent of American journalists joined the profession because they aspired 'to make a difference' (1996: 53). Such a disparity is not surprising considering that citizens of developing societies might be expected to see more physical deprivation and suffering in their local environs than those in wealthier nations, and thus might feel a greater calling to help redress imbalances and to overcome conditions of privation. Nor are such expressions of idealism unexpected, considering that the New Order frequently urged citizens to sacrifice individual or sectional interests for the sake of nation building and promoted the image of the press performing critical tasks of motivating, educating and guiding the people. The journalists in Weaver and Wilhoit's study, on the other hand, were primarily motivated by their own interests in writing or

Table 5.1 Reasons Indonesian survey respondents entered journalism[1]

Rank	Reason for joining journalism	No. of journalists	%
1.	Mission to help society	19	29.2
2.	Love of reading/writing	14	21.5
3.	Prior involvement with campus press	12	18.5
4.	Thirst for knowledge	10	15.4

Table 5.2 Reasons PWI candidates entered journalism[2]

Rank	Reasons for joining journalism	%
1.	Mission to help society	38
2.	Like reading and writing	25
3.	Economy	13.5
4.	Accident	11.5

(from Anwar 1977: 197)

their desire to use their perceived talents in the field rather than a burning need to 'set the world right'.

Love of reading and/or writing was the second most-commonly nominated reason for becoming a journalist, with 21.5 per cent of my respondents and 25 per cent of Anwar's (1977: 197) respondents nominating such a reason compared with 37 per cent of US journalists. A possible reason for the Indonesian figure being lower is that the country has not yet developed a solid culture of reading for information or pleasure, despite the successful campaigns to improve literacy (Wiradja & Bhaskara 1993: 6). The New Order also had a reputation for being 'profoundly philistine' (Anderson 1994: 139; also Schwarz 1994: 336–7), with relatively little emphasis on cultural development compared with infrastructural and economic development.

The third most-commonly nominated reason for joining journalism may be connected with the first. Almost 20 per cent of respondents mentioned their involvement in the bold and lively campus press as an influence on their decision to become a journalist. During the New Order, campus newspapers and magazines reported socio-political affairs in a far more forthright and spirited fashion than in the mainstream mass media. The audaciousness of the campus press was usually attributed to the politically aware disposition of students who were connected with it and also to the exemption of such publications from requirements to obtain publishing permits.

Many journalists joined because they sought a mentally stimulating work environment. Thirst for knowledge was mentioned by 15.4 per cent who sought an intellectual challenge, opportunities to be privy to first-hand information or to improve their personal insights and knowledge.

Watchdogs and *Pancasila* pussycats

The survey results cited above suggest that although Indonesian journalists have a variety of motivations for entering media careers, a substantial proportion were fired by a desire to improve their society. This leads circuitously to the questions posed in the last chapter – what kind of development did these so-called development, *Pancasila* journalists perceive as desirable, and what role did they see themselves playing in supporting that kind of development?

Todung Mulya Lubis postulated during the New Order period that Indonesia's journalistic community was split into three main groups over their role. The first group, supported by the government-endorsed PWI, mystified *Pancasila* in much the same way as described by Wonohito; the press is expected to implement and reflect the *Pancasila* democracy as it was defined by the New Order (Mulya Lubis 1993: 259–60). The second group advocated the colonial-era vision of the journalist as an 'independence warrior', who, following the achievement of sovereignty, should help to realise the dreams of autonomy by acting as a watchdog, monitoring development and critiquing human-rights' violations. Mulya Lubis (1993: 260) noted: 'Although those in this second group do not feel comfortable with the term *liberal press*, it must in all fairness be admitted that their attitude resembles the attitude of this type.' He proposed that a third 'more realistic' group compromised between these two attitudes. Journalists in this group tolerated some restrictions and avoid open confrontation 'in the name of responsibility' but also felt a 'duty' to minimise restrictions on press freedoms (Mulya Lubis 1993: 261).

The results of my survey, by contrast, identified five main perspectives among respondents about their positioning between the masses and the sources of politico-economic power. The most commonly described role was to be a watchdog who scrutinises and critiques the powerful; the second was agent of empowerment who seeks to enlighten and strengthen the masses; the third was nation builder who aims to build unity and develop the nation's social and physical infrastructure; the fourth was defender of the truth; and the fifth was entertainer (see Table 5.3).

Although few survey respondents used the word 'watchdog' to describe their role, just over half (50.8 per cent) described the press as ideally functioning like a sentinel who monitors the powerful and reveals misconduct so that the public can direct and change state policies and activities. Several journalists suggested that they would be indistinguishable from public servants if they did not uphold watchdog-style values. Even a journalist working for Golkar's *Media Karya* said that it was the role of journalists to expose the faults of the bureaucracy. 'If journalists strengthen the hand of government, there will be no difference between journalists and the government. If journalists are to expose the faults of government, journalists must maintain a gap – a distance between themselves and power.' While some agreed that journalists should promote programs that would aid development, even in cases when such programs were state-generated, they did not support the philosophy of a state–press partnership that compromised politically independent reportage.

The journalists in this group rejected the proposition that the aspirations, ideals and operations of development or *Pancasila* journalists needed to be substantially different from those of so-called watchdog journalists. As one explained:

> There is nothing that is out of anyone's common sense. The problems are different and more complex; you have to be more sensitive; it is less

Table 5.3 Journalists' opinions about their professional roles

Perceived role	Number of journalists	Percentage of journalists
Watchdog	33	50.8
Agent of empowerment	14	21.5
Nation building	12	18.5
Defender of truth	5	7.7
Entertainer	1	1.5

structured; you have to be more thorough and you have to know the whole picture. But there is nothing so complex that it can be thought of as a separate journalistic theory.

Another said: 'A watchdog is a watchdog. However, we should also consider the level of education [of our readers]. I think journalists should make it interesting and simple. Not development; not *Pancasila*.'

One third of these respondents also supported a courteous and refined style of criticism as culturally appropriate and desirable, but argued that it was erroneous to consider graciousness to be at odds with a watchdog identity. One reporter said: 'Maybe it is true that we are not so *kasar* (rough or coarse) as the foreign press, but we must report things that are wrong. I think there is little difference between truth and falsehood in different cultures.'

In sum, the journalists of this group argued that the difference between journalism in Western and developing nations lay more in the packaging than in the content of the news. The majority of respondents thus, consciously or not, supported the original conceptualisation of development journalism, as formulated in the Philippines, that aimed to distil news on complex events into language and formats that would be simple and meaningful to the indigent masses. They rejected demands to sacrifice watchdog functions. Media theorist Ashadi Siregar summarised the position by arguing that the press 'is a medium of the public' which should 'inform the public about empirical facts without adding their own perspectives and without attempting to influence the public'. Although he acknowledged the faults of the Western press, he argued that the Western press performed better than the New Order press which had to 'bow down' to both the government and the media owners, who were also 'government cronies' (*Jakarta Post* 5 Feb. 1995: 2).

More than half of this group, however, claimed that their watchdog role was endangered by numerous threats and legal mechanisms. In such a climate, some survey respondents stated that the press was 'castrated' and could only act as 'a slave', 'a courier' or 'an instrument of power'. One explained: 'The government has an intense strength in the press world. There are gaps that maybe allow us enough room to become small watchdogs of minor robberies only. If there has been a serious burglary, the watchdog becomes a pussycat.'

Only a small number of survey respondents (7.7 per cent) rejected the watchdog concept outright as too harsh, too dogmatic or too disruptive. One journalist said: 'I want to be the *nadi* (the pulse). I do not wish to be a fierce watchdog. I wish to be like [the prophet] Muhammad and to spread a good agenda. Muhammad was not fierce.' The arguments were not so much against the watchdog's role of investigating and exposing socially or politically significant misconduct, but rather at the incessantly disparaging and aggressive character that the survey respondents associated with the Western watchdog image. While journalists' fourth estate function does not necessarily have to be accompanied by truculent or bellicose behaviour, the respondents who rejected the watchdog role did not appear to divide the two elements.

Seekers of enlightenment, development and truth

Journalists in the second-largest group supported an agent-of-empowerment role, which contains elements of both the watchdog and the nation-building roles. This category was distinguishable from others because respondents often called themselves 'activists' and/or spoke of emancipation, social justice or development of citizens as human beings. They defined their function as educational, but in lyrical terms that involved awakening and arousing the individual rather than the simple provision of 'facts' or educative book learning. One reporter said: 'I think the press is not to teach but to move; to move the brain, to move the heart to see the world, to build humanity.'

This group emphasised development at an individual and a spiritual level. The agent-of-empowerment role involves uncovering corruption and misman-agement, and it supports the public's right to know. More significantly, however, the journalists also stated a goal to empower community members through education about the practical challenges of national development, their rights and their responsibilities. One subeditor said:

Just talking about [development] projects is not interesting. We would like to concentrate on the problematics that arise from development; for example the transformation of an agrarian society into an industrial society, the confusion of the people, how the classes cope and how the élite cope with power and the newly acquired wealth. We have had 20 years of physical development but the people are not happy. Development is not just physical but spiritual. It can be happiness with nothing more. Even if you are poor, you can have the wealth not to commit crimes and not to violate human rights.

The respondents suggested that such information does not merely educate but also liberates. In the words of one journalist, it 'frees the people from ignorance, frees them from misunderstanding'.

Despite the educational emphasis in much of these journalists' rhetoric, they did not define the top-down system of communications promulgated in the New Order in which the teacher-like journalist educates the childlike reader or citizen. They also described bottom-up and lateral communications in which the journalist was a medium for gauging public opinion, expressing the voice of the people and providing feedback to government. One journalist expressed a hope that more reporters would go into communities, in the same way that NGOs often do, to identify the needs of the people at the grassroots level and to understand and record traditional cultures as they change and, in some cases, disappear.

The journalists in this group had not necessarily intentionally drawn from liberation theories. The journalists' aspirations and approaches, however, have manifold similarities to that of Freire, whose methods declare death to traditional educational and communications techniques that are driven by the 'educated' professionals to maintain the political status quo. Instead the student becomes an educator and the 'subject' rather than the 'object' of educational processes (Freire 1974: 7–8; Freire 1997: 54). The ethnographic technique proposed by journalists resembles the Freirian strategy of educators or communicators spending time within an area to discover the living 'codes' and the major narratives of its residents (Freire 1997: 61, 92). Their rejection of the 'bread-before-freedom' doctrine also accords with Freire's perspective that development is transformation of the socio-political structure, not merely modernisation or having more material possessions (Freire 1997: 142). This position was, however, contrary to the New Order political style, which depicted development as economic growth, the president as the teacher/father of the child-like masses and state policy as the manifestation of popular consensus.

The respondents who supported the nation-builder function, the third most-commonly mentioned role, said that journalistic writings should help to foster national development, unify the nation and guard against threats to order. The journalists in this category differed from supporters of the agent-of-empowerment role by speaking primarily about infrastructural and physical development rather than individual or social development. They used key words such as stability, security, unity and prosperity rather than social justice. Proponents of nation building were also notable for their concern about inciting SARA hostilities. The respondents in this group implied that responsibility – manifested through self-censorship or extremely refined writing techniques – should be exercised in cases that would agitate social tensions. Journalists in other categories, by contrast, never directly mentioned SARA issues when speaking of the journalists' role although they occasionally mentioned broader concepts such as building tolerance.

Only one journalist in this group, a reporter from the state-run Radio Republik Indonesia (RRI), said that journalists should function as 'a mouthpiece of government'. The remainder said that watchdog-style investigation of political incompetence or impropriety and the correction of government faults were appropriate elements of the nation-building role. The members of this small group were thus closest to developmentalist and *Pancasila* press function as defined by the New Order, fitting the Army General Chief of Staff Tarub's description of the press as a 'stabiliser' and 'dynamiser' of community life. All but the one RRI reporter, however, differentiated self-censorship for community well being from self-censorship for government well being.

A minor portion of respondents nominated other reasons. A few (7.7 per cent) described journalists as defenders of the truth. The journalists in this category identified their main role as impartially providing accurate, balanced, comprehensive information. These respondents emphasised that journalists served a social function by providing 'facts', stripped of bias or opinion, rather than engaging in crusades. One new recruit to a Jakarta daily, for example, said: 'I do not think the journalist is there to set the world right or to change the world. They tend to remind people [of what is right and wrong] by giving the truth, although not all journalists write the truth.' The respondents in this group said that, as the eyes of the community, journalists have a responsibility to portray as many perspectives in as objective a fashion as possible.

Only one journalist described his role primarily as an entertainment function. His reply should be interpreted in the context of his position as a sports-desk editor; he was describing his own function on that desk rather than the function of journalists overall. Other journalists also acknowledged that journalism has an entertainment function, although they described such a role as subsidiary to or a component of the watchdog or other functions.

Captives of the system

Despite New Order assurances that *Pancasila* journalists differed from Western journalists in their role and perspective on press freedom, lack of autonomy was the most outstanding and consistent grievance of survey respondents. When journalists were asked about what they believed were the profession's strengths and weakness and what were their professional satisfactions and dissatisfactions, 80.0 per cent cited the restrictions imposed on press freedom. The survey results appear to be backed by a 1994 Centre for the Study of Democracy and Development (1994: 4) survey, which found that 95.9 per cent of the 49 journalists questioned agreed or strongly agreed that journalists engaged in self-censorship. Another survey of 100 Yogyakarta journalists conducted in 1996 by *Paradigma* bulletin in association with the Coordinating Commissariat of the National Indonesian Student's Movement (Korkom GMNI) similarly pointed to problems of press freedom. The survey found that 32 per cent of the Yogyakarta respondents claimed their news was often censored, 56 per cent said it was sometimes censored, while only 2 per cent said they were never censored (*Paradigma* & Korkom GMNI 1996: 5).[3]

In New Order discourses, journalists sometimes self-censored their news from a sense of responsibility, because Indonesian society was not developed enough to deal peacefully with controversial news. Respondents, however, often inverted this formulation. One, for example, stated: 'I do not think the political system is developed enough to encompass the truth.' Some felt that burying such news was 'fatal' for democratisation and social control. Fluctuations in political temperatures also led to uncertainty about what was safe to print. One disillusioned editorial writer said: 'They describe our system as free and responsible. This is a technical term for self-censorship. It is absurd. Here it is not clear which way you should go. We must decide by groping around in the darkness.'

Although Indonesian journalists are famous for their ability to negotiate restrictions on press freedoms by using a refined, between-the-lines writing style,[4] respondents had mixed opinions about how news written in a subtle, allusive fashion could effectively check abuses of institutional power. Journalists also complained that they were mainly educators and entertainers rather than true journalists, and their reportage was always strongest and most satisfying in non-political and human-interest stories.

Complaints about press freedom were connected with a twofold cord of dissatisfaction that the news industry was weak against the institutions of power and that there were few avenues of protection for journalists against physical threats. Many engaged in melancholy reflections on the small but real possibility of bashing, torture or other persecution. They saw the 1996 murder of Yogyakarta journalist, Fuad Muhammad Syafruddin – apparently in relation to his investigation of a bribery that was linked to the first family – as symbolic of the dangers that they and their colleagues might encounter.

Journalists were similarly concerned at the industry's weakness against non-physical threats. News offices had long experienced the *kebudayaan telepon* (the telephone culture), in which the military, the police and the bureaucracy telephone editors to 'advise' on whether or how to run particular stories. The *Paradigma* and Korkom GMNI survey found that 18 per cent of its Yogyakarta respondents said they received regular telephone calls while 60 per cent said they received them sometimes. Only four per cent said they never received them (*Paradigma* & Korkom GMNI 1996: 5).[5] Journalists were also concerned about the risk of their newspapers being shut down if their SIUPP licence was suspended or withdrawn. The 1994 banning of three prominent news weeklies, *Tempo*, *Editor* and *DëTik*, was a sore point with many. Speaking of the risk of being delicensed, one reporter said: 'If you are a little brave, hah, wiped out!'

Journalists had various responses to such pressures. Six younger respondents partially satisfied their need for expression by working with the underground and Internet press. Several older journalists said they swallowed their frustrations, working quietly to publish critical stories whenever they could, in the hope that their efforts might lead to a free press for their children and grandchildren if not for their own generation.

Although respondents nominated other concerns about their profession, no other issue rated so overwhelmingly high as their dissatisfaction with lack of press freedom. Other frequently mentioned complaints related to poor wages and working conditions (33.8 per cent); low professional standards (24.6 per cent); the inadequacies of managements of news organisations in protecting journalists against threats from government or business figures (23.1 per cent), and the so-called envelope culture (21.5 per cent).[6] It becomes clear from this breakdown that by far the overwhelming focus of occupational dissatisfaction related to the sense of constriction of freedom of speech. Questions of professionalism, wages and working conditions and the envelope culture relate indirectly to freedom of the press and are discussed further in Chapters 6, 7 and 11. The complaints relating to the unwillingness of news managements to protect journalists will be discussed further. This issue is important, because as one subeditor said: 'Journalists have a very difficult time because the government harasses them and the owners harass them. They are caught between two giants.'

The problem was connected in part to the economic weakness of the media, which left publications vulnerable to takeover by figures closely connected with the inner circles of political power. Even in organisations free of management links to political leadership, senior editors saw controversial stories as risks to their expensive and essential SIUPP publishing licences. Jakob Oetama, chief editor of the Gramedia publishing group, admitted in the early 1990s that: 'We are becoming less critical because we have to survive' (Vatikiotis 1990b: 47). Journalists described cases in which they believed stories had been too easily dropped or management had refused to defend them against threats of violence, legal action or withdrawal of publishing licenses.

Editors themselves rationalised their conservatism by explaining that while fiery reporters might have been willing to personally accept the hazards connected with sensitive stories, editors were responsible for the welfare of the dozens or hundreds of workers who might lose their jobs if the organisation was shut down. A standard response for editors confronted by reporters angry about censorship of their stories was: 'You don't have to think about all these people with families to feed.' One editor admitted that 'young and rebellious' reporters 'frequently abuse' him after he changes or deletes their copy, accusing him of being afraid. At the time, tensions at that editor's newspaper were so intense that one senior journalist had been suspended from duty for calling his editors 'cowards'.

Yesterday's heroes

The indication that journalists rejected the press-as-government-handmaiden role was further reinforced by the survey respondents' nomination of journalists and editors they saw as role models, heroes or admirable professionals. The three who were nominated most frequently – Mochtar Lubis (nominated by 41.5 per cent), Goenawan Mohamad (27.7 per cent) and Rosihan Anwar (26.2 per cent) – were all editors of publications banned by the New Order.[7] Lubis and Anwar are respected both as journalists whose reportage scrutinised both the Sukarno and Soeharto government administrations. Lubis, imprisoned for many years for his anti-government reportage, is particularly prominent as an intellectual who uncompromisingly opposed corruption and abuses of power. Mohamad is famous as a political activist, poet and editor of *Tempo* magazine, arguably the most respected investigative journal of the New Order period.

In defining what characteristics they admired about different heroes and role models, respondents most commonly mentioned the crusader-like characteristics by maintaining bravery in opposing authorities (38.5 per cent), integrity (20 per cent) and watchdog skills (18.5 per cent). The term 'crusader' is commonly associated with those involved in the national struggle for independence, and denotes a person of valour, fighting for change in the status quo. Integrity also included characteristics such as consistency and persistence. The respondents' support of these traits reflected their disaffection with journalistic colleagues who bent to suit the changing winds blowing from those in power. Journalists admired Lubis and Anwar because, in the words of one, even in their twilight years 'their zeal has not been extinguished'. One journalist praised Lubis's determination and resoluteness by repeating the words of the crusader's late friend, Mohamad Roem (1982: 116), who said Lubis had 'a head like granite. Harder than stone'. Although the government insisted that journalists were uncomfortable with watchdog philosophies, the respondents admired those who, in the words of one, 'opposed the flow of government'. Many of Lubis's admirers said they could not accept journalism that functioned like *Intel* (military intelligence). These commendations clearly describe traits more commonly associated with the liberal watchdog than with the positive and protective *Pancasila* press.

Lubis and Anwar retired from journalism long ago, and even Mohamad might be considered a figure of a previous generation. Although Mohamad still engaged in editing and column writing in the late New Order, he was more notable as the brightest journalistic talent of the 1970s. More than a dozen survey respondents volunteered opinions that no journalists and editors of the late New Order period could be considered as outstanding. One reporter observed: 'We do not have heroes from this age. The climate is not conducive to it.' Another respondent, an admirer of Lubis's willingness to face jail for his exposés of high-level corruption and collusion, similarly suggested: 'If you say he was brave, it is contextual. It was possible because of the times.'

Such comments exposed a common assumption of many respondents that the dearth of modern press heroes resulted from the socio-political 'climate' and state-fostered self-censorship. Observations about the greater pressures on New Order journalists are not strictly accurate; even the most rudimentary study of Indonesian press history shows that journalists braved considerably greater risks of imprisonment, torture and even death during the eras of Dutch and Japanese occupation. Lubis's personal history shows that imprisonment, harassment and unemployment through closure of newspapers were also regular threats in the Sukarno and early Soeharto era.

To understand why the generation of journalists who operated in the late New Order did not point to courage in its own ranks, it is of more significance to explore what the journalistic community means when it assigns the appellation of hero. The word denotes not only that the community applauds that person's clarity of purpose, priorities and persistence in the face of adversity but also that the community recognises the hero's mission as legitimate and pertinent. The journalist who boldly defies the wrath of the powerful to advance a clearly articulated and recognisable social good or ideal may earn the label of hero; those who boldly defy the wrath of the powerful for no apparent social gain will more commonly be labelled as deviant, foolhardy or simply foolish. The heroism ascribed to particular professional journalistic activities is therefore proportional to the socially perceived legitimacy of such actions.

The discussion above suggests that there was considerable confusion and division among journalists of the late New Order era about the appropriate goals and conduct of the development journalist or *Pancasila* press. Exposés on corruption, collusion and mismanagement were often not viewed as intrinsically commendable during the New Order; they were often criticised for being negative, socially disruptive and damaging to public faith in the delicate and still-developing institutions of state. The ambivalence surrounding the journalists' role and the uncertainty about what issues were worth taking risks for thus emerged as enormous disincentives to intrepid journalism.

Adjusting to the new paradigm

No normative press model perfectly represents any society, because there is always inconsistency, diversity and change within social value systems. However, the New Order model of the *Pancasila* press clearly had many shortcomings. The survey results suggest that although many respondents were driven by a desire to develop and improve their society, they were even more critical of government-imposed restrictions under the guise of supposedly culturally appropriate *Pancasila* values than they were of Western ideas.

The gap between the perceptions of grass-roots practitioners on the one hand and theorists, bureaucrats and politicians on the other points to the difficulties of creating utopian models that journalists are expected to fulfil. As was discussed in Chapter 4, defining a press model involves observing existing values and behaviours in all their complexity before attempting to decipher the cultures and structures of the journalists' relationship with the state and society. The New Order's rejection of liberal and emancipatory frameworks as 'antidevelopment' ultimately led to a model that was unable to encompass the complexity and diversity of journalistic aspirations.

In early 1998, when many elements of Indonesian society chafed over the perceived shortcomings of the Soeharto government's paternalistic policy, journalists showed mounting fractiousness over official restrictions on their freedom. Intellectuals and journalists called for the press to adopt a watchdog-style surveillance role (e.g. Badrie 1998; Ismail 1998; Ritonga 1998). Journalists also pushed at the boundaries of acceptable reporting. Almost each week, they published or broadcast critiques of state figures and policies in a fashion that would have been unacceptable the week before.

Soeharto's departure from the number one position in May 1998 was accompanied by an immediate increase in freedom to publish facts and opinions. In the first dizzying months of the post-New Order period, journalists released a bewildering array of stories, some of which had waited years and even decades for publication or broadcast. While some journalists published serious analyses and investigations of socio-political issues and events, others published sensationalist mixes of fact, speculation and rumour about everything from the sex lives of Soeharto-family members to sectarian violence in the outer provinces. Journalists and journalists' associations themselves acknowledged that much of the reportage was low quality and inflammatory, often being riddled with inaccuracies, half-truths and political manipulation. Journalists and non-government organisations established media-monitoring associations, which published journals like *Pantau* that regularly revealed the inadequacies of journalists who produced one-sided, inaccurate or even fictitious reports. Journalists and academics now frequently organise and address public seminars and workshops highlighting faults and insufficiencies in the news and current affairs.

Given the rapid change in the media environment, two tasks have become priorities for the professional and other associations that represent journalists.

The first is to establish mechanisms to protect freedom of the press and enshrine it as an essential element of the nascent press model. The second is to increase professional and ethical standards. The second priority results not just from a moral concern that substandard reporting can harm individuals and communities but also from a recognition that unless the media can regulate their own performance, then external powers such as the state may reclaim the authority to restrict press liberty for the public good. The two tasks are therefore intrinsically interrelated. Journalists' associations organised numerous seminars to talk about press freedoms and responsibilities and periodically issued statements or declarations on both issues. Attempts to build professionalism have also involved a boom in journalism courses, with investigative journalism and peace journalism among those with increased popularity.

The previously conservative journalists' organisation, the PWI, has evolved its concept of press freedom from a 'free and responsible' model to a watchdog orientation. For example, the PWI was a signatory to a 1999 Memorandum of Understanding, drawn up by ASEAN and Chinese journalists' associations, that pledged to urge governments 'to take strong measures to further practice good governance' and financial institutions 'to show more accountability and social responsibility'. The statement also commits journalists to 'undertake more pro-active and values-driven journalism' in investigating and interpreting events in the region.

The new paradigms are also evident among journalists, media associations and affiliated groups that have collaborated on efforts to revise the laws governing journalistic activity. These individuals and groups played a key role in contributing to the various proposals that ultimately led to the 1999 Press Law and to the draft broadcast law, which was still under parliamentary consideration in mid-2001. These groups have been adamant that their models be ratified without substantive modification to the central tenet of media autonomy. For example, several industry groups launched an immediate offensive when the parliament revised a draft proposal of the new broadcast act, which had initially been written by a coalition of journalists and media-industry figures. Several journalists' associations and other industry alliances protested outside parliament, called for boycotts of the DPR hearings, conducted a flurry of media interviews and engaged in other actions to pressure for further amendment of the bill.

The proposals of journalists and their associations were universally designed to minimise state interference in media activity and to promote self-regulation whenever possible. Initially, the issue of industry self-regulation was complex, because the many journalists' associations that operated in post-New Order Indonesia had different codes of ethics. The variation in codes meant that activities regarded as major misdemeanours by one association might not be regarded as punishable offences by another. To address this problem, 26 organisations engaged in protracted negotiations that led to them endorsing a compromise code, the *Kode Etik Wartawan Indonesia* (KEWI, Indonesian Journalists' Code of Ethics). The KEWI operates as an umbrella code, which all associations accept in addition to their individual codes. One aim of the unified code is to reduce the potential for future governments to claim that state regulation or corporatised status are necessary to standardise industry ethics and practice. Indonesian citizens can now bring complaints about the perceived misdemeanours of any journalist to the Press Council, which is elected by media-industry representatives. The Council uses the simple, seven-point KEWI as its basis for mediating and arbitrating cases. This self-regulatory philosophy was enacted in the 1999 Press Law, which removes regulatory powers from the state and shifts punitive powers to professional associations, the Press Council and the courts of law.

One step forward, one step back

The changes in the political culture mean that post-Soeharto political and bureaucratic figures are far less likely to pressure journalists to engage in the kind of self-censorship that caused so much journalistic dissatisfaction during the New Order. A great deal of liberty has arisen from the abolition of requirements for the SIUPP or other permits to print or broadcast news, meaning that governments can no longer close news organisations by withdrawing such licences. Despite this, the issue of press freedom remains paramount in journalists' consciousness. After completing a tour of regional PWI branches, Association Chairman Tarman Azzam described freedom of the press as the number-one priority of the membership base (Azzam 2001: pers. comm.).

One reason for continued emphasis on press freedom is that physical threats have become a far greater problem than before. Reports by AJI (*Aliansi Jurnalis Independen*, Alliance of Independent Journalists) and SEAPA (the South East Asian Press Alliance) have tallied the number of attacks on journalists and their newsrooms, and have found that the rate of attacks has escalated substantially since the end of the New Order and continues to rise. The incidents recorded include vandalism, assaults, abductions and murders.

Many attacks have involved the police and state authorities. In October 2000, hundreds of journalists rallied in Jakarta to protest the police beating of two photographers who were trying to take pictures during a demonstration. However, the largest sources of threats and violence against journalist are community groups and individuals. The propensity for community groups to launch assaults against journalists and news organisations has raised concern in the journalistic fraternity that the 'the masses prefer violence as a means to express their dissatisfaction' (SEAPA 2000: 3). Many journalists' forums and media articles have discussed the problem of the public 'taking the law into their own hands'. The Press Council and journalists' groups have tried to promote non-violent methods of revolving grievances with the media, such as the right of reply as stipulated in the 1999 Press Law, mediation through the Press Council or legal action through the courts. There are few ways of measuring whether such educational activities have significantly influenced behaviour in a society where state authorities have flouted official rules for decades and faith in the legal system is low.

Journalists have dedicated more energy to resisting state attempts to harass or coerce them. This is partly because state targets are easier to identify than potential community adversaries, and strategies for confronting official figures are well honed. For example, Wahid's moves to check journalists' activities through decree and the presidential palace's media watchdog team in 2001 (outlined in Chapter 4) were met by an immediate response by journalists and support associations. A Press Council statement (No. 6/DP/V/2001) argued that a state of emergency would cause suffering in the community, because of the severe security measures and the reduction in access to information that would follow. The Council and an array of senior media figures attempted to discourage Wahid from issuing the decree. They also objected to legal action by the watchdog team, on the basis that 'the powerful can easily scare the courts' into following their wishes. They urged the president's team to instead concentrate on the 'upstream' free-flow of accurate information, by using the right of reply to address reports that need correction. They also advocated that Wahid make better use of the Press Council's powers to act as a mediator in cases where journalists were perceived to have published erroneous information (Laksamana.net 21 June 2001).

The response to reports of the proposed rebirth of the Department of Information is also indicative the nature of the networks journalists employ to counter perceived threats. Details of the reports were posted by a journalist from ISAI (*Institute Studi Arus Informasi*, the Institute for Free Flow of Information) to several inter-related journalists' email discussion groups, such as the 'anti-New Order journalist' group (wartawan-anti-ordebaru@yahoogroups.com). By the next day, public statements were being issued and forums were being held to publicise the issue and organise an action plan. Support was summonsed nationwide, and even international groups, such as the Committee to Protect Journalists, registered concern with Megawati about the possibility of the Department being revived. Much of the action in the cases discussed in this chapter has involved journalists using their strategic position within the public sphere to issue reports and declarations and to ensure that they attract wide media attention.

Journalists' associations are sometimes criticised for over-relying on statements rather taking than firmer action against threats to professionalism and press freedom. Regardless of the flaws of this approach, it indicates the journalistic fraternity's faith in the watchdog approach and the self-righting powers of the socio-political system once problems are brought to public attention. Attempts to reduce community violence by calling for community members to use the right of reply, the Press Council or, at last resort, the legal system are unlikely to have immediate impact. However, they similarly point to journalistic commitment to rule of law and regularisation of the public sphere. In the unstable period of readjustment following the New Order's passing, the emphasis has been on cementing legal, professional and social changes that will enable them to establish and maintain a watchdog role.

6 Print professionals and ink coolies

For more than three decades, Indonesian journalists were unable to join unions to protect their wages and workplace conditions. During the New Order, both the government and media managements insisted that journalism must be defined as a profession. They argued that journalists were professionals because they worked in the realm of ideas rather than that of physical labour. They also contended that it was below the dignity of a professional class, such as journalists, to lower themselves to form unions as common labourers did. The logic of the approach is simplistic, at least on the surface, but it is bound in a complex fashion to the ideological precepts that propelled New Order politics. The assumption that journalists are not professionals is, in fact, somewhat ironic given that pre-WWII journalists often referred to themselves as *tukang berita*, tradesmen of the news, because the words reporter, *jurnalis* and *wartawan* were unknown to many of the young Indonesia intellectuals who entered the field (Kakiailatu 1997: 51). Journalists have long been colloquially referred to as *kuli tinta*, coolies of the ink, a term redolent of the drudgery of sweaty, unskilled labourers toiling in menial tasks. In the computer age, they are sometimes called *kuli disket*, coolies of the disk.

The rise of professionalism has been historically linked to that of corporate capitalism and the process of modernisation (Johnson 1972: 38; Perkin 1989; Larson 1977: 4–13, 136–158). 'For professions, the most significant "modern" dimensions are the advance of science and cognitive rationality, and the related rationalisation and growing differentiation in the division of labor' (Larson 1977: xvi). However, despite the emergence of 'professionalism' in modern society, various scholars note that 'profession' itself is a slippery concept (e.g. Freidson 1977: 14–15; Hoyle & John 1995: 1; Bucher & Stelling 1969: 4). The term profession may signify to some an understanding of professional norms, to others a proficiency in technical skills or a range of ethical workplace behaviours, and to yet others, a means by a certain group to control the marketplace in a certain field.

This chapter examines the symbolic significance of the New Order's assessment that journalists were professionals and not labourers, and how this definition helped to determine journalists' place in the socio-economic structure. It does not attempt to exhaustively categorise the attributes of journalists to determine whether the New Order's assessment was justified. Numerous phenomenologists have argued that such a strict definition of profession is artificial (e.g. Dingwall 1983; Freidson 1983; Hoyle & John 1995). This work instead follows in the tradition established by Everett Hughes (1958: 45), who first suggested that rather than ask whether a given occupation is a profession, it is often more consequential to ask what it means for an occupation to be identified as a profession and under what circumstances people will attempt to turn themselves into professionals. The chapter concludes with an exploration of how the New Order's categorisation of journalists as professionals and not workers continues to impact on life in the news media.

Professionalism and the right to organise

Arguments about whether Indonesian journalists are truly professionals or whether they might also be considered as 'labour' have usually arisen in the context of discussions about labour rights, especially in response to questions about whether journalists should have the right to organise collectively in unions or similar associations. During the Old Order, there was little argument about the issue. The 1955 PWI Code of Ethics describes one of the PWI's prime objectives as being to function like a trade union. By contrast, the New Order rhetoric promoted a view that it would be inherently demeaning to journalists if they were categorised as 'labour', and the PWI shifted its role to become a 'professional association' only and not a union. Despite a lengthy but low-key debate about whether journalists are workers who might require and legitimately claim union support, proponents of unionism achieved little success during the New Order period.

One of the earlier proposals to form a journalists' union emerged at a 1975 workshop, organised by the Publishing Companies' Labour Union in cooperation with the Asian American Free Labor Institute, with the aim of creating 'the core cadres to pioneer the formation of labor unions in printing establishments and publishing companies' (Dhakidae 1991: 393). The FBSI (*Federasi Buruh Seluruh Indonesia*, All Indonesia Workers' Federation) defined journalists as *buruh* who need their wages and social conditions protected, even though they also are professionals connected with the PWI. Hamidy, secretary general of the Newspaper Publishers' Association, rejected the proposal for a journalists' union in terminology that was to become exemplary of the New Order's position. Hamidy insisted that a journalist 'is not a *buruh*. A journalist belongs to a free profession and must service a certain ideal and, therefore, should not enter a union'. He advised journalists that they could 'leave at any time' if that ideal no longer suited them (Syukur 1975: 3).

Efforts to promote unionism in 1978 were also short-lived, but for different reasons. Parni Hadi, then an Antara news agency journalist, led a group that recommended to Manpower Minister Subroto that a *Serikat Sekerja Wartawan* (SSW, Journalists' Workers' Association) be established in individual news offices. Hadi recalls that Subroto accepted the principal that such an association could be formed under the provisions of manpower regulations requiring all workplaces with more than 25 employees to allow the formation of enterprise-level labour associations. Hadi says he and his partners abandoned the proposal when they became aware of the 1975 Information Ministry decree (Surat Keputusan Menteri Penerangan RI No. 47/Kep/Menpen/1975) that defined the PWI as Indonesia's 'only journalists' association'. Hadi's interpretation was that the industry-specific stipulations of the press regulation overruled the broad, normative provisions of the manpower regulations, thus forbidding the formation of any new journalistic association, whether it be professional or labour-oriented (Hadi 1998: pers. comm.). Then Information Minister Ali Murtopo strongly opposed the classification of journalists as either *buruh* or members of labour organisations. He argued that because journalists must idealistically struggle for community interests, it was incompatible that they belonged to unions that strive for the sectional interests of their members (Antara 15 May 1978: 7; *Sinar Harapan* 15 May 1978: 16).

An unexpectedly persistent advocate for journalists' labour unions was Admiral Sudomo. In 1979, while head of Kopkamtib, Sudomo explicitly defined journalists as *buruh*. He said that the press was being ruled by the *tauke* (employers) and that journalists were welcome to form *Serikat Buruh Lapangan* (Workplace-Based Unions) or to be organised under the FBSI (*Harian Umum AB* 8 Mar. 1979: 1, 8). The proposal was supported by the FBSI head, Agus Sudono, who judged journalists as being in the same category as labourers because 'they have no capital except the labour they sell through their writing' (*Harian Umum AB* 15 Mar. 1979: 1, 2).

Despite the lukewarm response he received in 1979, Sudomo again revived the idea in 1984 and 1985 after becoming Manpower Minister (Antara 15 Aug. 1985: A15; Antara 20 Nov. 1984: A8; Dhakidae 1991: 395–6). Information Minister Harmoko and *Kompas* newspaper both dismissed Sudomo's proposal, replying that journalists' interests and aspirations would be better served by establishing how to put into practice the terms of a new 'family-oriented' ministerial regulation and a ministerial decree on SIUPP licensing system for the print media (Permenpen RI No. 01/Per/Menpen/1984). The SIUPP regulation ostensibly aimed to protect news workers' welfare through cooperatives, workers' councils, pension funds and communication forums to represent and protect journalists' interests (Antara 21 Nov. 1984: A16; Dhakidae 1991: 396). Article 16 of the regulation stipulated that journalists and press workers should hold at least 20 per cent of shares in their publishers' companies. The regulation thus theoretically subverted Sudomo's arguments that journalists had the same status as labourers because they had no capital in their organisations. Article 28 further says that disputes between journalists/ workers and management should be settled through deliberative procedures involving familial-style compromise and consensus seeking. From 1984 until the end of the New Order, both the government and most media employers commonly opposed unions on the grounds that journalists, as company shareholders, did not need unions and that workplace concerns could be better negotiated via consensus-seeking mechanisms rather than the adversarial channels of labour organisations.

A series of attempts by journalists to renegotiate and strengthen their position as workers in the mid-1980s was also unsuccessful. One of the best-known attempts to initiate an in-house union was by a *Kompas* reporter, Albert Kuhon. Kuhon says that he found a discrepancy between *Kompas*'s critical reportage on corporations that did not have trade unions to protect their workers and the newspaper's own lack of protective union structures. Unlike Hadi, he argued that the 1975 press regulations defined the PWI position as journalists' sole *professional* organisation, but this did not preclude the possibility of establishing unions that protected journalists as intellectual *labourers* within the news industry (Kuhon 1997: pers. comm.).

Although Kuhon discussed the situation with management in 1985, the situation progressed little until 1987, when he and three office colleagues organised several meetings of up to 20 journalists to confer about the perceived inadequacies in systems for organising and evaluating professional work and the relative meagreness of journalists' salaries compared to *Kompas*'s high profits. *Kompas* management countered that the organisation's wages and conditions were the best in the Indonesian news industry. Kuhon conceded this point but maintained that workers were getting less than they deserved in terms of 'salary and social justice'. Kuhon argues that across the industry, issues such as staff promotions are generally determined by the employers' tastes and political needs because of the underdevelopment of formal work-evaluation strategies, wage-fixing mechanisms and other procedures for objectively evaluating staff performance (Kuhon 1997: pers. comm.). Kuhon's reformist agenda went beyond the mere protection of workers from potential exploitation. It explored the possibility of enhancing professional development through modern, merit-based decision-making processes rather than the authority- or affiliation-based decision-making processes inherent in the existing paternalistic hierarchy. The principles and systems of management that he identified as important for advancing journalists as professionals were intrinsically identical to those that would protect their rights as workers.

When union proponents circulated a petition within *Kompas* in 1988 seeking the minimum of 25 signatures required under Manpower Ministry regulations to form a trade union, *Kompas* management responded by threatening sanctions against union supporters. Kuhon's three key allies promptly apologised to management and were subject to disciplinary actions (*Berita Buana* 23 Mar. 1988: 6). Kuhon says that when he refused to relent or repent, management refused to publish any stories he wrote for more than six months. He finally left after being offered work by the rival *Sinar Kasih* newspaper group (Kuhon 1997: pers. comm.).

Replying to a request from *Kompas* for guidelines on the union issue, the PWI said that labour unions were 'against the essence and position of a journalist as a professional' (Dhakidae 1991: 409). PWI leaders said they endorsed the family-oriented 'principle of togetherness' as integral to newspaper management. They argued that the SIUPP regulations supported this togetherness principle and also proved that as capital holders, journalists were not workers in the normal sense.

Other journalists and photographers conducted small-scale attempts to form unions during the New Order in publications like *Pelita*, *Sinar Harapan* and *Jakarta-Jakarta*. In each of these publications, the instigators were either fired or given the 'option' of withdrawing from the union or leaving their jobs. None of the efforts progressed as far or were as well publicised as Kuhon's initiative.

As PWI Secretary General from 1993 to 1998, Hadi informally tried to promote within the journalists' association the idea of *Serikat Sekerja Karyawan Pers* (Press Workers' Associations) for all news-industry workers. In the dying months of the New Order, he admitted his proposal had not progressed far in a culture where 'too many compromises' were necessary (Hadi 1998: pers. comm.). At that time, Hadi's immediate superior, PWI Chairman Sofjan Lubis, continued to argue that as professionals journalists could not form labour unions or apply for protection under the Manpower Ministry regulations applying to *buruh*. Using the New Order's well-worn formula, he explained:

> It is not possible to form a labour union for journalists because journalists are professionals, the same as teachers, doctors and lawyers; they are different from factory hands or other *buruh*. Journalists have creativity and ideas; this is different from other jobs like laying roads. (Lubis 1998: pers. comm.)

Apart from maintaining a clear separation between the *modus operandum* and legal entitlements of the professional-intellectual classes and the labouring classes, Lubis also argued that, as company shareholders, journalists were responsible for developing their companies (1998: pers. comm.). By implication, he suggests that by exercising their rights as workers, journalists would hinder the progress of their organisations and thus hamper the growth of journalism as a profession.

Shareholding and the right to organise

Arguments that SIUPP legislation affected journalists' rights to form unions should be dismissed as specious. The 1984 SIUPP regulation was described as the basis of the family-oriented industrial system within the media (*Kompas* 16 Dec. 1994: 13; *Pelita* 21 Sept. 1984: 1). Under the regulation, all workers in print-media organisations, from journalists to janitors, are entitled to the shares that are owned and managed collectively through workers' cooperatives, foundations and other internal company structures. The logic of the 20 per cent workers' ownership was 'to create a **"sense of belonging"** to the company where the journalists work, thereby encouraging their motivation to actively participate in the upbuilding of their own welfare as well' (Sinaga 1987a: 22, bold type in original).

By implication, these shares rendered unionism counterproductive to the journalists' own interests as owners, but New Order officials were fully aware that media workers enjoyed few if any of the rights of media owners. Firstly, the regulation only applied to the print media. Secondly, even in 1997 – 13 years after employers had been given notice of their obligations to comply with the regulation and before the economic downturn had a dramatic impact on Indonesian business – Information Department figures show that 29 per cent of the print media's 15,164 workers were still waiting to be allocated any shares at all (Departemen Penerangan 1997/8: i–iii).

It is possible that the figure of 29 per cent is an underestimation. Journalists from several major publications claim that their companies had falsified the figures they provided to the Information Department, and accused them of 'spreading lies' in order to create the impression that they were fulfilling their legal obligations regarding workers' shares (*Kompas* 3 Jun. 1998: 10; *Suara Serikat* 20 Mar. 2000b: 8). Although senior New Order leaders threatened to punish those companies that did not meet their obligations under the regulation, (Antara 21 Nov. 1984: A16; *Kompas* 16 Dec. 1994: 13), the government displayed leniency on the basis that not all companies could afford to do so immediately. Government officials knew that many publications had neglected their duty under the SIUPP regulations, yet they still denied journalists the right to organise in unions regardless of whether the journalists concerned owned collective shares or not.

Even when companies provided shares that were managed by workers' representatives, the shares did not constitute the same form of ownership that individuals might obtain if they bought ordinary shares in a private company. Hadi (1998: pers. comm.) explains that:

> It is a token share. It does not pay anything. Only if the company makes a profit will the Workers' Cooperative get a dividend – a collective dividend. It is collective, not individual. And the workers do not pay financial capital ... only their expertise, which is considered a collective asset worth 20 per cent. If there is a profit, they get a share. If there is a loss, because they do not have financial capital, they do not bear that. It is very idealistic. It is so ideal. But it has not yet been implemented.

For such reasons, journalists who defected from *Tempo* in 1987 to establish a new magazine, *Editor*, bought 28 per cent of the company's shares with their own funds so that the 50 founders might have a real stake in the organisation rather than 'empty shares' (*Jakarta Jakarta* 24 Jul. 1987a: 4)

The workers' 20 per cent share holding also differed from regular shares because, even though under 1971 laws (UU 1971 No. 14) one share equalled one vote, newsworkers who owned collective shares did not vote directly on the company's board. Hadi (1998: pers. comm.) admits that even in the dying months of the New Order, workers' cooperatives and foundations rarely had representatives in their publication's supreme body, the *Dewan Komisaris* (Board of Commissioners). In Hadi's *Republika*, for example, the Workers' Cooperative had no board member. Therefore, even workers who were allocated 20 per cent rarely had an effective voice on the board, while a commercial investor with less than 5 per cent did. Because the collective shares allocated by news companies were not truly owned by individual workers, staff could not sell their shares or reinvest their assets in other companies. They lost their shareholding altogether if they left their jobs or their companies shut down.

In a systematic study of the Sinar Kasih, Jawa Pos and Kompas-Gramedia press groups in 1997, Kuhon noted that the administrators of the workers' cooperatives and foundations were usually also directors or senior editorial staff members of the news groups concerned (Kuhon 1998: 6–10). He concluded that shares donated and administered by executives and managers will not improve workers' positions. He advised that press professionals would only be empowered if they had an independent umbrella organisation through which to influence press owners and administrators (Kuhon 1998: 10).

Even those media organisations that gave their staff shares failed to operate under the provisions of cooperative laws. These laws specify that all members are equal, all have voting rights, rights are exercised in person and not by proxy, decisions are taken by majority vote, leaders and representatives are elected by members themselves, all have the right to dividend or interest on share capital and all have the right to claim repayment for their share of the capital contribution when they withdraw from membership (Hassan 1987: xxii–xxiv). Typical of the state of the industry was the situation at *Jakarta Jakarta* magazine. In the months before holding company Kompas Gramedia folded the magazine, staff complained that not only did the magazine's workers have no say in the choice of their *yayasan's* administrators, there was uncertainty about who the administrators were. The *yayasan* heads also never consulted with *Jakarta Jakarta* staff, nor did they provide reports on the progress of the shares (*Suara Serikat* 20 Mar. 2000b: 8–9). The 20 per cent share holding can thus only be compared to a family in that young children's welfare commonly depends on whether the parents act responsibly and benevolently when they decide how much they will give their children. Children's prosperity is rarely proportional to their investment of assets, economic influence or decision-making capacity within their families.

Dispute resolution and the right to organise

The first major advance for those who argued that journalists should have the same legal rights as other workers occurred in December 1987, when a *Sinar Pagi* newspaper journalist became the first journalist to win an unfair dismissal case in the *Panitia Penyelesaian Perselisihan Perburuhan Daerah* (P4D, Regional Committee for Resolution of Labour Disputes), which operates under the auspices of the Manpower Department. Abdul Jalil brought the case to the P4D after *Sinar Pagi* ignored 'family-like' appeals from both the Information Department and the PWI to respect his rights (Hastuti, Gantra & Almayan

1988a: 67). The *Sinar Pagi* case was promptly followed by a similar case, in which the P4D overturned the dismissal of a subeditor from *Merdeka* (Hastuti, Gantra & Almayan 1988b: 68). Journalists continued to use the P4D throughout the New Order. In one of the most prominent cases, the P4D in Jakarta found in favour of 10 *Suara Pembaruan* journalists, who had been asked by CEO Albert Hasibuan to resign in 1995 after they questioned the legitimacy and capability of the newspaper's senior executives and called for management restructuring.

The 1987 success of the *Sinar Pagi* journalist in the P4D prompted Sudomo to renew his advocacy for a journalists' union yet again. Sudomo said the SIUPP and the PWI were insufficient to manage workplace relations and that employers should respect labour laws and negotiate *Kesepakatan Kerja Bersama* (KKB, Cooperative Work Agreements) with workers (*Berita Buana* 3 Dec. 1987: 1, 9). Labour laws specify that workplaces with more than 25 workers cannot prevent staff from applying to the SPSI to form a workplace-based union, and such unions are particularly important for the negotiation process of the KKB. The General Secretary of the SPSI's Executive Council offered support by saying that the PWI was the umbrella for journalists' professional concerns such as press laws and ethics, while the SPSI was the appropriate umbrella for journalists' industrial relations and workplace concerns (*Angkatan Bersenjata* 11 Dec. 1987: 12).

Senior industry and Department of Information figures predictably rejected the idea. Information Minister Harmoko maintained his opposition to unions, claiming that journalists were not *buruh*. Even though the PWI had been unable to resolve the *Sinar Pagi* and *Merdeka* cases through family-like mechanisms, Harmoko and the PWI Chief Executive Zulharman Said both insisted that journalists should not go beyond the PWI and the provisions of the 1984 regulation (*Berita Buana* 3 Dec. 1987: 9; Hastuti, Gantra & Almayan 1988a: 67). *Sinar Pagi*'s lawyer reflected the official New Order positioning that professionals held a position distinct and superior to that of labourers by saying that if he were a journalist, he would be 'embarrassed' to form a labour association under the SPSI (Hastuti, Gantra & Almayan 1988a: 68).

Despite the utility of the P4D to some journalists, relatively few cases were resolved through this channel, because the systemic refusal to consider journalists as workers meant that few were aware of their options in resolving industrial issues. The difficulties encountered by staff affected by a mass sacking at *Pelita* are indicative of the problem. When *Pelita*'s management dismissed 64 staff in 1991 without notice and without consulting with the newspaper's *Dewan Karyawan* (Staff Council), the retrenched workers were refused assistance by the SPSI. Theo Sambuaga, deputy head of a DPR commission that had heard submissions from a delegation of sacked *Pelita* staff, called for new regulations governing press workplace relations. He found that the SIUPP regulations were unclear because they did not specify whether cases like that in *Pelita* should be handled by the Information Department, the Manpower Department or another institution (Firmansyah et al. 1991: 29). The New Order's policy, encouraging each publication to establish a *Dewan Karyawan*, consisting of staff members who might negotiate with management, left newsroom staff like those at *Pelita* with few clear legal avenues for defending their interests (Hill 1995: 71).

Workers and professionals in the New Order family

The New Order's refusal to recognise journalists' as *buruh* was consistent with its attempts to replace both leftist and liberal capitalist ideologies from labour relations with integralistic philosophies. Given the history of the ABRI's relations with organised labour and the New Order's developmentalist, corporatist construction of *Pancasila* Industrial Relation system (discussed in Chapter 2), the state was usually hostile or at least antipathetic towards unions, especially those in politically important sectors such as the news industry. Attending the 1975 meeting to promote the union concept (mentioned above), then Information Minister Mashuri and former Information Minister B.M. Diah drew on a wealth of existing state rhetoric when they talked extensively about a perceived need to break the old pattern of workers associations that supposedly pitted workers against employers (Antara 22 Oct. 1975: 9; KNI 22 Oct. 1975: 10; KNI 21 Oct. 1975: 8). In opposing 1978 proposals for a journalists' union, Ali Murtopo used similar discourses to claim that journalists must not organise into unions like *buruh*, because *buruh* create class conflict between workers and employers. 'This only can happen in socialist or communist countries,' he declared (Antara 15 May 1978: 7). In such a political context, it was unsurprising that journalists' unions were dismissed as confrontational or hostile to employers, and the PWI was defined not as a trade union but a professional association.

Senior New Order editors and journalists also commonly supported ABRI and other New Order ideologues in the *karyawan* versus *buruh* debate, because many had been involved in acrimonious personal and political relationships with the supporters of *buruh*-ism and labour rights during the Old Order. In the 1960s, Indonesia's press was split into two broad, opposing ideological alignments. The decades of Sukarno's leadership were marked by a progressively increasing animosity between those conservative artists, journalists and intellectuals who expounded the responsibility of artists to choose objective and responsible themes and those who advocated art as a servant of the revolution. Radical journalists were affiliated, through the PWI executive, with the PKI, SOBSI and related organisations. Conservative journalists were more commonly associated with the BPS, which was affiliated with ABRI's central command, SOKSI and associated political allies.

The hostilities between conservative and radical artists had been evident since the 1920s, but became notably pronounced when many of the former signed the Cultural Manifesto of August 1963. The Cultural Manifesto was written partly in response to the strident activism of left-leaning artists, who were often associated with the PKI artists' institute, Lekra (*Lembaga Kebudayaan Rakyat*, the People's Cultural Institute). Lekra's simmering antipathy to the Cultural Manifesto soon boiled over when Manifesto artists held the March 1964

All-Indonesia Conference of Writer *Karyawan*. The Conference, which aimed to form a *karyawan* organisation, the PKPI, within SOKSI (Reeve 1985: 231), resulted in journalists and other artists being drawn into the antagonistic binary discourses of *karyawan*–SOKSI versus *buruh*–SOBSI–PKI. In the 'political quarantine' that followed, Manifesto–PKPI supporters were sacked from government and cultural organisations and many found their writings were no longer published (Budiman 1973: 77; Ricklefs 1981: 263). Journalists associated with the Manifesto–PKPI were investigated by the left-dominated PWI (Reeve 1985: 232).

The tensions were further heightened with the September 1964 formation of the BPS by journalists intimately associated with those SOKSI figures who upheld the claim that 'the Doctrine for *Karyawan* is the Doctrine of *Bung* Karno [Brother Sukarno]' (Reeve 1985: 238). Sukarno banned the BPS in December 1964 by presidential decree (No. 72/KOTI/1964), following a series of mass anti-BPS demonstrations and accusations that the BPS was CIA-funded 'Sukarnoism to kill the tenets of *Bung* Karno and *Bung* Karno himself' (Oey 1971: 109–10; Said & Moelijanto 1983: 63–4; Sukarno 1965: 10). In 1964–65, the PWI expelled all 'counter-revolutionary' BPS supporters. Among them was Harmoko, a founding BPS member who not only later became a PWI Chairman but also served for 14 years as Soeharto's Information Minister, and Sofjan Lubis, also a subsequent PWI Chairman during the New Order period (Koesworo, Margantoro & Viko 1994, 26–8; Said 1988: 141–4; Said & Moeljanto 1983: 77–8, 90). Harmoko, Lubis and other BPS journalists were questioned by the public prosecutor's headquarters in Jakarta and Medan on suspicion of being counter-revolutionaries who had aided the Americans (Said 1988: 155–6). Increasing pressure against BPS journalists culminated when the information minister banned 29 BPS publications by decree (No. 17/SK/M/65) in 1965.

The battle between the BPS and conservatives against the PKI and other leftists was totally eclipsed by the national upheaval that followed the failure of the Gestapu coup of 30 September–1 October 1965. As is explained further in the following chapter, supporters of the BPS, *Manifesto* and PKPI led a purge of journalists and artists who had supported the PKI, *Lekra* and SOBSI in the post-Gestapu, anticommunist fervour of 1965–6. Those journalists who had been victimised by the polemicists of *buruh*ism would form the new generation of press leaders. Those who had supported the BPS, the Cultural Manifesto and *karyawan*ism would wield power and influence during the New Order as editors, PWI leaders and, in the cases of B.M. Diah and Harmoko, Information Ministers. It was thus entirely predictable that many of those who felt they had suffered at the hands of Lekra and the PWI would give short shrift to proponents of *buruh*ism and unionism.

Professional reward

Although the discussion in this chapter so far implies that professionalism was attractive mainly to the state and employers as an ideological tool for containing worker activism, the precepts of professionalism are also alluring to lower-level journalists. The New Order logic continuously described professionals as intellectuals above the status of the *buruh* who form the greater majority of Indonesian population. The term profession commands prestige and respect in most societies (Bucher & Stelling 1969: 4) and a sense of elevation over other workers (Larson 1977: xvi; Merton 1982: 112–3).

Larson (1977: 236) also argues that professionalism is an ideology that dissuades workers from identifying with those of lower status or from organising with them in unions. Discussing the news media in a global sense, Kunczik (1988: 96) argues that journalists generally succumb to an illusion of superiority as members of a 'free profession'. 'They refuse to see their work as what it really is: wage-dependent work. Instead one likes to think of oneself as a socially unattached intellectual, a kind of journalistic genius not concerned with material compulsions.' It might be expected that this general tendency for journalists to maintain the pretensions of professional and intellectual superiority would be particularly strong in Indonesia's historical framework. Indonesia's journalists were significant intellectual leaders of the national independence struggle and were later recruited during the New Order from various university faculties as 'an educated, intellectual class who could help in national education' (Surjomiharjo & Suryadinata 1980: 79).

Within the study of professions, it is acknowledged that professionals generally enjoy high pay, good working conditions and job security. Education and training, accompanied by testing, are the central tenets that allow professions to claim a monopoly of skills that cannot be reproduced by the untrained lay person and to guarantee the production of competent professionals. The professions and professional associations thus 'constitute and control' their market, in contrast to unions, which usually operate in subordinate markets (Larson 1977: 55–6).

Although journalists are called 'professionals', they have poor salaries and working conditions. These problems persist, in part, because journalists do not control entry to the market within which they operate. During the New Order period, the only restriction on entry into journalism was the obligation for all journalists to obtain PWI membership. The requirements for PWI membership were not demanding, as they were aimed at checking the journalists' status as a stable, law-abiding *Pancasila* citizen and not at proving knowledge or competency in journalism. All candidates had to pass an open-book entrance exam, which tested the journalists' knowledge of the code of ethics and their understanding of and loyalty to *Pancasila*. They had to submit a Certificate of Good Behaviour from a member of the police force, showing that they had never been connected with 'treasonable' or criminal behaviour. The minimum educational requirement was senior highschool. With the absence of any strict entry requirements, journalists lacked substantial workplace bargaining power.

The PWI could never realistically be expected to function as a representative of journalists' workplace interests during the New Order. Even when the PWI association worked 'to constitute and control' the market, it did so according to the vision of news industry management. Analyst Christianto Wibisono found that the PWI colluded with the *Serikat Penerbit Suratkabar* (SPS, the Newspaper Publishers' Association) and Department of Information to enable existing publishers to monopolise the market during the New Order through a strict licensing system that limited the number of new media organisations in the field (Wibisono 1994: 102; also Hutabarat 1993: 460; Wibisono 1993: 452). With this protection of the financial interests of news organisations, journalism became a capital-intensive, profit-centred industry during the New Order, compared to its function during the Old Order as a realm of crusaders (*Angkatan Bersenjata* 10 Jun. 1996: 1; Dhakidae 1991; Dhakidae 1993b: 376–380; Hutabarat 1993: 455; *Jakarta Jakarta* 24 Jul. 1987b: 13; Kuhon 1998: 10; Lubis 1992: 99; Siregar 1993: 399–403). The licensing system protected the commercial interests of proprietors and the political interests of the state, but it did nothing to support the journalists' claim to mastery over a specific professional jurisdiction within existing news organisations. The New Order was thus hypocritical in helping media proprietors to develop journalism as a sector of idealism to one of capital accumulation, while also insisting that questions of journalists' financial interests and rights as labourers were rendered subordinate, if not totally irrelevant, to the journalists' higher role as warrior for national development (Dhakidae 1991: 391).

The benefits of true professional status are not merely financial; the professional's claims to detached objectivity, cognitive exclusivity and service orientation allow them considerable autonomy, which can be used to defend themselves from the criticism of clients, employers and other external parties (Hoyle & John 1995: 8–9). Studies of journalism have long found that claims to journalistic professionalism and associated professional values, such as objectivity, usually provide journalists with an independent although limited power base, which helps to shield them from the interference of management and outsiders (e.g. Breed 1955: 333–4; Curry 1990; Osiel 1986: 170–3; Soloski 1989: 218; Tuchman 1978, ch. 5; Wibisono 1993: 443). Soeharto himself linked journalistic professionalism with autonomous self-regulation through a code of professional ethics. 'Certainly it is better if each profession administers itself and its own behaviour in a responsible fashion. Therefore, the community and the government do not need to interfere in the press's existence to guard the interests of people, race and nation' (*Angkatan Bersenjata* 10 Feb. 1996: 1).

Although the New Order defined journalists as professionals, it challenged their claim to 'cognitive exclusiveness' by rejecting any conceptualisation that development journalists were autonomous from the state. Head observed as early as 1963 that government authorities in developing countries would be unlikely to change the building specifications recommended by engineers or the medical prescriptions of doctors, but 'these same authorities do not hesitate to change the prescription of the journalist and thereby risk the failure of communication' (Head 1963: 598). Chapter 5 delineates the degree to which New Order journalists were dissatisfied with their inability to assert the superiority of their professional judgements against the state's encroachment on journalistic autonomy under the guise of protecting national development.

Raising the union banner

Discourses of professionalism fitted well with the modernisation-oriented developmental framework that legitimated the New Order state. This is because the task of turning an occupation into a 'profession' involves the application of scientific and rational principles in the division of labour considered integral to modern, industrialised society. The New Order's definitions of journalists as modern professionals, however, limited the journalists' ability to establish unions or other groups that protected them as workers. In return it provided few of the rewards that commonly accompany professional status, such as high pay and sovereignty over the occupational jurisdiction, and often obstructed the principles of autonomy on which professionalism commonly rests.

Unionisation finally entered Indonesia's family-oriented news firms in 1998, not because of a change within journalism itself but because of the collapse of the legitimacy of New Order policies following the resignation of Soeharto. When Habibie changed the regulatory structure to allow all workers to form unions and acknowledged a link between unions and professionalism (see Chapter 3), the official position regarding journalists' unions promptly reversed. Senior figures within the Department of Information responded to the climate of *reformasi* and actively advocated the concept that journalists needed to develop mechanisms to protect their wages and conditions. Dailami, who at the time was the Department's Director General of Press and Graphics, argued that the SIUPP stipulations regarding 20 per cent shareholdings were 'rubbish' and 'should be eliminated'. He asserted that journalists were ordinary workers and not professionals, 'even though they are offended if you say that', because there were no fixed educational requirements for entry into the market as there are in law or medicine (Dailami 1999: pers. comm.).

Several news-workers' unions were founded in the months following the relaxation of restrictions on forming unions. However, the PWI remains a professional organisation. Post-Soeharto era PWI Chairman (1998–2003) Tarman Azzam says it serves some union functions in that it will negotiate with employers, 'in a family-like way through *musyawarah*' if journalists ask for help, but the association does not automatically perform functions associated with unions (Azzam pers. comm.: 2001). The PWI's main rival, AJI, has associated itself with the International Federation of Journalists, an organisation the Alliance considers 'oriented towards trade unions' (Luwarso 1999: 25), in its efforts to increase awareness of the roles and functions of unions and to train potential facilitators for in-house rather than industry-wide unions. AJI adapted the Trade Union Training Australia guide to publish its own book, *Building Workers' Organisations in Press Companies* (Wisudo 2001). It has begun handling union complaints through mediation, legal proceedings and other action. From June to December 2000, for example, it handled 11 cases involving several hundred journalists.

The growth of in-house unions has been slow. Out of the hundreds of news organisations based in Jakarta in March 2001, only 18 have made steps towards establishing union-style organisations. Many of these are not truly unions but are, in the words of AJI's Trade Union Division Coordinator Bambang Wisudo, 'embryonic' union structures (Wisudo pers. comm.: 2001). These are usually the in-house *Dewan Karyawan*, *Yayasan Sejahteraan* (Welfare Foundation), cooperatives and similar structures that were set up during the New Order to administer workers' shares under the SIUPP requirements, but which are progressively adopting union functions.

Indonesian newsrooms are unlikely to witness rapid unionisation, partly because a strong culture of anti-unionism exists among journalists themselves. New Order thinking on the topic still pervades most newsrooms, even among very low-paid reporters. AJI has found that although the salaries of reporters are notoriously inadequate, they do not yet feel the need to organise. This is because they do not see themselves as common workers, and because so many opportunities exist for them to gain income through external means, such as the 'envelopes' discussed in Chapter 11.

Media employers who have been immune from a culture of animated unionism for decades are often suspicious of attempts to alter the employer–employee balance. One exception to the management culture of wariness of unions is the Antara news agency. During his brief period as Antara's General Manager, Hadi set up a *Majelis Karyawan* (Workers' Council), which was endorsed by management to undertake union functions. In contrast, most other union-style organisations have resulted from the initiatives of newsworkers, who have commonly faced what Wisudo calls 'resistence from above' (Wisudo pers. comm.: 2001). For example, some union representatives or proponents of unionism appear to have faced indirect sanctions, such as being transferred to their company's regional bureaus, where they have been too far from the main office to continue their activities. Although editors claim that the changes are unconnected with unionisation, repeated coincidences of timing has aroused suspicion among union activitists.

The director of the Jawa Pos Group, Dahlan Iskan, typified the response of employers with his comments in 1998 and 1999 that the industry was not ready for unions (Iskan 1999: 52). His list of potential barriers to unionism also indicates the degree to which New Order philosophies continued to influence media managers, even in the climate of *reformasi*. Iskan said that firstly, managements who were already good to their workers might see unions as destructive to their organisational cultures. Secondly, because many media owners were previously journalists themselves, it would be difficult to separate journalists from management. Thirdly, many workers own company shares (through the company cooperatives or *yayasan*), and thus it would again be too complex to divide 'worker' and 'management' issues. Fourthly, senior journalists, like the chief editor have to 'bow' to the company managers. Fifthly, union activism might be counterproductive, because it could put journalists out of work if previously strong media organisations were forced to comply with strong demands from their workers (Iskan 1999: 54–5).

Most of these perceived 'barriers' are based on conservative assumptions that unions induce antagonistic, avaricious and disruptive behaviours, actively seeking conflict for no particular reason. There is also a supposition that if companies have familial structures, such as workers' shares, or if they are owned or managed by former journalists, then the owner/managers become indistinguishable from other workers. As the discussion above indicates, these familial structures in no way alter the fact that real managers and owners have powers that most staff do not have in allocating wages, setting working conditions and in hiring, firing, promoting or demoting those who are truly workers. AJI members also note that there is a problem in those who fail to ask why there is no *serikat* (union) for journalists, when employers have enjoyed the benefits of a *serikat*, the SPS, for decades (Nurbaiti 2000: 33).

The price of workers' rights

Iskan insists that in a developing economy, unions cannot realistically improve journalists' incomes or conditions, because media employers face a problem of inability rather than lack of desire to pay good salaries or to share their profits (Iskan 1999: 59). Despite a measurable surge in television ratings and printmedia circulations in the period immediately before and following Soeharto's resignation from the presidency, inflation and industry instability has resulted in a decline in job secrity, wages and working conditions. Although hundreds of newspapers emerged in the months following Soeharto's resignation, when potential media proprietors took advantage of the relaxed interpretation of the SIUPP press licensing laws, most had poor financial foundations. Many analysts estimate that approximately 80 per cent of those new publications that emerged in the post-Soeharto era have subsequently folded.

Problems emerge not just with such publications offering inadequate salaries and conditions but also with managements that fail to pay salaries as promised. For example, when the *Perspective* tabloid, the *Suara Bangsa* daily and the *Suaka Metro* newspaper shut down, many staff were not given their final months' salaries and none received the requisite severance pay. Even prestige but low-profit publications, like *D&R* and *Jakarta Jakarta* magazines, owned by wealthy and well-established consortiums and companies, have shut in circumstances that led some staff to threaten legal action. Such problems such theoretically encourage unionisation, as occurred in the case of *Jakarta Jakarta*, which established the Serikat Karyawan *Jakarta Jakarta* (SKJJ, *Jakarta Jakarta Worker's Union*). In November 1999, the SKJJ became the first newsworkers' union to register with the Department of Manpower. However, AJI's North Sumatera representative notes that the union push has little support in a climate in which a journalist may easily be sacked from a financially unsound organisation but work is rapidly found the next day in another newly established organisation. The main consideration becomes simply having a press card that enables one to work and to obtain income through other sources, like envelopes (Meuraxa 2000: 38).

Unsurprisingly, a significant portion of AJI's union and other education programs have involved advising journalists on how to protect themselves in a volatile marketplace. AJI Jakarta chairman Imran Hasibuan, for example, warns journalists to follow the principle of 'buyer beware'; he observes that jobseekers have been uncritical of prospective employers 'who have only ever owned a shoe factory and suddenly decide they wish to found a media organisation' (Nurbaiti 2000: 33). Journalists are also taught to be appropriately sceptical of employers who claim that they cannot afford to increase salaries because circulations and advertising have not increased. Stanley, an AJI union trainer and former head of the now defunct SKJJ, says AJI's workshops teach journalists how to read their company's profit-loss statements and balance sheets and to estimate incoming revenues by analysing the space dedicated to advertisements (Stanley pers. comm.: 2001).

In concert with its efforts to promote unionism, AJI is also working to ensure that newsworkers' conditions are improved through the enactment of regulations requiring all print-media organisations to distribute shares among staff. Of the hundreds of news organisations that sprung up in the liberalised post-Soeharto environment, relatively few distributed collective shares to their workers. The Department of Information's figures for 1998 – the last year in which such figures were kept – showed that of the 871 print media organisations surveyed, only 34.9 per cent had distributed any collective shares to their staff (Departemen Penerangan 1998/9: i). In 1998, YLBHI and the Information Minister warned that media proprietors who did not fulfil responsibilities regarding shares would be taken to court (*Kompas* 3 Jun. 1998: 10; *Suara Serikat* 20 Mar. 2000b: 8). Although the sudden swell in newspaper numbers was seen as a positive sign for political reform because it represented an increase in the right to freedom of speech, the Department of Information figures indicate that new newspaper proprietors rarely protected the rights and legal privileges of journalists as workers.

The Press Law No. 40 of 1999 was meant to protect journalists' rights, but it has arguably failed to do so. Article 10 stipulates that: 'Press organisations provide social welfare to journalists and other press employees in the form of share ownership and/or net dividends and/or other forms of benefits.' The Elucidation states that 'other forms of benefits' are increases in wages, bonuses, insurance and other things, with the total package to be decided 'based on agreement between company management and journalists and other press employees'.

Bambang Sadono, the PWI's 1998–2003 Secretary General and a DPR member involved in the committee that worked on Law No. 40, says the new law addresses problems of press workers because the administration of the previous 20 per cent requirements was 'not satisfying' (*Kompas* 2 Sept. 1999: 15). AJI and other legislators complain that the stipulations lack detail, noting that a company that gave as little as one per cent of its shares to workers would be complying with the law (*Kompas* 7 Sept. 1999: 6, 14 Sept. 1999: 11). With no real policing of Article 10, the division of shares or other forms of company profits are unlikely to be distributed widely even among those organisations that make a profit.

The endeavour to increase workers' shares and rights to form unions will increasingly rely on legal action. Although AJI and the PWI have both pledged to defend journalists who are threatened or punished because they have agitated for their rights or the formation of unions, they have no way of compelling employers to act. The new labour laws shelter workers who seek to protect their rights and conditions through unions and similar groups, but many employers and employees alike are unfamiliar with the safeguards built into the law. AJI has hired a lawyer to help pursue employers who deprive newsworkers of their rights under the law. A case being pursued at the time of writing was that of a Semarang journalist from *Radar Semarang*, who had his employment conditions changed because he coordinated a union, called Kejora, and wrote regularly about unionism. If the legal proceedings continue, they could accelerate the incremental shift in the organic philosophies that have dominated workplace relations in newsrooms, making it too costly for employers to ignore the legal reforms that have followed political change.

7   Professional affiliation: politics and the PWI

Journalism was among the first major socio-economic sectors to be corporatised during the New Order. A series of decrees, regulations and laws defined the PWI as the only organisation legally permitted to represent journalists. PWI membership was made compulsory for all journalists. Despite initial division within the PWI about obligatory membership and its corporatised status, the association became a resolute and rigorous enforcer of the corporatist structure. Journalists who established rival organisations were actively pursued and penalised. PWI leaders claimed that despite the organisation's corporatised status, it was independent of politics. The following sections indicate, however, that all of the numerous groups have represented Indonesian journalists in the past century, including the PWI, have been influenced by the dominant political paradigms of their day.

Following Soeharto's resignation and the subsequent intolerance for ideologies and institutions flavoured by New Order approaches, the PWI's sole status has been abolished. This chapter explores the problematic attempts of the PWI to renew its image and the challenges and conundrums that the proliferation of competitors to the PWI has created.

Journalists' Associations and Political Culture

Many journalists' organisations existed prior to the establishment of the PWI, and as was mentioned above, their aims matched the political imperatives of their time. Among the earliest of Indonesia's journalists' groups were those that emerged, commonly with overtly political directives, in the period from the beginning of the twentieth century to the declaration of independence. The majority were established by the burgeoning nationalist movement as bases for campaigning for sovereignty from the Dutch colonial powers (Said 1988: 43–4; Soebagijo, Surjomihardjo & Swantoro 1977: 62–70; SPS Pusat 1971: 98–102). During the era of Japanese rule, the Japanese military controlled the press, the republican press associations were shut down, and many in the Indonesian resistance were jailed or killed (Said 1988: 48–51). Javanese newspapers and their publishers were represented by Japanese-instituted, corporatist-style bodies (Latief 1980; Said 1988: 79).

The PWI was born in 1946, after the October 1945 declaration of defeat by the Japanese military forces led to a scramble to ensure Indonesia's independence. The PWI was a centre for activating journalists to aid the ideological and armed struggle against the returning Dutch, who did not recognise the Indonesians' claims to statehood and who planned to resume their pre-war colonial administration (Soebagijo, Surjomihardjo & Swantoro 1977: 13–18; SPS Pusat 1971: 103). The independence movement used the PWI to maximise the limited human and physical resources of the scattered republican journalists against the Dutch press, which had higher circulations and better funding and resources (Goenawan 1987: 15). Many PWI founders, such as B.M. Diah, were significant actors in the fight for self-governance, autonomy and international recognition for the new Indonesian nation. The primary function of the PWI and other journalists' organisations in coordinating and encouraging the republican movement ceased in November 1949 when the Dutch formally agreed, under United Nations' pressure, to transfer sovereignty to all of the Dutch East Indies except West Irian. In subsequent decades, there have been marked mutations in the PWI's objectives, activities and membership base, which have also parallelled the dramatic shifts in national political cultures and bureaucratic organisational structures.

Chapter 1 described how most newspapers during the 1950s were usually directly or indirectly mouthpieces for political parties or the major ideological social streams. The PWI's first code of ethics, which came into effect in 1955, attempted to address the problem of political partisanship and bias, as identified by Tasrif (see Chapter 1) and others. The code encouraged professional self-correction by emphasising the separation of 'facts' from political polemic or supposition. It demanded that journalists be fair and objective, distinguish and divide reports of verifiable facts from editorials and opinion pieces, check the accuracy of comments and assertions, reject unfounded accusations and rumours, give the right of reply to those being criticised and cultivate personal honesty and tolerance (PWI 1955a: 55–8). The PWI's other self-declared aims were to defend freedom of information, to improve the quality of Indonesian journalism in harmony with community interests and to act as a trade union to improve the members' living conditions (PWI 1955b: 73–4). These aims were consonant with the preponderance of Indonesian political moderates in the PWI who supported the liberal, democratic political principles of the time (Oey 1971: 178).

When Sukarno later terminated what he deemed a failed experiment with alien 'Western-style' liberal democracy and introduced Guided Democracy, the PWI became a significant site of ideological struggle. The PWI was strongly influenced by leftist ideologies and was listed in 1962 as a member of the National Front, a mass organisation aimed at mobilising revolutionary forces. The PWI's constitution was revised to remove defence of freedom of expression and freedom of information as organisational objectives. The new constitution instead aimed to create a journalism corps 'capable and fully conscious of the tasks, functions and responsibilities of the revolution' (Oey 1971: 180). The

1963 code of ethics, while still maintaining many traces of the liberal philosophies of the 1955 code, obliged journalists to not 'diffuse news of a destructive character that may harm the Revolution and the people' (Oey 1971: 181). Compulsory PWI 'upgrading courses' involved lectures by Sukarno and other political leaders on topics such as the theory and practical application of Manipol and *Pancasila*, in order that journalists could appropriately disseminate the ideologies to their readers (Oey 1971: 188–9). The BPS provided an important centre for the struggle against the leftist dominance within the PWI. After the BPS was banned and its members expelled from the PWI, Sukarno declared that the procommunist PWI had 'truly become a tool of the revolution' (Sukarno 1965).

Communist influence in the PWI was annihilated during the nationwide anti-communist purge that followed the Gestapu coup. The PWI expelled 165 'socialist' journalists in Jakarta and at least 208 in other cities. Many, including the PWI's Chairman and General Secretary, were jailed or 'disappeared' (Goenawan 1987: 18; Said 1988: 165). It remained a stipulation until the end of the New Order that when applying for PWI membership, journalists born before 1955 – that is, those ten years of age or older at the time of the Gestapu incident – had to produce a certificate declaring that they were not connected with the G-30-S or the PKI (PWI 1995: 36).

The PWI adopted *Pancasila* as its ideological mainstay. Weeks after the coup, a transformed PWI formulated the Declaration of Indonesian Journalists, which affirmed journalists' identity as the 'supporters, guarders and defenders of the national [*Pancasila*] ideology and the 1945 Constitution'. The PWI rewrote its constitution, bylaws and code of ethics to add the *Pancasila*-ist rhetoric that suited the politics and form of governance being constructed by the New Order. In rejecting Sukarno's Manipol and Nasakom tenets, the PWI did not return to the liberal approach of the 1950s. While the 1955 Constitution defined the defence of freedom of information and freedom of expression as the PWI's primary aims, the constitutions and by-laws drafted during the New Order stress that the functions and freedoms of the PWI and press are based on and, by implication, limited by *Pancasila*.

Usage of the term *Pancasila* differed from that of the Sukarno era in that it was stripped of its revolutionary, socialist connotations and upheld as a supposedly 'non-political', family-oriented doctrine. The *Pancasila* philosophy, with its first tenet declaring belief in one almighty God, acquired anti-Communist, anti-Islamic fundamentalist, anti-*aliran* connotations that it did not possess during the Old Order. The declaration of allegiance to the *Pancasila* doctrine and a *Pancasila* nation in this chaotic period can be viewed as indicative of the ideological transformation within the PWI. Crawford (1971: 173) also suggests the many 'upgrading courses' sponsored by the PWI in 1966, ostensibly in-service training for working journalists, were actually 'reindoctrination courses, to counteract the residue of countless indoctrination seminars (also sponsored by the Journalists Association) in former years'. The position of *Pancasila* as the basis of the PWI was further strengthened in 1985 by the laws that obliged all other social organisations, including the PWI, to maintain *Pancasila* as their *asas tunggal*.

The one and only PWI

The PWI became increasingly subject to state regulation following the inception of the New Order. The 1966 Press Law, subsequently reinforced by the 1982 Press Law, stipulated that organisations for journalists had to be approved by the government. A 1969 ministerial regulation (No. 02/PER/MENPEN/1969) further ruled that all Indonesian journalists were 'obliged to become members of an Indonesian Journalists' Organisation which is authorised by the government'. Since the PWI was the only journalists' organisation approved by the government, the regulation was a circuitous path towards compulsory membership. Using the dominant political discourses, Information Minister Budiardjo said that the regulation would help to perfect the mechanisms of partnership and cooperation between the press and government and maximise the press's development function (Antara 20 Jun. 1969: 4–5; *Harian Kami* 7 Jun. 1969: 1).

The 1969 regulation provoked protest from a range of artists, intellectuals, journalists, politicians and public figures (Hartowardojo 1969: 3; *Harian Kami* 7 Jul. 1969: 1, *Sinar Harapan* 10 Jun. 1969: 1; *Sinar Harapan* 6 Jun. 1969: 1). Although the regulation had been drafted after consultation and approval from the PWI Executive branch, the PWI Central Jakarta branch heads, Zulharman Said and Harmoko, were among the leading protestors. They said the regulation ran contrary to the principles of journalism, subordinated the interests of journalists to those of the PWI and created an impression that the PWI was not sufficiently attractive enough to draw voluntary membership (Antara 24 Jun. 1969: 10; *Sinar Harapan* 24 Jun. 1969: 1; Zulharman 1969a: 3; Zulharman 1969b: 5).

A number of journalistic organisations were disbanded in the early 1970s (Dhakidae 1991: 340), and the PWI's position as the sole organisation for journalists was formalised through a 1975 ministerial decree (No. 47/KEP/MENPEN/1975). In contrast with the long, impassioned debate that had followed the 1969 regulation, the 1975 decree rated barely a mention in the news or the PWI organisational structure that was increasingly dominated by personalities with strong links to the state. The PWI reinforced its corporatised status in the 1980s with internal decrees (No. 009/PP-PWI/1989; No. 010/PP-PWI/1989) that described the association as the only body authorised to provide identification cards to journalists.

Despite numerous proposals to establish journalists' *unions*, there was little contestation of the PWI's position as the sole *professional* organisation until the early 1990s. An increasing desire by fractious young journalists, who felt that the PWI could not accommodate their aspirations at either individual or professional level, established a variety of small networks, discussion groups and counter groups (Amin 1998: pers. comm.). These journalists' groups emerged at a time in which a number of rivals to government-sanctioned unions and professional organisations were developing due to dissatisfaction with the ineffectiveness and lack of autonomy of other government-sanctioned, corporatist, 'professional' bodies (Budijanto 1993: 4). The journalists' discussion groups encountered occasional problems when attempting to gain permits for public gatherings and members were subject to some pressures from their offices, but were generally sufficiently low profile to avoid much attention (Marcellino 1998: pers. comm.).

There was no significant momentum to establish a true competitor to the PWI until June 1994, when the Information Minister Harmoko revoked the publishing licences of the three news weeklies, *Tempo, Editor* and *DëTik*. The closures prompted unprecedented expressions of concern and protest by news-industry figures, religious groups, parliamentarians, the military, non-government organisations and the wider society (*Buku Putih Tempo* 1994: 63–8; Romano 1996: 164). The PWI appealed to the government to resolve future problems connected with the press via legal channels or negotiation with the PWI and SPS, but did not publicly oppose the banning itself. Instead, it issued a statement that it 'could understand the government's reasons' for closing the news publications. Disillusioned with the PWI's failure to unequivocally support the three publications, a core group of 85 journalists and intellectuals, who contributed regularly to publications as columnists, created AJI in Sirnagalih, Bogor, in August 1994. Fifty-eight of the group also signed the Sirnagalih Declaration, which proclaimed their opposition to censorship and expressed disappointment that the 'caretakers' of the PWI had 'legitimised the minister's ban by saying they understand his action'.

As a competitor to the PWI, AJI was an illegal organisation. Members were subjected to ongoing state pressure and surveillance. Two AJI members, who ran the Alliance's unlicensed publication, *Independen*, and the organisation's teenage office assistant were arrested in 1995, charged and found guilty under article 154 of criminal code of spreading anti-government sentiment and under Article 19 of the Press Law for distributing an unlicensed publication. The two AJI members received jail sentences of 32 months, extended on appeal to 36 months, and the office boy to 20 months.[1] Legal action against AJI continued in 1997, when Andi Syahputera, the printer of *Independen*, was sentenced to 30 months' imprisonment for distributing material deemed to defame Soeharto.

The PWI endeavoured to neutralise AJI by isolating its supporters. Government sources were ordered not to provide information to AJI journalists. The PWI's Greater Jakarta branch passed a decree (No. 010/SK/PWI 2DJ/III/95) expelling 13 signatories of the Sirnagalih Agreement on the basis that they had sullied the good name of Indonesian journalists through their efforts to create a representative journalists' organisation outside the PWI. The PWI reportedly warned editors to sack employees involved in AJI, or it would rescind the editors' letters of recommendation (AJI 1995; *Bernas* 20 Mar. 1995: 1). The law required all the print-media editors to gain letters of recommendation from the PWI, and if the association revoked its recommendation, the publication would either have to replace the editor in question or shut down. The PWI withdrew its recommendation in 1996 for the chief editor of *D&R* magazine, which had conspicuously employed many AJI members. Other editors capitulated to PWI pressure. Some demanded AJI supporters leave the Alliance or resign their jobs, some transferred AJI members to positions in distant locations or non-editorial sections, and some 'invited' AJI activists to take study leave from their regular work (AJI 1994a: 103; Article 19 1995: 6; Human Rights Watch/Asia 1995; *Index on Censorship* 1994: 141; Reporters Sans Frontieres 1995). Some AJI journalists responded by writing under false names or working in rounds where they were unlikely to deal with government officials who might request PWI identification documents.

One organisation, double standards

Legal Aid Institute (LBH) director Luhut Pangaribuan has noted the paradox in the Information Department and PWI's harassment of AJI considering that, as was mentioned in the last chapter, Harmoko and Sofjan Lubis themselves were expelled from the PWI in the 1960s for their involvement with the BPS (1996: xii). The two cases were, however, fundamentally different. New Order regulations define the PWI as the journalists' association but they do not forbid journalists from joining other non-journalistic socio-political organisations. Many PWI members, for example, were also members of political parties and other groups, with a considerable number of PWI executives involved with Golkar. The BPS struggle was not about journalism. It was a case of journalists merely using their profession as an avenue to oppose communism. AJI, by contrast, was primarily a journalistic organisation, and its self-declared primary objective was 'to fight for freedom of the press in Indonesia' (AJI 1994b). The BPS merely used journalism as an arena in which to wage an ideological war, whereas for AJI, the ideological war was unequivocally about journalism itself.

The attack on AJI is more noteworthy for the total reversal it represents from Harmoko's 1969 position, described above, which decried the PWI's sole status as undemocratic. Harmoko was never questioned about the inconsistency of this shift from his earlier stance, possibly because few, if any, journalists remembered that he had adopted such a defiant posture 25 years beforehand. It is also possible that Harmoko's 1969 protests on the sole status were less connected with commitment to democracy than with the rivalry that peppered relations between Zulharman and Harmoko's Central Jakarta regional branch and the PWI's Executive branch, which had advocated the 1969 regulation. The PWI's action was also questionable because, although the PWI supposedly followed the doctrines of the 1945 Constitution, its repression of AJI contravened the principles of freedom of organisation that were enshrined in Article 28 of the Constitution (Arismunander 1997: 125; Muis 1996: 183–4; YLBHI 1995).

Questions can also be raised about the PWI leadership's insistence that their refusal to acknowledge of AJI was because they had to follow the principles of the law. Hadi (1998: pers. comm.), for example, says while he has friends in AJI and respects their basic human rights as individuals, AJI existed outside the law; therefore it would have been wrong for him as a PWI office holder to acknowledge AJI's position or to sit in a formal forum as PWI Secretary General beside AJI's Secretary General. This was not strictly true, because Article 2 of the 1975 on the PWI stated that any consequences that arose as a result of the organisation's status as the sole representative of journalists could be negotiated between the Information Department, the Press Council and the associated press organisations. The PWI was therefore authorised to mediate on AJI's behalf regarding the sole status issue had it so desired.

Corporatism and competition

Towards the end of the New Order, PWI leaders acknowledged that their organisation was flawed and in need of reform. Revision of the organisational structure, code of ethics and constitution were considered at meetings throughout 1998 (Hadi 1998: pers. comm.). The PWI leadership, however, tended to echo the catchcry of most of the New Order's sole organisations when they were contested, advising dissenters to reform the respective organisation from within rather than establish an illegal rival. PWI Chairman Sofjan Lubis (1998: pers. comm.), using a common Indonesian idiom, urged AJI members not to burn down the house merely because it has rats, but to work within the organisation to clean up the problems.

AJI members – in common with members of other independent professional groups that opposed the corporatist structure – argued that the New Order had too tight a grip on the corporatist organisations for them to be rectified. AJI members often pointed to Hadi as an example of a reformist figure, who toured news organisations at the beginning of his five-year term, fired by a mission to enlist younger journalists into the organisation and democratise its structure. Many journalists suggested that Hadi, in common with many others who entered the New Order political structure with hopes to improve the system, did not change his organisation but was himself changed by the organisation. While Hadi himself rejects such claims (Hadi 1998: pers. comm.), AJI members were sceptical of the possibility of working within the PWI without debasing or degrading their fundamental principles.

AJI was thus objectionable to the integralistic New Order élite, not only because it disparaged the PWI's performance and published critical reports about state leaders but because its members totally rejected one of the New Order's political mainstays. The PWI's positioning as the only body permitted to represent journalists was congruous with the corporatist structure that was fostered across all political, economic and social sectors. Noncompetitive collaboration was expected within and between officially sanctioned functional groups, that were meant to cooperate fraternally to advance the common goals of unity and development. AJI was essentially adversarial in nature, spurning any possibility of reforming the PWI from within. Instead it presented itself as a competitor and opponent to the older organisation and rejected the PWI's corporatised status as 'a politically motivated narrowing of constitutional freedoms' (Arismunander 1998: pers. comm.). Because of the high-profile nature of the news industry, AJI's continuing existence and promotion of competitive philosophies constituted a prominent threat to the New Order's ideological foundations.

Sofjan Lubis claimed that the PWI's corporatisation was essential for social and professional cohesion and that 'the lessons of history illustrated that no other alternative was possible'. In drawing such conclusions he stated that the PWI, from its birth in 1946, had an overriding mission of national unification and that the organisation could not afford the division that split journalists into conservative and leftist camps in the 1960s (Lubis 1998: pers. comm.). Gojek (1996: 2) similarly points to the PWI's one and only status as arising from its commitment to unity and integrity in the face of a society that is often characterised by religious or sectoral primordialism. Such arguments reiterate the New Order's rationalisation that the integralistic political structure was the only alternative to the perceived factionalism and disorder of the Sukarno era.

History does not support Lubis or Gojek's claims. The PWI was fractured in 1970 when the ABRI special intelligence body, Opsus (*Operasi Khusus*, Special Operations), tried to install its favoured candidate, B.M. Diah, as PWI head at the PWI Congress. After internal manoeuvring and lobbying, a rival PWI camp gained sufficient numbers to elect Anwar as General Chairperson. Diah's supporters convened a second meeting after midnight, declared the first election invalid and voted in B.M. Diah as the new PWI chief. The government initially recognised only the Diah board but, following threats of legal action, reached a compromise that allowed the PWI to operated two boards, chaired respectively by Anwar and Diah with separate managements (Anwar 1993: 243–4; Soebagijo, Surjomihardjo & Swantoro 1977: 39–40; SPS Pusat 1971: 104). The claim that the sole status of the compulsory professional association brought structural cohesion, political unity or familial harmony was disproved almost immediately after the corporatisation process began.

The jaded journalist

Despite the New Order's legal stipulation that all journalists had to be PWI members, the Department of Information's figures from 1986 to 1998 show that only approximately 60 per cent of print media journalists were PWI members at any time in that period.[2] The situation contrasts markedly with that of Indonesia's southern neighbour, Australia. Even though membership of the Australian Journalists' Association section of the Media, Entertainment and Arts Alliance is voluntary, 86 per cent of Australian journalists are members of their union-cum-professional organisation (Henningham 1996: 209).

In my survey of 65 journalists, 64 respondents discussed their views of PWI.[3] Of the 64, 39 (60.9 per cent) were registered PWI members, while the remaining 25 were not. The 39 registered PWI members in the survey included 34 current members plus another five 'lapsed' members, who had not paid their dues or received an up-to-date PWI membership identification card for several years. The 25 non-members included one former PWI member who was among 13 journalists who were expelled from the organisation in 1995 because of involvement with AJI.

The survey interviews highlighted the intensity of dissatisfaction with the PWI during the late New Order period (see Table 7.1). Almost three-quarters (71.8 per cent) of respondents were negative or very negative in their perspectives. Only 17.2 per cent were positive or very positive, while the remaining 10.9 per cent were neutral or ambivalent. The disaffection did not vary significantly according to the size of the media organisation that the journalists worked for, their age or their years of professional experience. It should be stressed that because the survey sample is so small, the figures are not absolute indicators of attitudes about the PWI. However, the consistency of responses suggests that deep discontent was entrenched across the profession. (See the Appendix for more details about the representativeness of the survey sample.)

The minority of respondents who made positive or very positive comments about the PWI spoke warmly of the protection afforded by the association for journalists who encountered threats from sources, its efforts to build the profession and its performance of necessary administrative functions. Evidently conscious that many of their colleagues were dissatisfied with the organisation, some volunteered defensive statements like: 'The PWI is not toothless.' Most members of this group expressed concerns about the PWI, and were sometimes strongly critical of the organisation, but they argued that the solution to its shortcomings rested on a committed membership and familial processes. In the words of one editor:

> Indeed we are not happy with the PWI but we must not go outside it. We must enter and fix it from the inside to make a different organisation, not one that blindly follows the government .... I see it as being the same as a family. If you are not a child in that family, how can you administer the house? [Those outside the organisation] can be big mouths and just talk.

Of the neutral journalists, one claimed she had little contact with or interest in the PWI, while the others balanced their critique and praise of the association quite evenly. One neutral journalist, for example, felt that the PWI was important because 'without such an organisation journalists would have to walk alone' but

Table 7.1 Attitudes of journalists to the PWI during the New Order

Journalists' attitude	Very positive	Positive	Neutral	Negative	Very negative	Total
Number	6	5	7	31	15	64
Percentage	9.4	7.8	10.9	48.4	23.4	100

also noted several deficiencies and evaluated that it had only been 50 to 60 per cent successful in performing its functions.

The majority of respondents spoke of the PWI in negative to very negative terms, commonly expressing at great length their sense that the PWI had failed them. Their innumerable criticisms included that 'the PWI is useless', it 'does not have any teeth or power', it 'does not achieve anything for its members', 'the PWI does not change anything', helping journalists 'is beyond its ability', and that 'work would be easier without it'. Respondents described the PWI heads as the *anak buah* (loyal subjects or assistants) of the government, who failed to adequately protect the journalists' physical safety and their news organisations' operating licences – all issues affecting press freedom. One, who became a PWI member because he was forced to, said:

> Since I became a member four years ago, I have never been invited to a meeting; I am only asked for fees. I have seen friends of mine become victims of police violence, but the PWI did nothing. In fact, they [the PWI chiefs] can make money from their polemic. They can negotiate with the government [over disputes involving journalists]. They get money while the case stops.

Speaking after AJI was first formed, the head of the PWI's Central Java branch claimed that it was only outsiders who complained of lack of democracy in the PWI (Elly et al. 1995: 48). The survey results suggest that the currents of discontent were also strong within the ranks of the fully paid-up, card-carrying PWI membership. The current PWI members were mainly negative or very negative (58.8 per cent for the two categories), although less so than lapsed (80 per cent) or non-PWI (88 per cent) members.

These negative PWI members had three key reasons for joining the PWI. Several had become members because they were forced to do so by their editors. Others reporters enrolled because they had difficulties dealing with government or military sources unless they carried a PWI identification card. Yet others observed that it was impossible to achieve high-ranking positions without PWI endorsement, so they had registered because it would be impossible to progress their careers without doing so.

The basis of discontent

While the PWI described itself as a *wadah* (an umbrella organisation), with attendant implications that it gathered, coordinated and sheltered journalists, by far the most frequently mentioned grievance of survey respondents (23.4 per cent) related to assessments that the organisation was not an umbrella but a tool of the dominant political forces. The second most voiced complaint (15.6 per cent) was that the PWI did not contribute to professionalism, either through building professional identity or professional training. The third and fourth most frequent criticisms were that the PWI was not capable of protecting or supporting publications whose licences had been threatened (10.9 per cent) or journalists at risk of physical harm (7.8 per cent). These complaints were inherently linked to the first judgement that the organisation serves state interests before those of its members. A comparatively small number also objected that the PWI did not improve wage or workplace conditions (3.1 per cent), caused conflict in the media (1.6 per cent) and was an inefficient administrator (1.6 per cent). Only a minority of journalists, therefore, complained about what might be called the personal and physical issues of financial recompense and welfare, while the majority expressed concern about more systemic ideological and political factors such as autonomy from the state, freedom of the press and professional identity.

Of the relatively few strengths mentioned, the most common (7.8 per cent) was that the PWI protected journalists' personal safety. Other perceived strengths were that the PWI fulfilled the requirement for a single, unifying professional institution (7.8 per cent), increased professionalism (4.9 per cent) and that it performed necessary administrative tasks, such as recording names and issuing identity cards (4.9 per cent). Only one journalist (1.6 per cent) expressed positive views about the PWI's building of the profession and its links with government.

The one surveyed journalist, from the state-affiliated Antara news agency, who described links between the PWI and the government as positive, argued that the organisation could act as a mediator between the press and government over complaints about news stories. The remainder who discussed the PWI's relationship with the state expressed concern, ranging from mild judgements that the PWI had 'lost its objectivity' to more strident assessments that the organisation was 'the henchman of the government'. Even during the New Order, many media theorists and observers treated it as a taken-for-granted fact that the PWI was a vehicle for the government to regulate entry into journalism and to monitor journalists' activities (e.g. ICJ 1987: 102; Rodgers 1982: 8).

Despite the New Order government's claim that it never interfered with the PWI's independence (e.g. Amirris 1993: 51), the 1970 Anwar–Diah case indicates otherwise. Anwar claims that almost all subsequent elections were subject to military or government manipulation (Anwar 1998b: 6). Speaking at the end of the New Order, Rosihan Anwar said that with the election of Harmoko to a senior post in the PWI executive in 1973, connections between the government and press became *mesra* (close to the point of fusion) and that since then 'the press organisation has lost its legitimacy as an independent body and, more sadly, its guts' (Budiyarso 1997: 646).

Positions on the PWI board were also seen as stepping stones to political power through Golkar connections. Among the most successful of PWI officials to establish political careers during the New Order were the former PWI chief executives, B.M. Diah and Harmoko, and the PWI Honorary Council member, Alwi Dahlan, who each held the post of Information Minister. The last PWI executive of the New Order was headed from 1993 to 1998 by Sofjan Lubis and Hadi, who were respectively seen as protégés of Harmoko and then Research and Technology Minister Habibie. In 1993, Harmoko and Habibie were considered among the closest of Soeharto's allies and potential future presidential aspirants, so Lubis and Hadi's promotion to the PWI's top postings attracted immediate comment (e.g. Haryanto & Toha 1993: 70; *Tempo* 11 Dec. 1993: 81). Both Lubis and Hadi were regarded as politically ambitious. The former was Deputy Chief of the Golkar fraction in the MPR, and both were judged as possibilities for a posting as Information Minister (*Tempo Interaktif* 5 Jun. 1997).

Few surveyed journalists complained of the PWI in terms of its failure to shelter workers in their relationship with management, but such comments would hardly be expected in the light of the PWI and news industry's rejection of the journalist as worker concept. The PWI Constitution did, however, identify a duty for the organisation to conduct efforts that were legally approved (*sah*) for the spiritual and physical welfare of journalists (PWI 1995: 11). The PWI consequently offered some health care, legal support and subsidised housing to its members. This, however, failed to turn the tide of dissatisfaction, and many newspapers provided more generous benefits to their journalists that those available from the PWI (Hill 1995: 70).

Another barrier to the PWI performing union-style functions is the composition of its leadership, which has for decades consisted almost exclusively of senior editors from major news publications. Additionally, many PWI heads have subsequently served in senior positions in the SPS, the representative of newspaper publishers. Kuhon (1997: pers. comm.), himself a former managing editor of the daily *Jayakarta* newspaper, describes the rotation of senior publishers on SPS and PWI board positions as 'a kind of lottery between them'. He notes that one consequence of this 'very tight consensus' between publication managements is that journalists who are fired or resign after disputes with their employers will experience considerable difficulties in finding alternative employment.

The comments by a substantial proportion of the surveyed journalists that the PWI does not build professionalism gain in significance considering that the PWI defines itself as a professional rather than a workers' organisation. The PWI has conducted programs to increase the education and professionalism of journalists. The surveyed journalists who criticised the PWI's role in professional development envisaged professionalism as something beyond the technical proficiency and official developmentalist ideologies usually emphasised by training courses. Issues they desired the PWI to address included the envelope culture, self-censorship, lack of astute issue analysis and superficial interviewing techniques.

Of the journalists who complained of the PWI's inability to shield them from the physical threats they encountered, more than half felt that, although the PWI tried to increase journalists' physical security, it was too weak to succeed. Paradoxically, those who held a positive or very positive orientation towards the PWI described the safety afforded by the PWI as a strength of the organisation and the journalism profession in general. Almost all the journalists who held such positive orientations could point to specific cases in which the PWI had helped them or other journalists they knew who had faced physical danger.

The reformasi roller coaster

During the New Order, there were few opportunities for journalists to oppose the dominant corporatist ideology implemented by the news managements and PWI chiefs who, as was pointed out above, were often one and the same. At a labour level, Kuhon and others who attempted to fight within individual news organisations were suppressed by their editors, with the PWI morally supporting the ideological basis of such suppression. At a professional level, the case of AJI and other small journalists groups shows that those few who attempted to fight professional corporatisation were repressed by the PWI and the state, with editors of individual news organisations providing (or being forced to provide) practical support for such legally based repression. The ideology of corporatism was thus self-sustaining for the life of the New Order.

The end of the New Order was accompanied by rapid deconstruction of this corporatist system in both journalism and wider society. In a conciliatory gesture, Andi Syahputera was released in May 1998, among the first of many designated 'political prisoners' to be released by the new Habibie government. Within weeks of Soeharto's resignation, Yosfiah revoked the PWI's 'one and only' status through a ministerial decree (No. 133/SK/MENPEN/1998), claiming that its exclusive position had to be eliminated to prevent the corruption and collusion associated with organisations that have monopoly status.

Some critics maintained that a ministerial regulation (Ministerial Regulation No. 2/PER/MENPEN/1998) passed the same day – stating that Indonesian journalists were 'obliged to become members of any journalists' organisation' – still violated the rights of journalists who may not have wanted to join professional groups (Astraatmadja 1998). In practice, journalists were not monitored to determine whether they joined professional associations or not. With the subsequent ratification of the Press Law in 1999, journalists have total freedom of choice as to whether they will affiliate, and if so, with which organisation.

In contrast to the slow emergence of journalists unions, professional organisations multiplied rapidly. There is no definitive list of all the associations, but in 2000, 33 journalists' associations registered an interest in participating in the election of Press Council representatives. Atmakusumah Astraatmadja, who was subsequently selected as Press Council head, says that since then, he has been contacted every month by new journalists' professional organisations (Astraatmadja 2001: pers. comm.). However, beyond the PWI, AJI and *Ikatan Jurnalis Televisi Indonesia* (IJTI, Indonesian Television Journalists' Association), no association appears to have a membership in excess of 500. Atmakusumah says that the executives of one association openly admitted to having 16 members. He suspects that many associations have no members apart from the founding executives. However, it is difficult to confirm this, because it is easy to manipulate names and data on membership lists (Astraatmadja 2001: pers. comm.). Many of these new organisations are very poorly organised, own scant resources and have no policies or agenda.

With the PWI no longer a regulator of entry into journalism, Habibie suggested that journalists, like doctors and other 'professionals', should be licensed. The proposal provoked instant criticism. Questions were raised about how the criteria for professional journalism would be established and which body would judge journalistic standards. In an indirect acknowledgement that professional standards were indeed low, the new *Serikat Pewarta* organisation said the move would probably only exacerbate problems of unemployment among journalists, because many would be unable to fulfil the criteria required to obtain licenses (*Indonesian Observer* 15 Jul. 1998). AJI supporters feared that the licensing proposal was an indirect attempt to re-establish the relevance of the PWI. Because the PWI had previously been the organisation that endorsed editors and organisations seeking the SIUPP publishing licences, it was seen as a strong possibility that the PWI would be chosen as the accrediting body for licensing journalists if such a plan was introduced (Suranto, Setiawan & Ginanjar 1999: 79–80). With the Indonesian government under heavy national and international pressure to deregulate the political and economic systems, the proposal was promptly dismissed.

Chapter 5 discusses how journalists' associations took advantage of the liberal philosophies of market self-regulation by lobbying for legislative changes that would end government powers to judge and discipline perceived breaches of journalistic ethics. Many initially hoped that journalists' associations would be in a position to regulate the conduct of members. However, members of the public could barely be expected to lay complaints with associations as they were unlikely to know which association, if any, an offending journalist belonged to, or what the code of ethics of that particular journalist's association entailed. A further problem was that once the legal obligation to join a professional association was removed, journalists could avoid sanctions from professional associations by simply not becoming a member of an association or withdrawing their memberships after complaints were laid. As was noted in Chapter 5, 26 journalists' organisations addressed this by drafting and signing a compromise code of ethics, the KEWI. The Press Council can use the KEWI to mediate complaints about any journalist, regardless of whether he or she is a member of a professional association or not.

Revitalising the PWI

Just as many New Order political players have reinvented themselves as political reformers, so too have senior figures within the PWI been keen to distance themselves from the organisation's corporatist past. In the post-Soeharto era, PWI executives readily agree that the association spent decades as 'an extension of the arm of government' and stress the importance of establishing and maintaining autonomy from the state. With Soeharto's resignation, Sofjan Lubis swiftly forsook his earlier insistence that one association was necessary for national or professional cohesion. He announced that the PWI did not have any pretension or desire to be the one and only journalistic association, and he welcomed other journalists' associations (*Suara Karya* 30 May 1998). Just as the PWI had issued a statement reflecting its renewed focus in 1965, the organisation issued the 'Semarang Declaration' in 1998. The Declaration pledged a commitment to all of the new paradigms of the *reformasi* press model – commitment to independence and idealism, freedom of the press, increasing professional standards, and the promotion of non-aggressive means for the community to resolve complaints with the press.

In the lead-up to the October 1998 Congress to elect a new national PWI executive, senior media figures expressed the hope that the poll would help the PWI to remove the smell of the New Order with a fresh, 'clean' leadership. The election results, however, stimulated months of intense complaint and ongoing suspicion. It was inevitable that the election would generate criticism, regardless of the outcome, given that all the key leadership candidates had been previously connected to contentious PWI decisions or activities. However, at a time in which the organisation was striving to dissociate itself from the corrupt culture of the New Order political system, it was not predicted that claims would emerge of election fraud. Rosihan Anwar claimed the winning candidate, Azzam, had been backed by a 'success team' of '*ninja* forces', who used 'ruthless' tactics involving attempted tradeoffs with rival candidates, the stymieing of debate in the PWI Congress, and hospitality and 'money politics' to win the support of the PWI branches. Anwar further claimed that Azzam's candidature had been part of a strategy to replace one 'Harmoko man', Sofjan Lubis, with another Harmoko employee (Anwar 1998a: 4). Azzam and his alleged 'success team' denied the claims (Amir 1998: 4; Azzam 1999: pers. comm.), and a PWI Honorary Council investigation found that procedures had been democratic (*Suara Pembaruan* 27 Oct. 1998).

Tarman was also repellent to AJI supporters because, as the previous PWI Jakarta branch chief, he was responsible for the 1995 expulsion of the 13 AJI journalists and the 1996 revocation of the PWI's recommendation letters for *D&R's* editor. Tarman says the true sources of blame are the former Central PWI branch heads, who issued the 1994 statement that they understood the delicensing of Tempo, *Editor* and *DëTik*. He says that he agreed with the Sirnagalih Agreement, but once disillusioned journalists established AJI, he was obliged by the PWI's organisational rules to expel them. He adds that AJI activists had publicly derided the PWI on a daily basis, and it was reasonable for the organisation to take disciplinary action (Azzam 1999: pers. comm.). AJI supporters have, in the main, been unmoved by such explanations. One of the 13 journalists to be expelled in 1995, for example, describes Azzam's rationalisation as characteristic of those implicated in controversial New Order political activities. He says PWI leaders mimic the New Order political leaders, who attempt to acquire credentials as reformists 'by pointing the finger at all of their former colleagues, seeking to reproach everyone but themselves' (Stanley 1999: pers. comm.).

Azzam and his secretary general, Bambang Sadono, were also unattractive to many because both are Golkar politicians. The former is a representative in the

Jakarta district parliament and the latter a DPR legislator. Many reformists, including those within the PWI, have unsuccessfully proposed that the organisation's constitution be changed to prevent individuals with senior positions in political parties from running for PWI executive postings. Critics claim that Azzam and Sadono's election shows that the PWI will remain irrevocably polluted by its links with the New Order and Golkar (*Kompas* 23 Oct. 1998a: 7; 27 Oct. 1998: 6).

Reformists are also concerned about Sadono's leadership. The Attorney General's office summoned him in the months preceding the PWI elections, to answer questions relating to several complaints of alleged corruption and collusion. No charges were laid, and the rumours remain unconfirmed. Sadono claims he was victimised because he was close to Soeharto's daughter Tutut and former justice minister Muladi, who were also named in the corruption and collusion allegations (*Bisnis Indonesia* 19 Sept. 1998). Despite this, an Extraordinary Congress of the Central Java PWI branch – the branch Sadono had chaired until he won the posting as Central branch secretary general – issued him a severe warning after it 'judged' him to be guilty in relation to two additional cases relating to allegedly inappropriate allocation of PWI member-ship cards and his appropriation a car that others claimed belonged to the branch (*Suara Pembaruan* 25 Apr. 1999).

The national PWI office therefore had an image problem at three levels. Many suspected that (i) the election process was corrupt, (ii) the leaders themselves had engaged in corruption and (iii) the association was subject to political cooption through the leadership's political affiliations. Months of vociferous complaints followed. Several demonstrations were held outside PWI offices. A rival professional association, the *PWI Reformasi* (PWI Reform), was formed. The PWI's Yogyakarta branch unsuccessfully called for a national PWI Extraordinary Congress to reconsider the election results. Through a regional Extraordinary Congress, the Yogyakarta branch also formally rejected Azzam and Sadono as the PWI's leaders and declared itself capable of operating independently of the Central branch if necessary. The Central PWI branch invoked democratic principles to try to placate its critics, saying that the election itself had operated according to democratic systems, and those who were chosen should be acknowledged as the result of democratic procedures (*Kompas* 23 Oct. 1998b: 7). The pattern resembles that repeatedly seen in Indonesian national politics, where protracted disputes over alleged political corruption and links to the Soeharto-era political structure have caused ongoing disruption to political life, and each side has attempted to claim victory and legitimacy through varied interpretations of 'democratic' procedures and rules.

The uproar has not substantially undermined the PWI's influence or power. It recorded 950 new members entering the association between 1 January 1998 and 8 March 2001. That was more than the entire membership in March 2001 of either of the PWI's largest rival associations, AJI or IJTI.

The changes that have occurred to the PWI's legal status are consonant with Larson's (1977: xii) prediction that since most recognised professions emerge by the grace of powerful political protectors, revolutionary social transformation should have profound implications for the organisation of professionals. This is because such transformation correspondingly alters the social status and positioning that established professional groupings had achieved in the previous regime. However, even though the PWI contends with rivals, it maintains a strong position in much the same way that Golkar does now that the New Order has ended. Both draw on a well-established national organisational structure, socio-political networks set up over the organisations' long history, considerable financial assets, substantial physical infrastructures and nationally recognised names. Both will continue to remain powerful forces because of this advantage.

8 No woman, no cry

The Indonesian term for journalist, *wartawan*, literally means 'news man'. Female journalists, referred to in formal contexts as *wartawati* ('news woman'), are a minority. The PWI's records for 1973 showed that only 2 per cent of its members were women (*Sinar Harapan* 1974: 4). Slow but consistent incremental increases were recorded in the numbers of female journalists since that time. In March 2001, women made up 10.4 per cent of the PWI's 9133 members (Azzam 2001: pers. comm.). In the same month, women made up 9.1 per cent and 30 per cent of members respectively of the PWI's smaller rivals, AJI and IJTI (Kuhon 2001: pers. comm.; Supriyanto 2001: pers. comm.). The higher figures in the IJTI reflect the comparatively high numbers of women that filled broadcasting positions following the proliferation of news programs in both television and radio industries during the 1990s and early twenty-first century. The average of women across the three journalists' associations was 12.1 per cent. Comparison with figures for journalism across the globe (e.g. Weaver 1998) reveals that Indonesian women's participation in journalism is not just substantially lower than in most Western countries, it is also in the low-to-middle range for Asia.

As is emphasised in Chapter 10, the reliability of statistics is limited in Indonesia, so the figures used in this chapter should be seen as guides for general trends and patterns rather than as definitive representatives of social realities. Caution is also required when considering statistics on women, because gender bias in survey techniques can lead to underestimation of women's performances in work and other activities (Ahooja-Patel 1996: 125; Manning 1998: 235–6). However, simple observation of Indonesian newsrooms corroborates the trends that the official figures show; although the numbers of women in journalism are increasing, especially in the broadcast media, they remain a clear minority.

During the course of my research, outlined below, the journalists and media analysts I met almost without exception attributed the relative scarcity of women in the industry to Indonesian 'culture' which supposedly dictates that a woman's role is in the home as mother and housekeeper. It is tempting to conclude that women's place in journalism is limited because Indonesian society draws dichotomous distinctions of men as reasoning, objective, strong people who engage in the productive (i.e. economic) functions of the public sphere and women as emotional, subjective, delicate people who engage in the reproductive (i.e. biological) functions of the private sphere. Such arguments are similar to those often seen in analyses of Western women. Numerous traditional feminist studies conclude that the male ontology of Western political theories excludes women from the public domain on the basis of the supposedly creative, natural and therefore non-rational character that arises from their fecundity (e.g. Clark & Lange 1979; Elshtain 1981; Lloyd 1984; Okin 1979; Ortner 1974).

It would be overly simplistic, however, to assume that few Indonesian women become journalists because culture forces them to remain housebound in the domestic sphere. Historians have long noted that Indonesian women have been markedly more mobile and economically active than their sisters in many other Asian countries. There has never been an assumption that Indonesian men are better than women in economically productive roles because of their presumed moneymaking skills. In the early nineteenth century, Thomas Stamford Raffles recorded that women alone conducted all the business of marketing, buying and selling because, according to a Javanese proverb, men were financial fools. 'In the transaction of money concerns, the women are universally considered superior to the men, and from the common labourer to the chief of a province, it is usual for the husband to entrust his pecuniary affairs entirely to his wife.' (Raffles 1978: 353; also Geertz 1961: 46, 124–5; Hull 1996: 87; Willner 1976: 119–20) In contemporary times, general workforce figures also belie the assumption that Indonesian women are less involved in paid labour than 'liberated' Western women. In 1999, Indonesian women formed 38.2 per cent of the total workforce (BPS 2000a: 42).

In contrast to their activity in the economic sphere, Indonesian women are conspicuously absent from formal politics. In 1999, only 9.1 per cent of members of the People's Consultative Assembly, 8.8 per cent of the Parliament, 26.2 per cent of Supreme Court judges, 2.7 per cent of the Supreme Advisory Council were women and 2.3 per cent of village chiefs were women (BPS 2000a: 60–6). Although women made up 36.9 per cent of the total workforce in the public service, they held only 7 per cent of the positions in the top three public-service echelons (BPS 2000b: 32; Johanson 2001: 4). Non-government organisations, with the exception of those devoted specifically to women's concerns, also appear to be male dominated. Academics have attributed the low representation of women in politics to socialisation that politics is men's business (Blackburn 1994: 171–2). A survey of Indonesian women also found that women felt they could only be political if they did not care about their domestic duties or women's *kodrat* (*Suara Pembaruan* 17 Sept. 1997: 5).

However, even women journalists who struggle and chafe against stereotypes that they belong in the home generally seem oblivious to the abundant evidence that neither Indonesian 'contemporary cultures' nor 'traditions' confine women *en masse* to household chores. Journalists who assume that culture locks women out of journalistic work are not considering the social cultures alone. Instead, their assumptions are flavoured by the news workers' location within Indonesia's 'modern' middle-classes and the integralistic political cultures that predominated during the New Order. This chapter examines how the New Order's strict definition of women's *kodrat* has contributed to the exclusion of women from the political sphere, including journalism, the so-called fourth estate of political life.

It is beyond the scope of this book to explore the influence of Islam. In the economic sphere, Indonesian patterns of female labour participation have traditionally differed markedly from those of other predominantly Islamic nations (Manning 1998: 233–4). In the political sphere, the state actively constrained or coopted Islamic movements during the New Order period. In recent years the interplay between religion and politics has become more notable. On the one side have been those who have contested the right of women to hold the presidency and the highest levels of power. On the other side, Islamic women's organisations, such as Aisyah, one of Indonesia's oldest women's groups, have worked at a practical level to emancipate women in Indonesian society. At an ideological level, many Islamic intellectuals have contested interpretations of the Koran that imply women have less rights in the family, workplace and political system than men (e.g. Munir 1999). The topic is an important one that warrants research and analysis. However, in the limited confines of this chapter, it is not possible to thoroughly explore such issues with the depth they deserve, and the discussion will focus primarily on mainstream political philosophy.

The double life of a female journalist

As was mentioned above, most of the journalists encountered in research for this book – whether male or female – claimed that women's participation in journalism was limited by 'cultural' proscriptions that women belonged at home while men worked outside to earn the family's income. One female reporter explained: 'Most women desire feminine activities managing the family and the children, which makes it difficult for them to go out [as reporters].' Most journalists work six days per week, most commonly finishing work between 7 to 12pm, but all are technically on call 24 hours per day, 365 days per year. Such workloads cause considerable problems for women aiming to combine work and family.

The married female journalists interviewed for this research described varying degrees of distress or frustration at the demands created by the *peran ganda*. One said that she sometimes felt like quitting because of the emotional pressures involved in leaving her child six days per week. Another admitted that she did not cope well, seeing her children 'for a few minutes in the morning and on weekends'. Others expressed uncertainty about how they would continue to manage their careers in the future against the conflicting demands of family. Priyo Soemandoyo's study of female television journalists reveals similar concerns (Soemandoyo 1999: 133–9).

The complexity of juggling both roles often increased as women moved higher up the career ladder. Dhakidae (1994: 36) agrees that for women, success as a journalist 'eats up the journalist herself'. He suggests that the late editor in chief of the *Surabaya Pos*, Toety Azis, resolved the dilemma between her public and private roles by virtue of physical geography. Her home was 500 metres from her office (Dhakidae 1994: 44). Another veteran journalist involved in the struggle for national independence, Herwati Diah, managed to combine the roles of mother, student and worker. This has been attributed to the fact that she is a woman 'who does not know exhaustion' (Hidayat 1993: xvii–xviii). Diah herself says that 'women cannot leave behind their femininity in the conduct of their duties', and while men are rarely confused about how to divide their home duties with deadlines, it would be 'strange if woman journalists were *not* confused in the same conditions' (Diah 1993: 123–4, italics in original).

Married women who work in journalism generally rely on the aid of female relatives or housemaids to care for young children. The dual position of journalist and wife–mother only becomes tenable because the large gap in incomes across Indonesian society enables all but the most lowly paid of journalists to hire cheap home help. A *Jakarta Post* reporter described the *pembantu* (housemaid or servant) system as the only thing that enabled her to cope, and said that she would have divorced long ago if she had not had domestic servants. In recent years, as access to the Internet has increased, some women are also working from their houses in the evenings by writing stories on home computers and filing by modem. The freedom of such women to pursue careers in journalism is tenuous, since it depends entirely on their ability to demand that other women fulfil 'feminine' household functions on their behalf or their ability to use technology to enable them to bring their office work into their homes. In calling on female *pembantu* and using Internet technology, these journalists do not substantially contest the discourses that the domestic sphere is intrinsically female nor do they challenge the gendered balance of power in the family structure. Although some women journalists talked of choosing husbands who were 'supportive', in the abstract sense that they endorsed the concept of their wives being journalists, none suggested that husbands should be 'supportive' in the practical sense of performing an equal share of domestic duties.

The gap between the female journalists' professional aspirations and general social expectations was also illustrated by the number of single women who bemoaned, both in formal interviews and social conversation, the problems that pursuing professional interests had created in terms of their relationships with men. A 31-year-old radio reporter, who married a fellow journalist one week after being interviewed, claimed that it had taken her many years to find a partner who was sympathetic to her career activities. Two women from the Semarang-based *Suara Merdeka* newspaper suggested that 'patriarchal' Indonesian men are reticent to consider any well-educated, career-minded woman as a partner. Academics generally agree that for Indonesian women 'higher education is often thought to be a liability in finding a husband' (e.g. Mulder 1989: 33). One of the *Suara Merdeka* women furthermore expressed doubt that she would find a man who would understand her either as a social individual or as a professional who needed to work for personal satisfaction.

Such women see marriage as a mixed blessing. One young probational newspaper journalist, in an unsolicited discussion, said she believed that marriage might save her from parental and other social pressures that limited her freedom of movement. However, a *Citra* magazine reporter, engaged to be married, hinted that wedlock might end her career. She admitted that her fiancé objected to her late hours and would want her to stay at home once they had children. This reflects the fact that marriage has traditionally been seen as a way for Indonesian women to obtain freedom from their parents (Coté 1992: ix–x; Woodcroft-Lee 1983: 183), but such freedom is short lived, being rapidly restricted by childbirth and consequent domestic obligations (Suryakusuma 1982: 14).

Both male and female journalists often mentioned the importance of 'time management' for women journalists. However, in such conversations, time management was not discussed as an issue important for the health and well being of the women themselves, but as an element necessary for maintaining relationships with boyfriends, spouses and/or children. By contrast, only two of the hundreds of male journalists who I met ever described the impact of their working hours on their private lives or indicated in any way that they were aware of or interested in the perspectives of their wives, girlfriends or other women about their work.

Unsurprisingly, a considerable proportion of Indonesia's few senior women journalists have remained unmarried. These include Annie Bertha Simamora and Agnes Samsuri from *Suara Pembaruan* (and its predecessor *Sinar Harapan*) and the late Threes Nio from *Kompas*. An official history of *Sinar Harapan* comments of Agnes Samsuri that: 'Her freedom without "traditional" ties is indeed an advantage in her journalistic duties' (*Sinar Harapan* 1981: 294). Such journalists, however, face considerable innuendo and other social pressures in ignoring social conventions. At one newspaper, for example, senior journalists sometimes point out highly respected, single female colleagues to the younger male staff and 'joke': 'Don't try to play around with her. She's a lesbian.'

Soft and helpless

The issue of working hours is not merely tied to women's family responsibilities but also to social and legal taboos on women working and travelling, particularly alone, late at night. Labour laws (e.g. Work Law No. 12 of 1948; Work Law No 1 of 1951; Ministerial Regulation PER-04/MEN/1989) tightly circumscribed the night work available to women until the late 1990s. The 1951 Labour Laws prohibited the employment of women between 10 p.m. and 5 a.m. except in occupations that particularly required 'feminine' skills, such as nursing. The 1951 laws drew from a conservative legacy of Dutch colonial conceptualisations about the weaker woman needing to be protected from the rigours of work outside the home (Locher-Scholten 1992). The restrictions on night work were only eventually extinguished in 1997 by new labour laws. This theoretically meant that women were legally prohibited from journalistic work until 1997, because night work is an inevitable part of the journalistic experience. Soon after the 1997 law was passed, Teten Masduki, then head YLBHI's Labour Division, agreed that the 1951 law had technically debarred women journalists from working at night, but that in practice the law had never been enforced (Masduki 1998: pers. comm.). Media organisations never complied with the now-defunct legal provisions banning women from night work. In fact, the journalists and editors I met seemed universally unaware that the legal provisions had ever even existed.

However, the 1951 law remains representative of the cultural conceptualisation of the Sukarno and much of the Soeharto era women need to be protected from the dangers of night labour. In discussions on the issue, male journalists often claimed that 'security' was the problem for women travelling late at night, although no male journalist ever described such travel as a danger to men. The journalists' stereotypes of female vulnerability match the New Order philosophies that promoted the image of women as the custodians of healthy and harmonious family and social life (e.g. Soeharto 1989a: 298–9). 'This perspective holds that women *should* be protected and confined because they are "natural" nurturers. They *should* be protected from the problems and dangers that men, the "natural" protectors, must face in the "outside" world, where they *must* obtain the means to provide for their dependants (Sullivan 1991: 74, italics in original).

The assumptions that women needed protection were not supported by the research at the time. AJI's records of 957 incidents of violence, both physical and non-physical, against journalists in the last five years of the New Order period showed that only 13 (1.4 per cent) involved women (Soetopo 1998: 4). It is possible that women journalists worked in areas less likely to involve danger or were more cautious than men, making them less likely to be subjects of attack, but the figures still indicated a considerable gap between the reality and the rhetoric of female vulnerability.

The women journalists I encountered never expressed fear or concern for their own 'security', a desire to be chaperoned or a wish to avoid such work and travel. They were concerned, however, that pressures from their protective families, neighbours and employers reduced their ability to engage in late night activities. Atmakusumah Astraatmadja, head of the Dr Soetomo Press Institute, noted that young women's parents usually oppose their leaving the house late at night in any circumstances, let alone to cover unrest or to go out of town with a male colleague (Astraatmadja 1997: pers. comm.). One *Suara Pembaruan* journalist says that if she works until 2 a.m., her younger siblings report the matter to older siblings living out of town, who then order her to be home before 10 p.m. An older reporter found that while her late husband had been sympathetic to her engagement in after-hours activities while he was alive, her now-adult son objects to her involvement in late-night work. Neighbours also pressure women who flaunt female stereotypes to develop their careers. Surveyed journalists reported that they were subject to community suspicion and gossip when going out to work at night. An LP3Y study of female journalists in four Jakartan and five provincial Javanese newspapers found similar opinions among interviewees about pressures imposed by parents, spouses and community members (LP3Y

1999: 180–9). My research found that even news organisations sometimes harass female journalists about night work. One survey respondent says that her bosses had warned her not to work late after she was observed in the office finishing a story at 2 or 3 a.m. The warning came even though male journalists also occasionally worked in the office after midnight, including the night in question.

Only one survey respondent, a female managing editor, dismissed suggestions that working hours and night travel were 'the core of the problem' limiting the number of women in journalism. 'The women I see in this newspaper do not have a problem with being forbidden by parents or husbands. They already know what the work is like [before they enter the profession]. When they know, there is no problem.' Her argument turned out to be flawed when subsequent conversations with women in her newspaper revealed that the majority faced family resistance to their late-night activities.

Another executive editor at the same newspaper furthermore indicated that his colleague did not see women being banned by parents or husbands, because the careers of women who were most susceptible to such problems usually ruled themselves out of working in journalism by admitting during job interviews that they faced such problems. 'They say to us: "My mother won't give me permission to come home later than 10 p.m."' The head of LP3Y, Ashadi Siregar, agrees that 'assumptions about the difficulties of journalistic work' prevent women from entering the profession (Siregar 1995b: xxxiv). Journalism teachers from five post-secondary educational institutions[1] argued that female students tended to favour public relations and advertising instead of journalism as areas for study, because the fields were stereotyped as more glamorous with easier work. Thus social taboos regarding the 'hard work' of journalism, involving late nights and travel, must be regarded not just as a hurdle that makes a long-term career more difficult, but also one that stops many women from even considering journalism as a viable career choice.

Journalism lecturers, male journalists and even a female student contemplating journalistic work also expressed the view that journalistic work was 'too hard' for women, although I never heard such complaints being made by women journalists themselves. The concerns about women being less suited to hard work again appear more based upon social stereotypes about the dependent, nurturing, housebound woman than observable realities. Statistics indicate that, on average, Indonesian women work 11.1 hours per day compared to 8.7 hours for men (Buchori & Bianpoen 1996: vi).

Limited career paths

The biggest factor preventing newsrooms from hiring women journalists appears to be simply the scarcity of women willing to apply for journalistic positions (LP3Y 1999: 14–19), but the problem is sometimes exacerbated by discriminatory employment practices. Siregar (1997: pers. comm.) claims to have encountered sexist attitudes when the LP3Y enters discussions with employers about training courses to prepare students for entry-level journalism positions. 'We ask them [the editors] how many journalists they need. If they say five, they will also say: "Please make those five men." They give priority to men.' All the editors interviewed for this research denied discriminative hiring policies. However, staff at two of the four newspapers studied indicated that some of their seniors were alert to the possibility that the women they hired might cost money by demanding maternity leave or by retiring early in their careers due to childcare commitments and thus 'wasting' the resources spent on their training.

A further challenge for women once they enter the profession is the possibility that their editors may seek to protect them from the *keras* (hard) news beats or rounds. Women have less chance for promotion if they cannot prove their mettle by covering major crimes, defence and security, politics or other 'hard' news. Studies of provincial newspapers and of commercial television found that the editors of these organisations were more inclined to post women to news beats that they considered *lunak* (soft) – such as arts, education, women's issues and social issues – because of concerns about women's ability to handle the workload, late nights and increased risks (LP3Y 1999: 45–56; 121–8; Soemandoyo 1999: 144–6; 234–5). One of the studies also found that in Jakarta-based newspapers, women were posted across the full range of news beats, but there were still some stereotypes about which beats were suitable and satisfying for women (LP3Y 1999: 56–61; 129–31). By contrast, in my research I found no evidence that Jakarta-based editors avoided sending women to 'hard' news stories, with women in such offices being assigned to cover events ranging from riots to army manoeuvres to drug seizures.

Siregar argues that the equity of women might be measurable by counting the number of female chief editors, particularly at daily newspapers where the pressures of deadlines are most intense. Department of Information data shows that in 1996 women made up 6.2 per cent of chiefs editors in the print and wire service media, 10 per cent of general managers and 15.3 per cent of chief executives. The Department data lists only three women as chief editors of Indonesia's 71 daily newspapers at the time – Toety Aziz at the *Surabaya Post*, the newspaper she founded with her husband, Abdul Aziz; Herwati Diah at the *Indonesia Observer*, the newspaper she created with her husband, B.M. Diah; and Ani Idrus at *Waspada,* the newspaper she established with her husband, Mohammad Said. All three – veteran journalists who were active during the colonial-era struggle for independence – took over the solo editorship of the newspapers they owned following the death (in the case of Diah and Aziz) or retirement (in the case of Idrus) of their husbands. Kartini Sjahrir posits that Indonesian women turn down offers to become editors because 'the work burden is too great with the responsibility of family' (Sjahrir 1994: 67).

Suryakusuma notes that the difficulty that women face is that 'they live in a world which essentially belongs to men. It is shaped, given masculine characteristics, ruled and dominated by men. Therefore the male world, the total social structure and masculine values, including male evaluation of women, is considered absolute' (Suryakusuma 1982: 7). Despite the official rhetoric about women being 'equal but different', women journalists are primarily judged by male editorial staff on their ability to fit themselves into a male-dominated work environment, which has historically been defined and controlled by males to suit the performance needs and characteristics of men. While many editorial staff suggested that they did not discriminate by evaluating female journalists and their work with different criteria than they use for men, only one indicated that he had taken steps to adapt the male-oriented newsroom organisational and social structures to be more accommodating of the needs arising from women's dual function.

Strength in 'weakness'

Regardless of the challenges women might face in their working environments, both editors and reporters almost universally regard women to be superior to men in the area of source relationships. It is a commonly accepted wisdom in the Indonesian news industry that sources seem to prefer associating with female journalists. Both male and female journalists described occasions in which sources repeatedly rejected requests for interviews from male reporters, but later agreed without objection to talk on the same topic with a woman from the same news organisation. One managing editor insisted that he believed the women he had observed were often 'more aggressive with their questions because they knew that the officials would be more responsive'.

Patriarchal stereotypes of women being neat, decorative, passive and non-aggressive – as befitted the New Order's domesticated image of the good wife and mother – can work to women's advantage. The women journalists found – and journalists worldwide might agree – that paternalistic sources are often more accommodating with reporters that they believe to be naïve, submissive and non-threatening. Many women journalists, both senior and junior, said that sources expected the female approach to be sweet and submissive. In the words of one: 'Sources think women will not cause trouble because they are pretty.' A Jakarta-based foreign correspondent said that men often adopted the approach of: 'Let me sit you on my knee and explain things to you.' She acknowledged that although it can be limiting and irritating to be treated less seriously than men, 'it does give you an access which you might otherwise not have simply because you are seen as less of a threat'. A foreign correspondent from Australia's Nine Television Network, Andrea Thompson, similarly said that the patriarchal attitudes and 'lack of sexual equality' advantaged women journalists, because male sources were not accustomed to saying 'no' to women. She felt that male news sources believed politeness required them to accommodate women as much as possible (Thompson 1996: pers. comm.).

Sources' preference for dealing with female journalists is also consistent with women's position as mediators. Women have traditionally mediated relations within families and village communities. They also organise the ceremonial *selamatan* meal and other social rituals that are important for maintaining the alliances that sustain economic relationships, client-patron connections and social harmony (e.g. Cooley 1992: 231–4; Djajadiningrat-Nieuwenhuis 1992: 44–6; Geertz 1961: 26–7; Manderson 1983: 7; Oey-Gardiner & Sjahrir 1991: 106; Sullivan 1994: 156–74; Suryochondro 1984: 164). Such characteristics might easily be extended to allow women to become mediators in political culture, allowing them to more easily develop the intense relationships required to open the mouths of Indonesia's sources who (as is discussed in Chapters 9 and 10) have traditionally been tight lipped.

The organic woman and ideological compromise

The evidence indicates that women's ability to participate in journalism and their experiences with sources during the New Order mirrored prevailing socio-political understandings of their *kodrat* and associated motherhood roles. Suryakusuma is among many scholars who conclude that these policies combined 'the most regressive elements of *priyayi* and Western gender politics' (1997: pers. comm.). A welding of patriarchal Dutch and Javanese values was evident during the Old Order (Djadjadiningrat-Niewenhuis 1992: 43). However, the were further entrenched by the same conservative, post-WWII Western discourses that shaped New Order economic development programs (Jhamtani 1991: 98–9; Noerhadi 1982: 30–1; Robinson 1985: 56; Soetrisno 1997: 65; Sullivan 1994: 127). The definitions of women's rights and roles enshrined in laws and policies, 'which emphasize women's roles as wives and mothers whilst ignoring the realities of women's lives, suggest bureaucratic myopia and/or an unwitting acceptance of Western values, the legacy perhaps of both colonialism and neo–colonialism regarding sex, behaviour and power' (Manderson 1983: 2).

It is easy to understand how conservative discourses about the appropriate role of women as mothers may work to limit women's activities outside the home. However, in order to determine why Indonesian women are so active in the economic sphere and yet so under-represented in journalism and other political activities, one needs to study the synchronicity of foreign organic ideologies with *priyayi* conceptions of power. Chapter 1 explains how Hegelian and *priyayi* conceptions of statehood overlap. In both Hegelian and *priyayi* philosophies, leadership and power rightly flow to those who withdraw themselves from the particular and from 'natural' feeling and emotions towards an unselfish, 'universal' consciousness. Hegel proposes that the state should balance, unite and regulate the family and civil society, binding all subjectivities together, not on the basis of immediate feeling, economic needs or the relations of production, but on the interests of the community as a whole. In this formulation, the bureaucracy is the universal class and rational, fully ethical civil servants act self-consciously, without reference to private emotional or economic interests. Women are thus viewed as less suitable for public service because, incidentally, emotion and attachment to the particular are elements that are inextricably associated with the practicalities of women's lives as wives and mothers.

Despite the perceived deficiencies of women in organic and *priyayi* philosophies, discrimination against women in the workplace and the public sphere was banned by the 1945 Constitution and various laws (e.g. Workforce Law No. 14/1969; Law No. 7/1984 on Ratification of the Convention for Elimination of All Forms of Discrimination against Women; Manpower Minister's Circular No. SE-04/MEN/1988). Pragmatism also called for women's regular and active involvement in the public sphere for the wellbeing of both individual families and of national economic development. The New Order resolved these inconsistencies between Indonesia's laws, physical needs and organic/*priyayi* ideologies by devising the philosophy of the *peran ganda*, which allowed for some adaptability in the translation of ideology into cultural practices.

The *peran ganda* enshrined in government policy what Djajadiningrat-Nieuwenhuis (1992: 43) defines as 'ibuism' (motherism), an outlook which 'sanctions any action provided it is taken as a mother who is looking after her family, a group, a class, a company or the state, without demanding power or prestige in return'. The New Order allowed mothers to act freely as full adults in the public sphere because their actions were accepted as stemming from their duty to family welfare (Sullivan 1994: 145) rather than their desire for satisfaction or stimulation from careers or public activities.

Djajadiningrat-Niewenhuis's formula needs to be extended, however, to clarify that the prioritisation of family, group, class, company and state occurs *in that order*. A woman's service to a particular company, for example, would usually be seen as untoward if it came at the expense of her family. In defining family as women's first duty, the New Order gave women the autonomy to act as they saw fit to fulfil family needs, and then in turn to fulfil group, class, company and state needs. However, it also reduced women's chances of escaping the base-level emotion and earthy particularity of close family life. The New Order thus limited women's potential to achieve ethical universalism or power by promoting a definition of women's *kodrat* that is inherently incompatible with the organic-*priyayi* notions of power.

Patterns of industrialisation from the 1970s – where men were increasingly recruited to a work domain outside the home and nuclear family units lived further from the traditional support networks of relatives and village community – also meant that the greater burden of household duties fell upon women as their families moved out of an agrarian lifestyle (Robinson 1985: 52–4). The higher social and economic status that followed a family's rise into the emergent middle classes was often accompanied by reduced freedom of physical movement and participation for women in non-domestic matters (Hull 1996: 93). Many women, however, saw diminished autonomy as a small sacrifice to pay for the elevated status, prestige and comfort that accompany an 'emancipated' middle-class lifestyle (Manderson 1983: 8–9). There also appeared a strong influence of the *priyayi* ideology that work done by women symbolised lower class status and exploitation (Hull 1996: 84; *Prisma* 1985: 2). The definition of the housewife role as privilege for middle-class women had ramifications for journalists, who themselves come predominantly from the middle classes.

If women are to serve their families, they must also optimise their earnings per hour in order to limit their time away from their principal responsibilities in the home. Regular employment, self-employment and piecework usually involve a certain income rate for a predefined number of working hours or units produced. Labour time can be limited to an agreed number of hours, although there is the potential to gain more money by working longer and/or harder. A woman working in the higher levels of civil service, a political appointment or journalism may be obliged to devote long working hours towards ensuring a quality performance, but longer working hours in such cases are not accompanied by a higher salary or direct benefits to her family. On the contrary, they take her away from her family longer than absolutely necessary. The poor woman working all night in a factory might therefore be lauded for her self-sacrificing nature, while the middle or upper class woman working late into the night in journalism or political projects might be criticised for putting her career ahead of her family. Philosophies of 'ibuism' thus encourage women to confine their work to the purely economic rather than the political sphere in order to minimise the time spent away from their families. The philosophy of *peran ganda* validated women's participation in the public sphere, but it also contained their involvement through the politically loaded proviso that 'secondary' occupations of paid work be consistent with women's *kodrat* and 'primary' duty to their families.

Life on the thinnest edge of the wedge

While there are innumerable cultural influences that affect Indonesian women's lived experiences of their 'womanhood' and 'femininity', women are not generally shackled to their homes. Journalists, who are trained to seek verifiable 'truths' and to separate 'facts' from falsehoods and stereotype, should be better equipped than most people to deduce from the evidence around them that the scarcity of women in their profession cannot be reduced to a simplistic formula of 'woman equals mother, childcarer and housewife' while 'man equals father, provider and worker'. Perhaps journalists, even those who contest such a view, believe that the formula represents the wider public understanding because journalists usually belong to the educated middle class that is heavily influenced by *priyayi* aspirations and world views.

The difficulties that women experience in journalism, with regards to the difficulties of leaving their children and travelling at night, can be seen to represent the types of problems that Indonesian women commonly encounter in many occupations. Although such obstacles may be faced by innumerable women workers, women journalists might be seen as working at the thinnest edge of the wedge because their duties to cover the news may require lengthy absences from home at little or no notice, may involve long and unpredictable work hours and may oblige them to rush headlong into dangers that all others are attempting to flee.

News editors appear to appreciate women's superior skills in dealing with sources, but not so much that they prefer to hire women before men. Women are employed on the assumption that they will perform equally to men in the male-oriented structures of both their news organisations and the political structures they report on. Women journalists compete with men on a disadvantaged basis, attempting to fulfil family duties in addition to their work, or attempt to equalise their position by coopting *pembantu* or relatives to perform their share of the nurturing household functions. With the possible exception of the few women journalists who did not marry at all, there appeared no effort to contest the underlying organisational and ideological structures that perpetuate the 'man worker, woman homebody' divide.

The New Order's argument that good public servants must be freed from family tensions is typical of the integralistic ideology that those involved in political life must be freed from the time and emotional drain of passionate, particular home life. The *dual function*, which specifies that women's duty belongs first to their family, indirectly repudiates the notion of women's direct involvement in the political apparatus, except in the lower ranks of the civil service where staff generally work regular office hours. The predicament of women journalists, as described above, seems indicative of those faced by women in the other 'estates' of politics. A study of 104 female politicians in the late New Order shows they faced similar problems of family pressures (Wardani 1999: 19).

Considering the inextricable entanglement of women's housebound position within integralistic philosophies, it is unsurprising then that Philip Eldridge notes that during the New Order, both government and non-government organisations generally avoided questions relating to women's position in the household, the gender-based division of labour and the construction of social roles as 'too complex and sensitive to confront in any direct way' (Eldridge 1995: 153; also Cooley 1992: 238; *Inside Indonesia* 1996: 12). Even though journalists struggle to expose social inequities, they too appeared unable to confront such issues. Perhaps journalists were unaware of the revolutionary potential in changing the patterns of gender relations; widespread reform of power structures within the home must logically have precipitated or been precipitated by changes that would reach as far as the state and military apparatus that relied intensely for so long on the 'man worker, woman homemaker' dichotomy.

Female journalists in the post-Soeharto era

Any discussion of the improvements of the position of women in journalism in the post-Soeharto era is bound to be short, simply because there has been no notable net improvement. Chapter 3 explained that there has been a substantial change in the official rhetoric regarding the role of women in society, but that the practical process of relinquishing integralistic paradigms has been wavering. Post-Soeharto political leaders have talked much about breaking down the patriarchal structure, but there has been no acknowledgement that women cannot easily step out of their homes unless men support them by spending more time in the private sphere as men commonly did in the pre-New Order, pre-industrialised era. Habibie, for example, declared that women must have the same legal and political rights and opportunities as men, but spoke only of women's rather than both parents' roles in the home and in childrearing (*Republika* 27 Nov. 1998: 12). Wahid's wife, Sinta Nuriyah, typifies the approach of the era when she says that she advises her daughters that can have a career, 'as long as they can become good housewives who can maintain a harmonious family and raise their children to be useful people' (Endah & Kleden 2001: 71.)

Given that the government's new rhetoric of women's empowerment is yet to impact on many aspects of their maternal and domestic commitments, it would not be expected that there would be significant erosion of the barriers that face women in journalism or any other political domain. Unsurprisingly, the PWI's figures for 1998 to March 2001 show a zero net increase in the percentage of female members since the end of the New Order (Azzam 2001: pers. comm.). This is lower than the rate at which women were recruited into journalism compared to men during the New Order. Records for both PWI membership and Department of Information data on the print and wire-service industries showed the percentage of women in journalism rose by an average increment of 0.3 per cent per year during the New Order period.[2] It is too early to determine long-term trends, but short-term figures suggest that the end of the New Order has not heralded a mass rush of women into either mainstream politics or journalism.

The leaders of the PWI and AJI are aware that there has been no improvement in the rates of recruitment of women into journalism. Both the PWI and AJI claim to support reform of the old patriarchal political system, but neither organisation plans to organise campaigns or activities to address the low participation of women in journalism, which is the practical legacy of patriarchal government. Until the practical issues relating to women's 'double burden' at work and home are addressed through more workplace or social support for women, it is unlikely that women will choose to enter journalism or be able to maintain long-term careers in substantially increased numbers.

9 News sources in the political labyrinth

The topic of press freedom in Indonesia has inspired innumerable reports from scholars, free-speech organisations, human-rights activists and journalists themselves. Most of these reports study issues of censorship and self-censorship that result from legal and other intimidatory powers of the state. Such reports expose and analyse the state's attempts to either conceal information that a journalist has already discovered or to justify such concealment through the discourses of development journalism and *Pancasila* values. Throughout the New Order, the Indonesian government engaged in direct censorship or promoted indirect censorship through mechanisms such as threatening journalists with the risk of job loss, jail, fines or physical violence.[1]

Reports on press freedom rarely address the less visible issue of concealment of information through source unwillingness to talk to journalists. A journalist who is obstructed from obtaining information about issues of public importance is just as much censored as one who has obtained the information but is prevented from using it. In recognition of this general principle, UNESCO has declared that one of the most important rights of journalists is the right to access both official and unofficial sources (MacBride et al. 1980: 239). This chapter explores how the New Order's patriarchal political culture limited journalists' access to government sources, creating an information environment that was regularly described by journalists and analysts as closed, opaque or lacking transparency. The chapter also shows that most of Soeharto's successors have been anxious to establish their credentials as political reformers, and openness to the media has been an important part of their attempts to prove their responsiveness to public concerns.

The forbidden city

During most of the New Order period, journalists were frustrated by the political structure that shielded the president from direct systems of accountability. Soeharto, at the very pinnacle of the political ladder, was the most remote source of information for journalists. He was not directly answerable to the electorate through popular mandate, and the Parliament never attempted to significantly alter his or his cabinet's decisions. His engagements with the media were similarly managed in a fashion that prevented direct accountability through public interrogation of his actions or policies.

Soeharto was constantly quoted in the news, but those statements tended to come from secondhand or staged contacts with the media. These included speeches, comments at formal, preorganised events, or reports from ministers and friends who relayed announcements to journalists as they left his office. Australian Associated Press's Tom Hyland (1995: pers. comm.) says Soeharto was akin to a king 'who issues pronouncements – but never directly, never himself – to somebody else who then comes out and says, "The president told me this."' As president, Soeharto rarely agreed to press conferences or direct interviews. The Index on Censorship group (1975: 83) reports that he held the first press conference of his presidency seven years after he was formally appointed to the nation's number-one position. The 1974 conference was held only to deny claims in a popular magazine, *Pop*, that he had an aristocratic background, in contrast with the official family tree that shows he hails from peasant stock.[2] The Information Department observed as early as 1975 that journalists wanted regular press conferences with Soeharto 'so that they could truly and fully comprehend the thoughts of the President as the highest decision maker' (Departemen Penerangan 1975: 66). This wish was never fulfilled. Soeharto's press conferences were so infrequent that when they were held, reporters were inclined to lead their stories with the fact that he had agreed to talk directly with journalists rather than what he had actually said (e.g. *Berita Buana* 2 Dec. 1987: 12; Goh 1998: 4).

The few journalists who were granted audiences with Soeharto interviewed him in a respectful fashion with only the mildest of probing (Berry et al. 1995: 18; Tiffen 1978: 195). One presidential reporter told me that on the rare occasions they interviewed Soeharto, regulars at the Presidential Palace were 'very careful' to only ask 'questions that do not hurt his feelings, that do not trigger his emotions'.

Journalists required special security passes to work in the Presidential Palace. Soeharto's security staff vetted and groomed applicants for security passes to ensure that the journalists who covered the president's activities would confine themselves to merely reporting verbatim quotes from his official visitors. One subeditor described the Palace as 'the forbidden city', because the process of obtaining access was so demanding.

> They ask you questions like: 'If you were in danger and you knew that the president was in danger too, what would you do?' Of course you would save yourself. A friend told me that she replied: 'I would fight to save my president with the very last drop of my blood. Because the 200 million people in this nation need him, but who am I? I am nothing.' She got the job.

Another reporter, with 12 years experience inside the Palace, said that many reporters spent their first year confined to the Palace press room before they were given the permit to enter the Palace itself.

There was no place for investigative reporting skills, because it was understood that there was no such thing as journalistic competition or 'scoops' in the Palace. One editor described 'high stamina, conscientiousness and responsibility' as the prerequisites for a Palace posting, because the position primarily involved the 'boring' task of waiting for hours for meetings to conclude and remaining alert enough to take meticulous records of the end results (Departemen Penerangan 1975: 84). Palace reporters said they scrupulously compared notes with their colleagues to ensure that their transcriptions of source quotes agreed 100 per cent. This protected them in cases in which Soeharto's visitors subsequently claimed that they had been misquoted. Stories containing inaccuracies or politically contentious material could lead to individual reporters or entire news organisations being banned.

Although Soeharto never courted the media with invitations to *wayang* performances or for chats over coffee in the style of the flamboyant and gregarious Sukarno, senior journalists remember that the New Order leader was not always so formal with journalists. *Jakarta Post* editor Susanto Pudjomartono (1996: pers. comm.), who began his journalism career in 1966, remembers that during late-night cabinet meetings during the first year of the New Order, waiting reporters served themselves *nasi bungkus* (rice parcels) from the same table in the same room as Soeharto.

> We talked to *Pak* Harto [Father Soeharto] and he was willing to talk to everybody. Then they served the food on different tables. After two or three years, they moved the journalists' food table outside. We ate with the adjutants and not the ministers.

One senior journalist, with professional experience of both the Old and New Orders, attributed the brittleness of relations between journalists and Soeharto to the latter's formative experiences in army combat.

> Everything in the system was orders: 'Do as you are told.' They [the generals] had the habit of staying in jungles, in the front lines. You were either one of their own or one of their enemies. If you speak differently, then you belong to the enemy group. Soeharto has no tradition of speaking to enemies.

Army sources have similarly noted that Soeharto did not tolerate argument, with one quoting him as saying during his army years: 'My politics are at the end of a bayonet.' (Jenkins 1984: 33)

The change in Soeharto's accessibility corresponded with a general alteration in his relationship with Indonesia's small civil society. During the initial years of the New Order, the press along with non-leftist student, religious and other social groups might have been seen as functioning collaboratively with Soeharto. The newspapers that survived the mass post-Gestapu press shutdowns were anti-Sukarnoist, sympathising with the New Order's military proponents (Hill 1987:

27). A new sense of press freedom became apparent in the late 1960s, marked by open discussion of political affairs (Crawford 1971: 169–70; Anderson 1976: 29, 40–1). Some have attributed the tolerance of Soeharto and the Armed Forces (ABRI) to their need to consolidate support for and legitimise the new leadership (*New Journalist* Aug. 1982: 21). Although there were some press criticisms of economic and other policies, the New Order's major ideological foundations were relatively immune from attack because of the anti-leftist makeup of the press. Leftist analysts argue that the press was even rather servile, publicising propaganda on behalf of the New Order (Southwood & Flanagan 1983: 69–72).

Strong press critiques of the New Order started to emerge by 1969. Although the government apparently initially believed it was prudent to endure sporadic press condemnation (Hill 1987: 28), its tolerance had evaporated by the early 1970s. In 1973, veteran journalist Rosihan Anwar (p. 5) noted that 'with the power the military have in government today, the generals are also able simply to ignore what the press reports or comments upon, as it does not affect the position of generals'. Soeharto's distancing of himself from the press thus accompanied a general reduction in press freedom in the face of increasing criticism from the centres of civil society.

The guardians of the city

The military were semi-denizens of 'the forbidden city'. They were both literally and figuratively the Palace guards who protected and preserved the power and privilege of the New Order leadership but who also wielded power in their own right. ABRI maintained a mini-citadel, the Mabes (*Markas besar*) ABRI in Cilangkap, which was the headquarters for land, air, sea and police operations. Procedures for admission were less rigorous than at the Palace, but journalists who were stationed to cover the Mabes ABRI were similarly screened and usually waited about one month to receive an entry permit. Unaccredited reporters could attend occasional functions at the Mabes by official invitation. One ABRI-specialist reporter said the armed forces had only two basic stipulations for journalists, the first 'to guard the good name of ABRI' and the second 'to follow the 1945 Constitution and *Pancasila*'.

Mochtar Lubis argues that ABRI's dominance of political activity during the New Order was accompanied by an unwillingness to share power with other sources, ultimately creating 'a very closed society' in which the press was 'completely intimidated' (Hill 1987: 33). Despite this, military leaders were more accessible and open than the president. Press conferences were held at the Mabes ABRI every few weeks, or more regularly during events of public concern. The ABRI information culture was less monolithic than that in the Palace, and reporters were able to gain information and even scoops through cultivating personal contacts and exploiting the vested interests of different factions. Seasoned reporters suggested that they required about one year to develop a range of informal contacts, and that it was important to take a long-term approach by socialising with low-level officers who might be promoted to positions of power in subsequent years. ABRI sources were more likely to cooperate with journalists when there was the competition and division between rival ABRI groups, when certain factions wanted to advance their own strategies and when certain officers aspired to be promoted. Information from such sources was most commonly off the record and thus had to be checked and rechecked numerous times before publishing.

The culture opened notably when certain groups within ABRI – often discontented with and disenfranchised by the circle of power around Soeharto (see MacIntyre 1994: 111–15) – began promoting greater social and press freedom in the 1990s. Survey respondents noted that ABRI-press relations improved during the period of *keterbukaan* (socio-political openness) in the early 1990s, when the army became more accommodating about providing information. The openness was motivated, at least in part, by the desire of certain ABRI groups to facilitate criticism of the Soeharto government (HRW–A 1994: 5). In this context, the increased accessibility and openness was the result of a political desire to use the public sphere as a zone for élite power contestations rather than any commitment towards the long-term renegotiation of power between the élite and the masses through the mass media.

The political citadel

Ministers and first-level bureaucrats were also visitors to 'the forbidden city', and as temporary tenants of the citadel of power, they too kept journalists at a distance. Even though there was never any shortage of formal functions and speeches at which ministers and other public officials would deliver what one foreign correspondent described as 'sterile pronouncements', both local and foreign journalists found it difficult to obtain personalised audiences within the top echelons of the Indonesian bureaucracy. Many ministers preferred to minimise their media-relations work by talking to groups of journalists (Departemen Penerangan 1975: 38) or by making comments through speeches at formal events (Departemen Penerangan 1975: 30) rather than granting individual interviews, in a pattern opposite to that of their Western counterparts.[3] By the mid-1970s, editors admitted that they were disinclined to request interviews because they had to wait a minimum of three weeks for an answer, if they received any reply at all. One editor estimated that only 40 per cent of requests succeeded (Departemen Penerangan 1975: 41).

Ministers were urged in the 1980s to 'open themselves to healthy criticism' (Antara 22 Mar. 1988a: A24), but for the remainder of the New Order, reporters could expect to wait several months for responses to requests for interviews. From his experience in the mid-1990s, former AAP correspondent Terry Friel (1995: pers. comm.) explained that:

> To organise an interview it took a good hour or so just to get through to the secretary and put in your request. Then often a day, or two days, or three weeks later you'd suddenly get a phone call saying there would be an

> interview in the minister's office in half an hour. It was generally an hour
> and a half trip in the traffic to the minister's office ....

The story was no better for local journalists. When requests were approved,
journalists had often waited so long that the original topic they had proposed to
discuss was too outdated to consider.

From a reporter's perspective, the restricted access to ministers was
professionally frustrating. Journalists worldwide generally prefer individualised
interviews with sources, because it enables them to be more probing in both
obtaining new information and rechecking existing information, to engage in
debate, and to take greater initiative in directing the range and depth of topics
discussed (Bell & Leeuwen 1994: 8–9; Departemen Penerangan 1975: 37; Tiffen
1989: 37). However, Indonesian editors appeared sanguine about the unwillingness of ministers to submit to individual interviews. Some accepted that
although news organisations would never obtain exclusive stories from group
interviews or from coverage of ceremonies, there was the advantage that the
ministers could not subsequently deny saying what they had said to so many
witnesses (Departemen Penerangan 1975: 38–9).

Like Soeharto, ministers were freely accessible during the beginning of New
Order. During the early New Order years, editors were invited to regular
background briefings and critical discussions with state and military bodies, like
Kopkamtib. Such meetings constituted an important feedback mechanism, in
which the chief editors had high-level input into decision-making processes
about how to change or develop government policy (Departemen Penerangan
1975: 26). The Information Department's 1975 study of government-media
relations indicates the pattern of ministers distancing themselves from journalists had become entrenched by the early 1970s. Pudjomartono (1996: pers.
comm.) similarly notes:

> In 1966 to 1967, there was no such thing as PR in the ministry. We could
> talk directly to anybody, including the Cabinet officials. We would wait
> outside their room chatting to the secretary. Some ministers regularly
> invited journalists to lunch. Now public relations tries to stop you from
> talking to them.

These limits on access appear to result from the unwillingness of ministers to
speak 'off the cuff'. While a few ministers, such as former foreign minister Ali
Alatas and former environment minister Sarwono Kusumaatmadja, were
confident in making *ad hoc* comments to press questions, most were considered
hesitant to deviate from comments already made in formal speeches or from
other standardised responses. Former minister/state secretary Moerdiono, one of
Soeharto's most loyal colleagues, admitted that he was 'very cautious in making
statements' because he 'worried that they might impact negatively on society'.
He advised fellow ministers to think twice before talking publicly, especially on
sensitive issues (*Jakarta Post* 17 Mar. 1998: 1). Most ministers expected

journalists to accompany requests for interviews with written copies of the questions they were likely to ask, in order to prepare themselves.

Journalists were not required to display the extreme delicacy with ministers and senior bureaucrats that they did with the president, and could be incisive and probing, as long as the questions were 'proper and polite'. When foreign correspondents attended, they were 'envied for their incisive and unrestrained way of getting to the core of problems', but they were also 'reproached for their lack of tact and aggressiveness in their straight, inconsiderate ways of "information grabbing"' (Makarim 1978: 262). Of the 65 journalists who participated in my survey, only one claimed to be as bold and forthright as foreign journalists in his questioning of ministers. He admitted that such behaviour had resulted in one government office placing his name on a blacklist of 'journalists who ask direct questions which the ministers do not like'.

Cross-examination of ministers through the basic journalistic interviewing tool of devil's advocate questioning was thus avoided. Instead of depicting political and military leaders as defending themselves directly or indirectly against antagonists, the Indonesian media portrayed such leaders in ways which suggested stability and unity (Berry et al. 1995: 18). *Tempo*'s Dewi Anggraeni (1994: pers. comm.) suggests that rather than challenge the statements of such high-ranking individuals, journalists were more likely to keep them talking and then screen the information carefully once the interview was completed.

The exception was when ministers, generals or other dignitaries were obliged to brief the press after meeting with Soeharto. Senior figures could be confident in talking, knowing that there could be no negative political repercussions for parroting the words of the nation's number-one figure. One Palace reporter explained: 'They are different after meeting with the president. He is obviously the king. We take advantage of that. You can interrogate the ministers, and they will usually answer you more politely than they would in their office.'

Even when journalists were able to access and question ministers, senior bureaucrats and other political leaders, such figures were frequently unaware of important policies or activities within their portfolio or area of responsibility. Foreign correspondents attending a media briefing on the 1998 presidential elections, for example, were bemused to find Golkar politicians studying piles of textbooks and holding emergency consultations in huddles because, even as participants in the political process, they did not have enough information to answer basic questions about political procedures. One politician was greeted by 'a roomful of laughter' when, following a question about special powers that were about to be granted to the president, she replied: 'It's a special power, but nobody knows what kind of power this is' (*Jakarta Post* 20 Apr. 1998: 2).

The information provided by the top echelons of political power at official speeches, ceremonies, project launches and anniversary celebrations was thus often not very newsworthy. Despite this, news organisations were compelled to prioritise such events with front-page coverage or the lead position in television or radio broadcasts. Journalists and editors admitted that if stories about a particular minister were not given prominence by their news organisations, officials from the minister's department would sometimes call to question why. Verbatim quotes from Soeharto's speeches were published in lengthy front-page reports that were rarely accompanied by contesting viewpoints.

The rubber stamp of officialdom

This top-heavy domination of the news was criticised by other New Order political institutions, such as the DPR, that had been weakened by the omnipotence of Soeharto and his executive. During the early 1990s period of *keterbukaan*, during which the DPR and other political groupings became increasingly active, members of parliament complained that journalists paid vastly more attention to the activities of the executive than to the legislature (*Kompas* 29 Apr. 1991: 1). One parliamentarian surmised that the 'imbalanced' reporting in favour of ministers and bureaucratic officials resulted because 'the press was entangled in political feudalism' (Bernas 7 Jul. 1993: 1; also Abar 1994b: 4).

Journalists described parliamentarians as 'accommodative' and my own observation was that members were very accessible to journalists roaming the DPR building. While journalists agreed that the approachability of parliamentarians to be high, they found fault with the quality of information. One senior journalist said:

> Most just come, sit, keep really quiet .... and receive money. The five Ds.[4] That's a blessing because once they open their mouths, they seem to come up with stupid questions .... There was a legislator from a house commission in charge of the environment who asked the minister about the greenhouse effect. He thought that it was caused because people build a lot of glass buildings. Of course there are also good people there. But it is hard to be generous.

Many parliamentarians were also loath to be critical because the state could pressure their parties to recall them (Mas'oed 1994: 62), as happened in the mid-1990s to outspoken MPs Sri Bintang Pamungkas and Bambang Warih Kusuma (*Asiaweek* 14 Mar.1995: 37).

The low quality of the members of the 'rubber stamp' parliament was not solely responsible for the poor coverage. The DPR's Deputy Head, Saiful Sulun, argued that journalists only attended DPR meetings when they were almost finished, thus missing the nuances of the debate, and that journalists had the courage to criticise the legislature in a way that they lacked when criticising the government (*Kompas* 29 Apr. 1991: 1). My personal observation of journalists' activities in the DPR suggested that both were reasonable comments. One example was journalists' unwillingness to cover students' submissions before a DPR committee in April 1998, which included strident criticism of Soeharto. One journalist told me that although public records were kept of activities in the parliament, and such events were technically 'safe' to cover, he did not think that parliamentary privilege provided protection on issues relating to Soeharto. The case is mentioned to provide context. Although journalists were frustrated by the hesitancy of Indonesian sources to speak fully, frankly and on the record because of fears of repercussions, the tendency towards self-preservation before openness was equally manifest in journalists themselves. 'Censorship' of news through source silence occurred within a general culture of direct and indirect censorship that took many forms.

The bureaucratic maze

Information flow was also disrupted by a bureaucratic culture, in which public servants had greater obligations to demonstrate loyalty and accountability to their superiors on the institutional ladder than the masses they served. The large and unwieldy bureaucracy was like a maze outside the political citadel, which journalists had difficulty negotiating to access official sources and documentation. New Order bureaucrats classically employed three responses when journalists contacted them. The first was to pretend to be out of the office or 'busy' when journalists called. The second was to hide information through superficial answers during interviews. The third was to talk candidly but off the record. Foreign correspondents who covered Indonesia through the New Order found that, as a general rule, public officials were less forthright and confident than their Western counterparts in dealing with the media.

Journalists and media analysts acknowledge that such responses arose because those in the New Order bureaucracy often thought of journalists as *hantu menakutkan* (a frightening ghost) (*Kompas* 9 Apr. 1998: 3: Kusnadi 1996: 4). Their trepidation arose from concerns that social problems would be uncovered within their jurisdiction and, as a result, their social credibility and careers would suffer. Survey respondents had innumerable stories about how bureaucrats had been intimidated, passed over for promotion or prematurely retired for the well-meaning sharing of apparently innocuous information that later turned out to have some indirect political connection. The Information Department's 1975 report (Departemen Penerangan 1975: 61–2) similarly found that lower-echelon bureaucrats were afraid to talk with press even though they were permitted to give background information within their competency (*Berita Buana* 22 Oct. 1975: 12), indicating the long-term perpetuation of bureaucratic opacity throughout the New Order.

A consistent finding among journalists was that bureaucrats were easier to talk to once they knew a higher authority had already commented on a topic. Once the minister had made a broad pronouncement on an issue, the director general and lower officials would more readily provide the details. One journalist attributed this to the culture of *kebapakan* (paternalism), in which bureaucrats had the right to speak but did not feel confident to until they had 'permission' from higher authorities. This culture thus mirrored the Palace culture, in which ministers were freer to speak once they had been authorised to by the president.

Breaching the citadel

It is a truism in any country that the journalists who cultivate close relations with their sources are those who produce the best copy. Journalists who confine their activities to press conferences and brief liaisons with official institutional representatives are less likely to produce stories of great depth, reveal new insights, or uncover new issues. It is, however, still possible for journalists in Western nations to perform creditably through relatively impersonal contacts with sources who, in the age of tele- and computer communications, they may never meet.

Journalists and public relations sources noted that New Order officials were less inclined to give information to journalists over the telephone than their Western colleagues. Both foreign and local correspondents stressed that it was far more important in Indonesia to develop personalised relations with news sources than in Western countries. Despite the time-consuming nature of travelling to sources' offices or homes for interviews, journalists usually tried to conduct face-to-face interviews. This was important not just because it was necessary to gain the confidence of the source through person-to-person contact. Physically locating oneself in a bureaucrat or businessperson's office was also often the only way to get around the secretaries and junior officials, who commonly acted as if it were their life mission to protect their bosses.

Because of the limits of formal access to news sources, journalists also made greater efforts to establish extended informal networks through the social circuit. Cocktail parties, celebrations, seminars, business launches, diplomatic functions, *buka puasa* (the fast-breaking meal), *halal bihalal* (a gathering at the end of the fasting month to ask forgiveness) and other social occasions were and still are important venues for establishing, renewing and widening connections. News organisations receive dozens of invitations to such events each week. One journalist described such gatherings as a key means by which 'the Indonesian élite keeps its channels of discourse flowing .... It's the substitute for the telephone'. Journalists noted that sources who had been difficult to contact also became more approachable after a meeting, even a brief one. The Australian Broadcasting Corporation's (ABC's) Michael Maher observed that: 'Even if you speak to them for five minutes and thrust a name card in their hand, it's worthwhile.'

Despite the usefulness of one-off contacts, the process usually requires considerable effort towards building and sustaining existing connections. The time-consuming process of integrating with sources meant that stresses arose around the journalists' need to obtain information within time frames that suited the deadlines of news corporations. Time delays in obtaining interviews and information increased the difficulties of operating within the deadlines. For example, a daily complaint of the hundreds of foreign journalists who converged on Jakarta and Bogor for the 1994 APEC forum meetings was that they were unable to arrange their deadlines to accommodate the vagaries of their Indonesian bureaucratic sources (Kakiailatu 1994: 71). In the West, the journalists' routine is generally organised around presumptions that the bureaucracy will respond instantly to their requests for information; the journalists covering APEC were unaccustomed to a less information-centred bureaucracy that tended to reply eventually, rather than immediately. Such problems were faced by local journalists too but were less intense for journalists from larger organisations, such as *Kompas*, because the general reputation of their prestigious companies made it easier for them to ingratiate themselves with sources.

Media theorists note that reliance on intimate source-journalist relationships is generally problematic, because it increases the tendency of reporters to mute criticism in order to avoid offending and thus losing the input of important information providers (Chibnall 1977: 156–9; Herman & Chomsky 1988: 22; Sigal 1973: 54). Both participants in and observers of the Indonesian news-making process acknowledged that journalists who built bonds of confidence with military and government leaders could be admitted to an 'inner circle' with such sources, but they risked the possibility of jeopardising their relations with that circle if they published or broadcast critical reportage (Jenkins 1996: pers. comm.; Jenkins 1986: 156; Milne 1989: 446). Such close affiliation may furthermore lead journalists to become so empathetic with the sources that they 'lose their critical capacities' and begin to 'think like officials and forget their function' (Departemen Penerangan 1975: 87).

Dancing with wolves

Although the information presented in this chapter may make it appear that New Order journalists were totally reliant on charm and social skills, they also wielded blunter weapons to gain access to aloof sources. Reporters could not ultimately invade the offices of unwilling sources and prise open their mouths, but they did use the media's public position to challenge the source's right to remain silent. Journalists sometimes published details of particular sources' refusal to answer questions, placed boycotts on certain sources (e.g. *Kompas* 1 Jun. 1998: 11), took legal action against others (e.g. *Jakarta Post* 5 Oct. 1995: 2) or prompted ministers and other influential figures to publicly condemn the sources concerned (e.g. *Jakarta Post* 29 Sept. 1995: 2; *Kompas* 18 Nov. 1994: 17; *Republika* 6 Oct. 1995). Such pressures sometimes forced apologies and backdowns from the officials involved (e.g. Antara 22 Nov. 1984: C4; *Jakarta Post* 20 Apr. 1998: 2; *Suara Pembaruan* 25 Apr. 1998: 5; *Suara Pembaruan* 22 Apr. 1998: 5). There is no evidence of journalists daring to use this kind of publicity against senior New Order figures, such as ministers or army generals, but sources with more limited power such as governors, regents, mayors, middle-level bureaucrats and police officers were subject to such journalistic pressures.

Journalists were also creative in mining for scraps of valuable information from lower-level sources. Reporters turned to senior officials' drivers, office assistants and even cleaners for useful information that such sources discovered serendipitously through their incidental access to the halls of power. More creatively, some journalists used the intimidatory *kebudayaan telepon* (telephone culture) to their advantage. Telephone culture involved politicians, bureaucrats or members of the armed forces calling journalists to 'advise' that a story be covered a particular way or not be published at all. Such appeals were often disregarded if they came from lower-level officials who did not wield sufficient power to affect the news organisation's activities (Orentlicher 1988: 224). Sometimes the warnings could be useful 'tipoffs' about incidents that journalists had not previously been aware of.

From the citadel to the circus

With the collapse of the New Order, the obligation for Habibie's caretaker government to appear to be responsive to public interest impacted immediately and noticeably on journalists and their sources. As the New Order crumbled, many sources who had previously been hesitant to speak to journalists began to regularly court the news media. The change was most obvious in the upper echelons of political power, with Habibie among those making conspicuous attempts to woo journalists. Habibie's adviser, Dewi Fortuna Anwar (1998), says that Soeharto had advised his protégé not to talk with the media. She claims to have counselled Habibie that journalists would write about him, regardless of whether he spoke to them or not, so he had best accept the opportunity to present his point of view.

Habibie surprised journalists in the first days of his presidency by seizing the microphone to make impromptu speeches at public gatherings. Following complaints by Palace journalists about problems with access, Habibie granted a 'dialogue' with print-media editors (*Kompas* 7 Jun. 1998: 1). He regularly met with foreign journalists and conducted question-and-answer sessions with local journalists (Kelly 1998: 23; Price 1998: 9; Richburg 1998: A23). Admitting that many people regarded him as 'the puppet of his former master', Habibie told journalists that he intended to separate himself from the culture of the Soeharto era. 'You have transparency. You could never talk to President Suharto the way you can talk to me .... I am not the king,' he said (Mydans 1998).

The media's characteristic 'Javanese' refinement in dealing with élite sources also slipped. *The Jakarta Post*, for example, castigated Habibie for granting his first interviews to CNN journalists ahead of the Indonesian media. In an editorial, the newspaper criticised Habibie for 'his pretentious show' on CNN, his 'lamentable' manners and his inability to listen to others (Greenlees 1998: 7).

Some of the élite initially protested the unfamiliar rough treatment. For example, after Home Affairs Minister Syarwan Hamid was accused by the newly emboldened press of involvement in a 1996 raid on the Indonesian Democratic Party (PDI) headquarters, he complained: 'I've become frightened and worried about whether my statements are understood and written as they are, without being changed by the press. My other fellow Cabinet ministers are also frightened to talk to the press.' (Associated Press 14 Aug. 1998) Another minister suggested, however, that power holders became accustomed to the new culture. 'It used to hurt, but not any more. Every newspaper is trying to outdo each other. We're growing used to it.' (Chew 1998)

Wahid, a favourite source among many journalists during the Soeharto era (see Chapter 10), provided many colourful soundbites as president. He developed a reputation for being a joker and a clown, as he attempted to cover his lack of policy and political strategy with humour and light-hearted sallies. Journalists' preoccupation with slick presentation, wisecracks and one-liners reflected the paucity of the Wahid government's performance. Although journalists enjoyed the lively repartee of the comedian president, the public rapidly became frustrated with politicians who relied on personality rather than policy to address Indonesia's financial and social problems. One example was the picketing of the August 2000 MPR session by protesters demanding an end to what one placard-holder called 'the political circus'.

Wahid-era politics were strongly influenced by the president's propensity to issue bold public statements with little apparent reflection on their implications, and for journalists to circulate them, with little evident analysis of their worth. Regularly, public outcry forced the president to retrospectively revise his on-the-spot pronouncements. His pattern of stirring domestic unrest, by making controversial remarks to the media about Indonesian politics while abroad, has been much criticised (e.g. *Jakarta Post* 8 Feb. 2000, 14 Feb. 2000). A characteristic example was his on-again, off-again suspension of General Wiranto from his portfolio as Coordinating Minister for Political Affairs and Security, which was played out via the media in February 2000. Much of the debate about Wiranto's future occurred while the president was on a two-week overseas trip and the General was back in Indonesia, with both parties issuing alternately hostile and appeasing statements to journalists.

In October 2000, Wahid introduced a new posting at the palace, that of chief presidential spokesman. From the start it was assumed that the 'greatest challenge' for the spokesman, Wimar Witoelar, would be to 'find ways to limit opportunities for president Abudurrahman to speak' (Bektiati, Fibri & Prabandari 2000: 30). This task rapidly proved beyond him.

Megawati's attainment of the presidency provides potential for another major redirection in the political culture and state–media relations. Following several instances of poor treatment from journalists, she was not disposed to grant regular interviews or press conferences during the Soeharto, Habibie or Wahid eras. While he was still president, Wahid publicly described his relationship with the publicity-shy Megawati as being like 'older brother and younger sister for many years', but he also reputedly joked privately that she was 'mute' (Greenlees 2000: 10). After the garrulous, shoot-from-the-lip leadership of Habibie, Wahid and many other politicians, her reluctance to speak was sometimes lauded as a desirable strategy (e.g. Sudradjat 1999: 1).

Megawati's first day as president suggested that the media could expect limited direct contact with her. Immediately after being appointed as president, she read a brief statement from a Presidential Information sheet to journalists at a press conference and left without time for questions and answers, despite reporters' robust entreaties for more information. Megawati's media style undoubtedly stems from her cautious, conservative and reserved nature. Some journalists and analysts suggest that her advisers compound her reticence to address journalists by preventing her from engaging too closely with the media in order that she does not expose any limitations in her political vision or grasp of national affairs.

Megawati is not the only notable source who remains silent in the new era of transparency. It continues to be as difficult as ever to obtain reliable information about Soeharto. A typical example was the confusing jumble of conflicting 'facts' that journalists gathered from unforthcoming sources in the days after the former president was hospitalised after apparently suffering a stroke (Stanley 2000: 42–6). Additionally, some high-profile politicians and prominent individuals or groups have at times refused to speak to certain journalists on the basis of their gender, religion or attire (*Pantau* 2000: 79; *Kompas* 11 Jun. 99: 3). Others have refused to speak to any journalists at all (AJI 2000), while the Governor of East Java became notorious for punching a journalist in the stomach for asking a question he did not like (*Merdeka* 12 Apr. 1999). In general, however, high–ranked official sources have been more inclined to portray themselves as open and accountable rather than refusing access to journalists. The culture has filtered to a small degree to lower echelons, but most cultures change slowly, and lower-level bureaucrats often lack the skills to find information and to present it rapidly even in cases where they have the will to do so.

Because the more things change …

The breakdown of the New Order has correlated with increased freedom of expression for journalists, enabling them to boldly publish free and frank criticism in a style that had been unthinkable for decades (see *Jakarta Post* 3 Jun. 1998: 2). In conjunction with this, the élite's ability 'simply to ignore' the press has diminished. Sources cannot afford to wait months before returning calls or to evade the waiting packs of journalists. In an example from 1998, the then Information Minister, Yunus Yosfiah, submitted to journalists' queries as he entered a human-rights conference, even though he was 'clearly annoyed' by their questions about his alleged involvement in the 1975 deaths of five Western news men in Balibo, East Timor. (Williams 1998: 20). Louise Williams (1998: 20) notes that six months previously:

> under the press restrictions of the former Soeharto regime, Indonesian journalists were unable to call their ministers to account and General Yosfiah could have merely walked past. But paradoxically, as Minister for Information, General Yosfiah has presided over the freeing up of the media, and so he was forced to stop.

Chapter 4 explains that many journalists feared that Habibie's bureaucracy was merely interpreting the legislation in a more moderate fashion. They believed new laws were required to ensure that the interpretation did not become stricter in future if political circumstances enabled a return to a more organic system. In evaluating whether there is a serious need for such legislation, it is instructive to consider observations from *New York Times* journalist Seth King about the way in which Indonesian journalists broke out of their previously 'subservient' behaviour, demonstrating 'new freedom and daring' in their reporting. In an article for the *Times*, King quotes editorials in the nation's leading newspapers warning that they will be ready 'to hit' politicians and bureaucrats 'whenever they deviate'. He also cites the Information Minister's promise that he will not attempt to dictate to the press. The *Times* article, however, was not written in 1998 but in 1966, during the dying months of the Sukarno presidency when the Minister of Defence, Lieutenant General Soeharto, was seen as part of 'the fresh wind' blowing economic and political reform into the nation (King 1966: 12).

As was mentioned above, Soeharto was characterised by greater accessibility to the media during the early period of the New Order, when the government relied on the support of a broad coalition of sociopolitical groups. Rosihan Anwar (1973: 4) notes that the 'honeymoon' was over within a few years, with Soeharto and ABRI 'tightening up' controls on the media and the civil society once they had 'the self-confidence that they could well go alone without too much reliance on civilian co-operation'. The openness of source relations during the politically fragile early post-Sukarno and early post-Soeharto era throws into sharp relief the closed nature of sources during periods of greater stability. In such a historical context, enacting legislative reform was perceived as essential in order to prevent politicians from returning to the old opaque political and information culture once openness was no longer in their vested political interests.

Article 4, Section 3 of the 1999 press law makes some progress towards recognising that the right to access information is an important component of press freedom. Section 3 states: 'To guarantee press freedom, the national press has the right to look for, obtain, and disseminate ideas and information.' Sofjan Lubis describes the new law as a major advancement in official consciousness, as it recognises the right to information as being tied to basic principles of popular sovereignty, democracy, justice and the rule of law that are laid out in the Constitution (Lubis 2000: 4).

Chapter 4 discusses the call for the law to be reinforced with FOI law. The call for FOI legislation identifies the weakness in the 1999 Press Law, which predominantly defines press freedom in the negative sense. It provides freedom *from* harassment, by legislating against factors that lead to censorship or self-censorship. It is weaker in providing freedom *to* engage in journalistic work. Although the 1999 law endorses the rights of journalists to seek information, it does not include a more positive, active conceptualisation of press freedom that compels the state élite to share information and be accountable to journalists and the wider public. Azzam argues that the 1999 Press Law could be used by journalists as FOI legislation, but that journalists have not to date been brave enough to test the act by taking action against sources who obstruct press freedom by refusing to provide information (Azzam 2001: pers. comm.). There is, however, no guarantee that the courts would accept the interpretation that the journalists' right to seek information sources is matched by a reciprocal legal obligation for sources to provide what is being sought.

The new, independent Press Council formed under the 1999 Press Law (Article 15, Section 2) is seeking to address this uncertainty. The Press Council voted in May 2000 to form a Commission for Law and Legal Issues that will lobby for an FOI act that would oblige government to reveal information requested by journalists or citizens and for a Shield Law that would protect sources at risk of retaliation for sharing information (Astraatmadja 2000: 4). The latter proposal recognises that bureaucrats will remain disinclined to release information while they face risk of reprisal. Complex questions of how to ensure the safety of sources are unlikely to be resolved quickly. Issues of source vulnerability have been highlighted by the sacking of the outspoken, reformist ABRI general, Agus Wirahadikusumah, in August 2000. His dismissal occurred just days after he exposed a Rp 173 billion (US$19.3 million) corruption scandal involving Kostrad, the Army's Strategic Reserve. Development of a draft law on freedom to access information has been officially listed as a priority for the government and DPR. However, at the time this book was completed, the impetus towards progressing such a law had been slowed by the logjam of legislation awaiting the consideration of parliamentarians, who had been pre-occupied for more than a year with fighting over the fate of Wahid.

Conclusion

This chapter has traced the practical ways in which Indonesian journalists' ability to access sources and gather information is inhibited or enhanced by the dominant political philosophies on the appropriate degree of accountability between the élite and the masses. The integralistic New Order culture was one in which information was not perceived as an openly accessible communal possession, but something dispensed at the discretion of state guardians. Sociologist Gaye Tuchman (1978: 3) notes that 'news imparts to events their public character as it transforms mere happenings into publicly discussable events'. In integralistic ideology, many of the events and issues the media might consider worth bringing into the public domain – such as issues related to the system of authority, the processes of decision-making and the merits of government policies – were, in the words of one journalist, 'not up for discussion' (Byrnes 1995: pers. comm.). This is not to imply that all actors in the New Order state apparatus were characterised by withdrawal and secrecy regarding their functions and activities, or that they did not perceive the media as a site of hegemonic struggle. Rather, it observes that the New Order ideology tended to naturally submerge those social realities that those in a more liberal culture would assume should be displayed for the public good. Foreign correspondents from western countries – where journalists generally saw it as a right and not a privilege to interview public figures – estimated that difficulties relating to source accessibility and openness meant that completing an original story requiring multiple sources and checking could take up to three times as long as it would in their home countries (Romano 1996: 50).

With the collapse of Soeharto's political regime, the culture mutated, and sources began seeking rather than shunning the attentions of journalists. Moments of contestation and challenge across and between different political factions have typically led to greater activity in the Indonesian public sphere. At such moments, élite alliances shift, contract or break, creating new needs for factions to win media attention and public support. Examples of these moments include the beginning and end of the New Order, the 1974 Malari affair, the 1978 period of student and intellectual action and the period of *keterbukaan* during the early 1990s. Reporters have exploited such moments, using the changes in political allegiances as opportunities to drill for information in the cracks that emerged in the closed communications culture. It was in the interests of the Habibie and Wahid governments to solicit the media spotlight. However, New Order history suggests the environment could easily close again, requiring journalists once more to play against the different lines of communication that constitute the civil society. Journalists' organisations and other groups have been moving rapidly to ensure that new legislation is enacted, to force a substantive rethinking of the political culture and journalists' position within it, in an attempt to entrench enduring changes that will survive once the factions have realigned and stabilised.

10 Information broking in the public sphere

Journalists had mixed success during the New Order with their attempts to access sources outside the personalities of the political and bureaucratic sector. In the economic sphere, for example, business leaders were often reluctant to share information with journalists. Documentary information – a fundamental alternative for journalists when human sources cannot or will not provide trustworthy information on a given topic – was hard to obtain. By contrast, journalists have found Indonesia's intellectuals to be both more easy to contact and more reliable than most other news sources. In the integralistic system, which allowed no formal opposition to government, such intellectuals played an important role in advocacy and activism. They were able to play on the New Order's constant invocation that it embodied true Indonesian culture, by identifying themselves as playing the roles held by *resi* (ascetics) and *kyai* (Islamic scholars) in critiquing the state over the centuries. This historical identification also holds true in the post-Soeharto era, although it is often not as well deserved. This chapter details the news media's unsteady relationship with intellectual, business and other sources in Indonesia's civil society and the accessibility of documentary information that might normally be considered a possession of the public domain.

Pretty girls, public relations and private enterprise

In many countries, private enterprise try to counterbalance the power of the state through a number of means, one of which is attempted management of public debate and business image through the media. During the New Order, however, private companies were averse to building relationships with the media, even in cases where publicity might have produced positive outcomes for them. Companies regularly declined to release rudimentary information about apparently inoffensive topics such as new business opportunities, business expansions and mergers. This culture only started to change in the last decade of the New Order, corresponding with the increasing power of Stock Exchange supervisory bodies and the trend for listing companies overseas. The requirements of company listing forced the appearance of increased transparency in the economic arena, encouraging many businesses to publicly disclose more about their activities (Caplen 1995: 58).

Symptomatic of the private sector's aversion to dealing with the media was the apathy demonstrated by public relations companies, which worked mainly for private businesses. Both foreign and local journalists criticised the poor performance of PR personnel, although the foreign correspondents' international experience made them more acutely aware of the potential for adept media management and the relative absence of proficient PR practitioners in Indonesia. A BBC correspondent described Indonesian PR as:

> basically a bunch of good-looking women walking around and trying to promote their clients, usually through lunches, or if a press conference is held, by pressing little envelopes of money into the hands of journalists in order to ensure their client gets some column inches.

Although some survey respondents could name individual PR practitioners who performed in a competent, constructive fashion, PR officers were generally smeared as 'naive', 'ill-informed', 'tight-lipped' and 'useless'. Problems included PR consultants who knew so little about their clients that they were unable to provide information as simple as the correct spelling of names.

Journalists also complained that many PR consultants were worse than just incompetent or ill informed about their clients. Their activities constituted, in the words of one, 'running interference' (McBeth 1995: pers. comm.). PR practitioners indicated a poor understanding of both the basic skills of PR and the operations of the media. One example survey respondents gave was of PR officers, in both government and business, who telephoned journalists to complain if their press releases were not published in full. Such conduct indicated that they had seriously overestimated what they should realistically expect their work to achieve.

PR practitioner Renville Almatsier admits that many of his colleagues had 'an allergy to news', because they were afraid of being misquoted or because they felt their only function was to deny incorrect information. They thus engaged in GTM (*Gerakan Tutup Mulut*, a Closed Mouth Movement), refusing to go on the record or claiming not to know about the problem, consequently thwarting the news process (Almatsier 1994: 4). The chairman of the Gemala Group, Sofyan Wanadi, says that PR in large companies was so 'very bad' that journalists were inclined to go straight to company executives rather than persevere with ineffectual PR officers. He says that as a consequence, businesspeople were unprepared for journalists' calls and could not answer in a satisfactory style, creating an impression that the companies were avoiding the media (*Republika* 31 Aug. 1995). Private companies resembled government organisations in that most did not recognise the strategic position of public relations in management and did not include PR staff in decision-making processes (*Kompas* 27 Sept. 1994: 16).

The deputy head of the Perhumas public relations professionals' association, August Parengkuan, points to the inability of PR officers to handle the mass poisoning of instant noodles in the early 1990s as a case reflecting the lack of professionalism within the industry. Cases such as these are considered a standard test of PR practitioners' skills in Western countries where sabotage or internal production problems have led to numerous cases of contaminated batches of food or medicines being publicly distributed. Good PR personnel have repeatedly demonstrated the ability to maintain the affected producers' reputation by displays of public concern and good corporate citizenship, with the famous 1983 Tylenol case in the US being considered an early, textbook example (Murray & Shohen 1992). Parengkuan says that in the noodle poisoning case, journalists found it difficult to contact or obtain information from the company's PR officers. Instead, in a situation that typified the New Order's congested information flows, journalists provided more information to the public relations officers than they received (*Kompas* 27 Sept. 1994: 16).

Skilled practitioners from larger companies specialising in PR acknowledged that the industry as a whole provided few services beyond press releases, launches and special-event management. With the economic boom of the early to mid-1990s, hundreds of small public relations consultancies burgeoned, often with only one or two staff attempting to provide a limited range of publicity functions. IndoPacific's Tracey Adamson noted in 1996 (pers. comm.) that the public relations industry was 'just moving out of that phase of being nothing more than parties and connections – providing connections with the media or the government'.

Most PR practitioners have little formal training. No professional qualification is required to register an individual practitioner or a company with the Association of Public Relations Companies. Although public relations courses are offered at tertiary educational institutions, many practitioners have no qualifications other than three-month training programs offered by personal development centres such as the London School of Public Relations and John Robert Powers. The 12-week, 12-lesson courses at John Robert Powers devote as much time to lessons on the social graces (conversation etiquette and table manners), appearance (hygiene and wardrobe) and personal growth (self-confidence and personality) as they do to media relations, public relations planning and crisis management. Miriam Tulevski from Nama Corporate Communications questions how graduates of courses that teach them good posture and nail-filing techniques will understand how to address communications problems, plan proactively and overcome obstacles (1996: pers. comm.). Although Tulevsky and similar operators are sceptical of the charm-school elements of PR courses, such training appears consistent with market expectations. A perusal of job advertisements sent by employers to John Robert Powers showed that the employers' universal and often primary demand of public relations' personnel was *penampilan menarik* (attractive appearance).

It should be acknowledged that the performance of PR personnel in government was no better than those in private enterprise. Throughout the New Order, numerous government ministers, officials, consultants and even the president himself recognised the need to improve the knowledge, skills and operating speed of information and public relations officers (e.g. *Berita Buana* 10 Oct. 1983: 3; *Harian Umum AB* 1 Aug. 1985: 1; 3 Mar. 1982: 8; 7 Jan 1982: 1;

Suara Karya 15 Jan. 1982: 1). Intermittent calls by senior figures for public relations officials to be more open and proficient never had any lasting impact, because the organic culture did not support change. Even in the later years of the New Order, when 'openness' had become a political buzzword, government organisations were still more inclined to limit their public relations staff to collecting newspaper clippings than to engage them in management activities such as news analysis, decision-making processes and strategic planning (*Kompas* 27 Sept. 1994: 16). Press releases were still commonly written in unappealing bureaucratic language and neglected news values, so that they were rarely suitable for publishing (*Kompas* 15 Oct. 1992: 12). Tulevski noted in 1996 that ultimately: 'The government doesn't feel it has to do PR because it doesn't have to win votes.' A public relations person I met at the DPR in the dying months of the Soeharto era agreed with my assessment that journalists rarely sought information from government PR officers if there were opportunities to address ministers, politicians or other officials directly. However, he implied that he believed such a situation was appropriate, saying his main duty was 'giving out press releases, not acting as a facilitator'. The poor culture of public relations in private enterprise thus reflected the underdevelopment of PR in both the state and civil society, and there were few models of good practice for practitioners to follow.

It should also be noted that difficulties in accessing news sources in private enterprise cannot be blamed on public relations personnel alone, since Indonesia's biggest businessmen have expressed reluctance to expose themselves to the press in case it results in critical news. Despite claiming that the apparent reticence of businessmen to speak to journalists results merely from lack of preparedness, Sofyan Wanadi also acknowledged that his big-business colleagues were fearful of encounters with the press (Elison 1995: 40). In a report on Bob Hasan, the *Jakarta Post* saw nothing unusual in the way the timber tycoon 'cunningly' managed 'to sneak past a pack of lingering newshounds' to avoid press attention. Hasan only differed from the norm in that: 'If an encounter with the media is unavoidable, he is not shy about make [sic] brash remarks, sometimes launching personal attacks on reporters, instead of remaining tightlipped as most of his equals would.' (Asmarani 1998: 7)

Shamdasani (1996: pers. comm.) notes that when businesspeople did agree to be interviewed, they resembled government sources in that they liked journalists to forward a list of questions so that they could prepare and regulate the process. 'Some of these businessmen have other businesses that they don't want to highlight. Some of them have maybe had an affair or have two wives. They're trying to control that part. They have too much information that they want to hide.'

The culture of business

The apparent reluctance of business to engage with journalists was connected to the New Order's philosophy that national development required close integration of the economy with the state. Although from the 1980s onwards, the New Order government progressively deregulated the economy, most economic activity remained in the control of state and military institutions. Chapter 2 discusses how the private enterprise that existed was heavily reliant on state support and market control, and the culture of building connections with the political–military machine was important for the development of new large-scale private business enterprises and the prosperity of existing ones. The New Order state regularly offered large development contracts or monopolies to members of the first family or other well-connected businesspeople without undertaking formal tendering processes, thus denying other equally or more capable businesses the opportunity to bid for the contracts through a merit-based competition that might be subjected to public scrutiny.

The 'game of contacts and interchange' revolved around networking to obtain information, protection and contracts (Raillon 1994: 176). It was often noted that with commercial interests mainly advanced through personal contacts rather than a competitive political or economic system, business enterprises relied less on the kind of organised lobbying activities and institutions found in most Western countries (Mackie 1993: 89–91; Raillon 1994: 176–7; Schwarz 1994: 296–7). Businessmen also appeared to have greater value for a culture of silent allegiance than public displays of skills or competence. For example, leading businessman Liem Sioe Liong's proclaimed practice was to be 'loyal to business associates and employees, supportive of friends and quiet' to the point of invisibility (Raillon 1994: 166).

It is thus unsurprising that during the New Order, Indonesian organisations apparently did not perceive sufficient benefits to warrant substantial investment in the publicity and promotional activities of the PR sector any more than the state did. In this climate, the PR industry's central activities of organising parties and providing connections adequately fulfilled the minimal needs of the businesses that it served. This contrasts with western political systems, where government officials and business people are subject to greater pressure to maintain an image of public accountability and more emphasis is placed on public relations and other structures that provide communication links between government/business bureaucracies and citizens/journalists (McNair 1998: 145–7).

The ascetics

Groups and individuals outside the government and business bureaucracies, who had less access to bureaucratic decision-making processes or who opposed the bureaucratic hegemony, were usually notably more accessible as news sources. Journalists found it far easier to approach and obtain information from NGOs, academics, religious leaders and even certain retired generals than from politicians, public servants or businesspeople. This broad category of non-government intellectuals was the only category of sources to be nominated as good information providers by any significant number of journalists.

The *pakar* (the experts) were the most respected and most frequently accessed sources from this intellectual community. This broad category of *pakar* included leading scholars, authors and journalists. *Pakar* who have become popular public figures include sociologist Arief Budiman, Islamic intellectual and socio-political commentator Nurcholish Madjid, poet Emha Ainun Nadjib, economist Soetjipto Wirosardjono, lawyer Todung Mulya Lubis and editor Goenawan Mohamad. The media profile of these *pakar* is such that Riwanto Tirtosudarmo described the leading newspapers as 'vehicles for the ideas of intellectuals'. Intellectuals and activists were not only regular media sources but also 'prolific writers whose articles and columns always appear in the press' (Tirtosudarmo 1992: 134).

Religious leaders were sources for intellectual critique whose voices were usually respected even among those outside their own religions. For many years during the late New Order period, one of the most universally popular sources was Wahid, in his position as NU chairman. The then *Muhammadiyah* chairman, Amien Rais, and the late Catholic priest, Y.B. Mangunwijaya similarly stood out as religious intellectuals and social reformers with high public and media profiles. Islamic leaders were also important informal community leaders (Gaffar 1992: 20, 133) and mosques were venues that allowed Indonesians to critically discuss political and cultural issues with relatively little state interference (Ramage 1994: 157–8).

Other vocal intellectuals were retired generals and bureaucrats who had previously been key players in élite political circles, such as the late Gen. Sumitro, Lt. Gen. H.R. Dharsono, Lt. Gen. Ali Sadikin and former home affairs minister Rudini. Such figures were the guiding force behind reform groups such as the centre-right *Petisi 50* and the liberal-democratic *Forum Pemurnian Kedaulatan Rakyat* (FPKR, Forum for the Purification of People's Sovereignty) (Uhlin 1995: 100–1; Ramage 1995: 34). The trend to become more outspoken only after being safely pensioned or forcibly excluded from political realms was evident across the full range of civil servants, not just among élite army commanders. One *Kompas* political reporter I met expressed frustration that it seemed impossible to encourage sources in official positions to communicate candidly until after they had left the channels of power, at which point they suddenly developed a passion to challenge those remaining in the government and military structure.

The NGOs were also popular media sources because, even though most were not comfortable with action that might be directly labelled 'political', they played an important role in promoting counter-hegemonic viewpoints and addressing economic, socio-cultural, political and environmental issues (Eldridge 1995: 1–2, 13; Uhlin 1995: 102–11). These advocacy and activist groups frequently centred around the activism of students who, as is discussed further below, shifted their political interests off campus due to restrictions in the late 1970s on political activities in university grounds. It is estimated that there were several thousand NGOs in Indonesia in the late New Order period (Lele & Tettey 1996: 45). The government-funded Komnas HAM was the only state-instituted organisation that came close to NGOs in terms of the respect and attention it received from journalists, even though questions were raised at the time of its formation about its capacity for independence and objectivity (Baskoro & Riza 1993: 94).

It should be acknowledged that only a relatively small percentage of students and other intellectuals were politically active during the New Order, and many intellectuals worked with the state apparatus to help design or legitimise its policies. Therefore, there was not a large pool of critical, vocal intellectuals to become news sources. Even the small proportion of intellectuals who were critical and vocal could not always be used as quotable news sources, because they too were subject to pressures and threats, just as sources within the bureaucracy were (see LCHR & ELSAM 1995: 46–8; HRW–AFC 1998; Mulya Lubis 1993: 253–8). Additionally, lectures and public activities involving outspoken intellectuals and artists were often cancelled by the authorities (e.g. *Asiaweek* 2 Nov. 1994; Supono, Rismansah & Junaedi 1995: 64).

Journalistic willingness to access these sources also fluctuated with political pressures. Coverage of sources with strong mass support bases, such as Wahid and Rais, remained relatively steady. However, journalists were disinclined to regularly access more vulnerable figures, such as leftist labour activist Budiman Sudjatmiko, especially when élite dissatisfaction with such sources was high. One *Jakarta Post* journalist explained that the topic of the story and general political climate also affected decisions about which intellectuals would be interviewed.

> For some articles you would choose Juwono [Sudarsono, then a soft-line political analyst], because he's considered more respected by officials and that would help to get the message through. You would use Ariel [Heryanto, a postmodernist university academic] when you need a critical voice on an issue. But in a sensitive time, such as when warnings are issued, you would not pick him. And when [lawyer and head of the Independent Election Monitoring Committee] Mulyana Kusumah was branded a communist, we stopped interviewing him for a few months.

Certain intellectuals were not accessed because they had been blacklisted by the government.

The voice of common wisdom

Because the New Order absorbed opposition political parties and most adversarial groups into the corporatised, integralistic state apparatus, the NGOs and the intellectuals played important quasi-oppositional roles to government and big business. Heryanto (1996: pers. comm.) says that the masses relied on these figures 'to legitimate their cause. Intellectuals say nothing new, but by saying it they give authority to the common wisdom'. These intellectuals attempted to express the views of the largely silent polity and expand the limits imposed on mass engagement in political processes. The willingness of NGOs and intellectuals to cooperate with the media thus corresponded with their own involvement in socio-political activism and their endeavours to legitimise a wider range of interactions between the state and civil society.

In a study of environmental reporting, George Junus Aditjondro (1992: 12) finds that New Order journalists over-relied on non-government institutions and prominent intellectuals for commentaries and information about social movements and community problems. He is less positive than Heryanto about their role, and he concludes that journalists neglected important social problems that could make interesting cover stories in their own right unless the cases were taken up by prominent NGOs (Aditjondro 1992: 12). The 'little people' who could also have provided such information were rarely accessed to set news agendas, offer alternative interpretations and angles on issues, or provide information and quotes.

This reflects the worldwide tendency for news organisations to optimise the results of their news-gathering efforts by locating their reporters around the pulse points of bureaucratic activity such as ministers' offices, government departments, police headquarters and the stock exchange. Fishman (1980: 143) dubs this 'the principle of bureaucratic affinity: only other bureaucracies can satisfy the input needs of a news bureaucracy'. 'Efficiency' becomes a major consideration in source selection, because journalists must balance the need to check 'facts' against the obligation to seek large quantities of fresh news each day and to meet deadlines (Departemen Penerangan 1975: 79; Gans 1979: 128). Journalists conventionally satisfy the conflicting demands of time and accuracy by grounding their stories in 'objective' and 'authoritative' statements from 'accredited' sources with 'cultural collateral' (Hall et al. 1978: 58; Ericson, Baranek & Chan 1989: 3–5). These accredited sources tend to come from the government and other dominant social institutions that are seen as 'representative' bodies with 'legitimated' status to represent community interests (Fishman 1980: 51–2; Herman 1986: 172; Herman & Chomsky 1988: 18–25; Sigal 1973: 120–5; Tuchman 1978: 91–2). Limitations on accessing the accredited sources of the government and business bureaucracies led Indonesian journalists towards the 'intellectual bureaucracies' of universities, religious groups, artistic centres and NGOs. These organisations can summarise and package enormous quantities of information into manageable portions. Aditjondro's research demonstrates that the news bureaucracy is not sufficiently flexible to allow journalists to regularly invest time and other resources into seeking information in a more raw form through direct interaction with a range of social groups.

The constituents of these intellectual bureaucracies have high credibility and social importance arising from the historical political influence and high status of intellectuals. Anderson notes that this predates the arrival of Islam in the late 1200s, with intellectual power being expressed by the *resi*, who lived with their students in remote locations and studied the secrets of the cosmos, developing psychic powers and practising clairvoyancy. The intense charismatic and spiritual power of the *resi* rested upon their sacrifice of self-interest and their withdrawal from the politics of Indonesia's various kingdoms. The *resi* only returned to the centres of power to warn of faults that threatened to fracture or annihilate the political kingdom (Anderson 1990: 63; Budiman 1978: 616). With the spread of Islam, the Islamic *kyai* scholars were seen as continuing this tradition, again removing themselves from the political regime, only reintegrating themselves to herald the downfall of the dynasty (Anderson 1990: 64–5). A ruler could crush critics who acted from political self-interest, but attacks on a selfless and spiritual *resi* suggested that the ruler was dominated by personal passion, itself an indication that his/her power was failing and that the political structure was disintegrating (Budiman 1978: 616–17).

Given that only a small portion of intellectuals were politically active during the New Order, their identification as noble ascetics may have been based more on romantic notions of the *resi* and *kyai* than observable reality. However, Budiman's analysis of the student movements of 1966 to 1974, in which he was actively engaged, indicates the way that intellectuals were able to draw social cachet and political power from the mythology.

> Within such a culture, students, in order to play the role of social critics, should stress their lack of interest in power and personal ambition. There is no debate about the class origin of students or intellectuals in Indonesia, since they are not supposed to serve the interests of any social group. Thus when they talk about exploitation of the poor, they do so only to serve the nation and warn the ruler beforehand that something is wrong and that if no action is taken social disturbances may occur.... Suharto, by saying that there were political interests behind the students, was trying to say that the students were not *resi*. So he felt justified in crushing them. (Budiman 1979: 622)

Students, intellectuals and NGOs also gained cultural collateral and newsworthiness due the work of some as strategic leaders during the formative moments of Indonesia's modern history. During the colonial era, unemployment and limited career opportunities among the intellectual class led to greater activity in social movements (Legge 1988: 19). Student organisations and key intellectuals like Sukarno, Hatta and Sutan Sjahrir became central directors of political struggle during periods of both Dutch and Japanese governance (Legge 1988: 43). During the 1950s, political parties sought students and academics to become the thinkers, leaders and driving impetus of political organisation (Legge 1988: 20; Sanit 1989: 21). During the turbulence of the post-Gestapu era, conservative students and intellectuals were prominent social actors in the formation of the New Order, demanding the removal of leftist members from government, the Sukarno's resignation, the PKI's banning and socioeconomic reform (Bresnan 1993: 36–8; Budiman 1973: 77–8). Despite this initial support in founding the New Order, student groups emerged as critics of the new government's economic policies from the late 1960s onwards. However, the post-1978 policies of 'campus normalisation' seriously restricted the political activities on campus (Sanit 1989: 23–4, 58; Vatikiotis 1993: 109), forcing increasing off-campus organisation and activism, including alliances with workers, farmers and other grass-roots constituencies (Lane 1991: 18–19; Uhlin 1995: 113). This enhanced their tendency to speak as though they were channels for the voice of the common folk.

Those intellectuals who engaged in political activity enjoyed respect because of the conceptualisation that intellectuals were mobilisers of social change. Intellectuals who critiqued and challenged the status quo were not considered mere social commentators but politically important actors in their own right. Many newspapers consequently have at least one reporter who specialises in covering universities and similar institutions, not for news about education *per se* as reporters do in developed countries but to draw from the pool of intellectual activity that such institutions represent.

Lies, damned lies and statistics[1]

Western studies have indicated that journalists tend to limit themselves to a circumscribed range of information sources, such as news releases and quotes obtained from interviews, rather than accessing an array of other possibilities such as official documentation, academic texts, survey data and trend statistics (Ericson, Baranek & Chan 1989: 1). Despite this, such official documentation does become important for journalists in circumstances where cross-checking information is otherwise impossible. Cross-checking information is a staple of journalistic practice, enabling the journalist to support and justify new or contentious facts by amassing additional facts that, 'when taken together, present themselves as both individually and collectively self-validating' (Tuchman 1978: 86). This section explores the availability and reliability of research, statistics, written histories, company records and other such data that allow journalists to seek new information or cross-check existing information through means other than interviews or eyewitness accounts.

Because the New Order political system did not maintain an ongoing, open dialogue between the state and citizens over the management of the nation, there was only a slow development of the infrastructure, administrative procedures and personnel skills for gathering, storing and sharing information. Journalists' complaints about the limitations of systems for filing and retrieving documentation date back to the 1970s (Departemen Penerangan 1975: 54–5). The opaque information culture permeated both the government and private sectors, so that even sophisticated organisations often lacked records and documentation about their activities and were reticent to circulate documentation about themselves. Similarly, there was little support for libraries and other centres for storing and distributing information. The National Library of Australia's Indonesian-based Asia Officer, Oliver Mann, said that in the Indonesian context: 'Libraries are not important. Books are not that important. So, in that context, the standard of librarianship is woeful by Australian standards but is probably adequate for Indonesian needs.' (Mann 1998: pers. comm.)

Indicative of the New Order's relationship to statistics and information was the 1996 drafting of a law on statistics which attempted to regulate opinion polling and surveying, ironically at a time when the state was working to deregulate the economic sector (Mulya Lubis 1996: 35). The new law was designed with the intention of obliging all researchers to inform the Central Bureau of Statistics of their research plan, aims and methodologies. During the drafting stage, senior figures from private research bodies, universities, legal institutions, non-government organisations and the mass media raised concerns about the potential for the law to make surveys more difficult and expensive, to breach the confidentiality of contracts involving clients who commissioned research and to create opportunities for the government to veto certain kinds of research (e.g. Dhakidae 1996b; Muntohar 1996; Tjondronegoro 1996).

Todung Mulya Lubis, borrowing Herbert Feith's terminology, described the law on statistics as an extension of the 'politics of regularization' that was also evident in the New Order's progressive corporatisation of political parties, trade unions, primary producers, professional groups, public servants, students and NGOs. The legal provisions were described as mechanisms to turn the Bureau of Statistics into a 'state apparatus' and 'ethics police' to force the achievement of the state's desire (Dhakidae 1996a: 8; Dhakidae 1996b: 44). The attempt to monopolise control of statistical research reflected the New Order's basic assumption that the state is the one and only body that guards and administers all rights (Mulya Lubis 1996: 34–5).

The New Order's attempts to control the research culture in both state and civil institutions was also indicated by its requirements that researchers obtain permits for research activities within the country. Foreigners were also legally obliged to submit a research application through the Indonesian Embassy or directly via the Institute of Sciences (LIPI) in Jakarta, so that both the researchers and their research plan could be vetted in a six to 12-month process by the Institute and the defence authorities. The Human Rights Watch Academic Freedom Committee (1998) argues that the New Order's research permit procedures gave 'government and military officials effective veto power over proposed academic field research and invite corruption'.

Even when information and statistics were available, the reliability of such data was often questionable. Leading researchers voiced concern that incomplete and inappropriate procedures and low budgets rendered the results of many major statistical surveys on socio-economic issues weak, misleading and irrelevant (*Kompas* 21 Apr. 1998: 2; *Kompas* 2 May 1991: 1; *Kompas* 1 May 1991: 1; Wirosardjono 1993: 36–7). Such faults are political in an indirect sense because unremitting demand on government institutions to provide statistics *en masse* has not been matched by appropriate funding, training of personnel and other forms of government or big-business commitment and support. Dhakidae (1998: pers. comm.) furthermore warns that government statistics, were often consciously inflated by at least 15 per cent. He advises that statistics by themselves are not reliable and should only be used to study proportions and trends. Others similarly complain that the New Order's research data was 'notoriously wrong, often exaggerated or invented for the sole purpose of pleasing a superior' (Beutler 1982: 28; also LCHR & ELSAM 1995: 47–8).

External political pressures also led to restriction, if not outright censorship, of statistical and survey data. In a study of poll and survey researchers who have been censored or punished, Dhakidae (1993a) found that such cases have always involved research topics that touched on the image and the legitimacy of power of authority figures. The best-known case was one in which *Monitor* magazine's editor was jailed for publishing an opinion poll listing Soeharto, Saddam Hussein and the editor himself as more popular than the prophet Mohamad. On the surface, the case was a religious issue, but it also had strong political undercurrents (Amnesty International 1992: 142; CPJ 1991, p.1; HRW 1994: 4; Kingsbury 1992: 64; Vatikiotis 1990a: 23–4).

Because of government pressures, the news industry rarely conducted polls. *Kompas* found that in deciding whether to conduct a poll, newspapers had to weigh up the risk of being delicensed or threatened by political powerbrokers and public demonstrators (20 Jan. 1997: 20). Opinion polls attempting to measure the popularity of politicians were considered an especially 'negative priority' during the New Order; a powerful individual's real popularity rating was something that 'should be safely concealed and never be made public' (Dhakidae 1993a: 14). Dhakidae notes that for these reasons, it was impossible throughout the New Order period to obtain permits to conduct public-opinion polls on voter intentions. 'To know beforehand that a big party like Golkar will be kicked out of track had a free election been conducted is a sort of nuisance.' (Dhakidae 1993a: 17)

Statistics and figures were sometimes available from private enterprise, but they were as unreliable as government data. Even figures from large private research institutes had to be read with caution, taking into account the political orientation and business connections of the research centre. Similarly, the figures that companies released to the public about their business activities often varied markedly from those provided to the tax office, which doubtlessly differed considerably to the figures kept for internal use. Public records such as stock market reports or tax figures were useful for journalists, not for their inherent reliability but for the way they provided opportunities for observing general trends or cross-checking claims made to the public against those made to government.

Research from NGOs was a major alternative to that from government and economic powers, but much of it also had limited integrity. One survey respondent commented that research from Goenawan Mohamad's *Institut Studi Arus Informasi* (ISAI, Institute for the Study of Free Flow of Information) was useful, but that he found it to be as strongly and conspicuously influenced by the politics of the organisation's pro-democracy activists as propaganda material from the government. A reporter who specialised in covering NGOs found that the smaller organisations were especially inclined to exaggerate or inflate their findings because of desire to gain publicity and the attendant public and financial support that accompanied a higher profile.

This overall absence of extensive, reliable record systems forces reporters to be guarded about the information they published or broadcasted. In Western societies, journalists whose copy is censured can often refer to written documents and records to indicate the accuracy of their stories. Former *Far Eastern Economic Review* correspondent Adam Schwarz points out that in an oral society, like Indonesia, journalists may only have the source's testimony to corroborate their assertions. He found that as reporters developed sufficiently intimate contacts with senior sources, they started 'edging into the paper trail' and gaining access to documents unavailable to the general public (Schwarz 1996: pers. comm.). Once such documentary backup becomes accessible, journalists can write in a more forthright fashion about delicate subjects. Those who cannot obtain such documentation must weigh the risk associated with the story against the potential of proving the claims within the story.

In the era of reform

In the 1970s, Rodney Tiffen (1978: 139) observed that the operating environment in Southeast Asian countries did not encourage dependence on a few institutionalised sources. Tiffen's observations were made in reference to the activities of foreign correspondents in the region but were no less applicable to local journalists in Indonesia. Because of the difficulties of gaining information from government and other institutions during the New Order, reporters redirected their efforts away from reliance on accredited institutional spokesmen towards the development of personal relations with an array of sources both within and without the bureaucracy.

In the years preceding the economic downturn, the business community showed increasing awareness of the advantages of improving their PR techniques. Connections and networking could only provide a power base for a very small group. The discerning middle class comprised an estimated 25 million people before the 1997 economic decline, and it was impossible to reach that group through contacts and parties alone.

The economic crisis has been followed by both international and domestic pressures for increased transparency in business and economic activities, deregulation of monopolies and limitations on state-based protections and incentives for big business. Many state and private institutions involved in business enterprises have been forced to expose themselves to public scrutiny, but it will take many years before they develop an organisational ethos of openness, let alone the staff skills and infrastructure needed to facilitate better communications. Journalists still regularly complain about business figures being reluctant to meet with journalists or speak on the record.

Initially, the PR industry suffered during the financial crisis because the related cuts in business expenditure forced many closures and amalgamations. Many of the international personnel in larger PR companies left Indonesia when the currency plunged, thus draining an important pool of expertise in the area. Some PR companies, however, have emerged stronger and more efficient as a result of the restructuring within organisations and industry regrouping.

Overall, the capacity of the PR industry to improve media relations and facilitate information flows is still weak. My experience as a journalist trying to obtain information from the Indonesian Bank Restructuring Agency (IBRA) in 1999 typifies the problem. Banking-industry reform is seen as important to revival of all other economic sectors, so theoretically, IBRA should be acutely aware of the need for responsiveness and accountability. When I sent my questions by facsimile to IBRA's PR person, as he had requested, he replied: 'These are very good questions, but unfortunately I don't know the answers.' He promised to contact those who had the information, but six months later he was yet to answer or even acknowledge my repeated requests, and I had long since obtained the data through other means. Supriyanto further claims that many in business and PR maintain the attitude that if they provide envelopes of money (as is discussed further in Chapter 11), journalists should not attempt to dig for information beyond that the sources are willing to offer (Supriyanto 2001: pers. comm.).

In the post-New Order environment, stories based on statistics and documentary sources of data have increased. Chapters 4 and 9 explain that there is no FOI law and journalists still rely mainly on their personalised contacts if they wish to conduct paper chases through the internal documentation systems of bureaucracy. However, opinion polls are conducted freely on the full range of political topics. Just weeks after the disintegration of the New Order, the *Jakarta Post* was able to report that a University of Indonesia and Soegeng Sarjadi Syndicated poll had found that 46.2 per cent of respondents thought Habibie's presidency was flawed because of corruption, collusion and nepotism (*Jakarta Post* 24 Jul. 1998: 2). News abounds with official statistics measuring social, political and economic changes during the economic crisis and the unsteady process of recovery.

The reliability of the polls varies considerably, with many news organisations lacking the expertise to assess what constitutes a statistically reliable sample, appropriate questions or a suitable survey methodology for the given set of circumstances. For example, many of the public-opinion polls reported in the news have limited relevance because most are conducted in urban centres, and sometimes solely in Jakarta. They neglect the opinions from Indonesia's rural citizens, who form the vast majority of the country's population. Researchers also sometimes have difficulty obtaining information from respondents. An example was a 1999 pre-election opinion poll by the University of Indonesia's political science laboratory. Thirty-two per cent of respondents would not reveal their voting preference on the grounds that their votes were secret, and a further 21 per cent told researchers they did not know how they would vote (Dodd 1999: 4). Reporters also frequently demonstrate little skill at analysing the significance of the results, sometimes leaving out key figures or reaching conclusions that appear to contradict the nature of the figures.

Towards the final months of the New Order, an increasing number of intellectual activists and NGOs joined attempts to stretch the bounds of debate and to reformulate the ideologies that underpinned existing socio-political relations. Intellectuals openly disparaged Soeharto, his family and his cronies in a style rarely heard in a culture that only previously had permitted subtle, between-the-lines, indirect critique of the president and his closest allies (e.g. *D&R* 7 Mar. 1998: 21–5). Even intellectuals within the government apparatus became more directly critical, with 17 LIPI scholars obtaining much publicity for their daringness in signing of a petition critical of the regime. University students became the most prominent leaders of the anti-Soeharto movement. They organised demonstrations, a five-day occupation of the DPR/MPR, and on-campus activities involving rectors, deans and other academic staff in addition to students (Aspinall 1998: 9). A largely sympathetic media played up the *resi* role, with *D&R* for example stating that 'The Voice of Students = The Voice of the People' (*D&R* 8 Mar. 1998: 27).

Many of the old-school intellectuals have moved into the centres of mainstream politics itself. Wahid is the most prominent example, but so many other intellectuals took up senior positions in parliament or political parties that it became the subject of newspaper commentary (e.g. Alfian 1999: 6; Zuldarnis 1999: 6). In common with Wahid, almost all promptly lost (or indeed squandered) their pure, *resi* image once they shed the disinterested position of external critic and were faced with the daily realities of decision-making and compromise.

Students continue to be active, albeit to a lesser degree than in 1998, but their critiques have lost much of their power. After years of almost-daily student demonstrations, their street protests are often not met with respect for this *resi*-like conduct, but with public complaints about the traffic jams and disruptions that they cause. During the Wahid era, much of the populace returned to the philistine but pragmatic and critical interests that dominated the early New Order – such as rebuilding the economy and putting rice on tables.

The so-called age of *reformasi* has enabled a growth industry for those who act as *pengamat* (observers or commentators) or who establish NGOs. Many supposed 'experts' with 'reformist' zeal emerged from diverse corners, claiming the capacity to talk on every topic conceivable. There is very little transparency about the qualifications of these experts to talk, whom they represent and by whom they are being paid. This new phenomenon has prompted claims that many intellectuals are in fact '*intelektual musiman*' (seasonal intellectuals) (Hasbullah 1999: 6). As Chapter 3 discusses, innumerable new NGOs have also emerged, and this created a new array of sources for reporters. However, many journalists often fail to adequately scrutinise the performance of such organisations before publicising their activities or opinions, in the same way that they often forget to examine the qualifications of *pengamat*. Journalists could reduce their reliance on these NGOs and *pengamat* by locating sources within the community with salient stories and experiences to provide insight into issues or set new news agendas. However, they commonly lack the time, experience or initiative to undertake such activities on a regular basis.

Like all other elements of journalistic practice, journalists' relationship with non-government sources and their access to reliable documentary or statistical information was transformed when the political culture was altered. During the New Order, they differed from Western journalists, who spend much of their time merely processing the floods of information that constantly pour from the major politico-economic organisations. Indonesian journalists' labours were instead directed into tapping the trickles of data from individuals in business and government who had access to strategic information. Alternatively, they worked at finding independent observers within the intellectual domain. Information is far more easily attained from a greater number of sources in the post-Soeharto era, but the challenge remains for journalists to critique it carefully. Transparency has become a buzzword, but ironically journalists must be more vigilant than before to evaluate the trustworthiness of both sources and their data.

11 The envelope please

When Indonesian news sources call press conferences or invite reporters to functions, they do not just offer the journalists information or the opportunity to build a better journalist-source relationship. They also often offer *amplop* (envelopes) containing money to cover 'transport costs' or to express the source's 'appreciation' for the journalists' attendance. The amount of money contained in the envelopes can vary considerably, depending on which news round or beat the reporter covers. News desks, like the economic desk, are considered *basah* (wet) while others, like foreign affairs, are considered *kering* (dry). Such terminology is not unique to journalism. Other institutions, such as government departments, are informally described as wet or dry depending on the tendency of and opportunities for bureaucrats to accept payment in return for facilitating document processing, decision making and similar activities (Young 1990: 154).

The envelope culture is largely a clandestine one, as neither sources nor journalists openly flash envelopes or bundles of money around at press conferences. Sources or their public relations personnel regularly conceal envelopes between press releases, copies of speeches or other documents that they provide to journalists. In government departments and large business organisations, the source may hand a bulk sum of money to the head of the press gallery, who divides and distributes the cash among the round's reporters. Some state institutions make monthly allocations of rice and money to the local PWI branch, which coordinates distribution of the resources to journalists, although some branches refuse to undertake such tasks (Budiyanto & Mabroer 2000: 59–61). At other times, reporters may be offered 'souvenirs' or be invited to 'sample' the source's wares or services, such as mobile phones, electronic equipment, hotel accommodation, travel and restaurant meals. Envelope culture entered the realm of the 'cashless society' in the late 1990s and early twenty-first century, with some larger corporations and government departments making direct deposits into reporters' bank accounts or offering shares to journalists who regularly cover their institutions.

The 'envelope culture' creates ethical quandaries for journalists and sources, with the potential for either party to exploit or be exploited by the other. At the extreme, envelope culture involves bribery, extortion and use of false identity for financial gain. This chapter explores the conduct of journalists, sources and others involved in the culture, the origins of the practice, and the ways in which the culture has historically been tied to patrimonial political cultures. Some individuals and organisations have led concerted campaigns to eradicate the envelope culture, but considerable conundrums face those who attempt to pursue such efforts in the post-Soeharto era.

The history of the envelope

Although many sources suggest that there were no envelopes in the early independence era (e.g. Anwar 1977: 19; Departemen Penerangan 1975: 101), former *Indonesia Raya* journalist Atmakusumah Astraatmadja suggests that a type of *amplop* existed in the 1950s in the form of general patronage (Astraatmadja 1996: pers. comm.). Due to the shaky economy, newspaper subscriptions were low, advertising income was negligible, and media proprietors were driven more by political ideals than profit motives (Anderson 1984: 155; Hasibuan 1957: 37–45). Hill (1995: 28) notes that 'in a sea of financial insecurity', newspapers only managed to stay afloat 'by virtue of the editors' ability to call upon sympathetic monied supporters to tide them over'. Although newspapers relied on military or political patrons for credit and other assistance, neither the patrons, the journalists nor their readers were likely to conceptualise such patronage as improper or corrupting, because most newspapers of the time were attached to one of the plethora of political parties and factions. Gifts of money and other aid from politically aligned sources would therefore not have been seen as an 'external' influence in the normal sense.

Some ministers and big businessmen also started to give 'transport money' or allotments of rice to journalists in the 1960s and early 1970s (Anwar 1977: 19; Daud 1998: pers. comm., Makarim 1978: 260; Gintini 1992: 16). Rosihan Anwar suggests that these early forms of envelopes were offered to help struggling journalists in 'an era in which inflation had gone berserk. Journalists only accepted that money for the sake of filling their rice bowl without thinking further about the need to defend their self respect, dignity and journalistic integrity in the conduct of their profession' (Anwar 1977: 19).

However, the envelope is primarily a New Order phenomenon, both in the sense that the envelope culture started to boom during the early years of Soeharto's rule and also with the implication that the envelope arose from New Order politico-economic culture. The increasing frequency of envelope journalism was observed and documented both by journalists and sources at the time (e.g. *Harian Kami* 22 Jan. 1970: 2; 5 Jul. 1969: 1; Departemen Penerangan 1975: 92–101).

Hadi argues that the envelope emerged in the politically pragmatic and utilitarian atmosphere of the New Order, which focused on the fundamentals of economic growth and physical development compared to the political idealism of the Sukarno era in which 'politics was ruler' (Hadi 1998: pers. comm.). Siregar traces the explosion in the envelope culture in the 1970s to the New

Order's tendency to offer 'transport money' to journalists covering functions marking the completion of development projects and initiatives. He describes a 'pattern of partnership' that followed the rapid increase in both local and foreign investment and the subsequent burst of major infrastructure developments under the New Order's economic strategy (Siregar 1997: pers. comm.). Development project organisers had considerable funds at their disposal and were inclined to cover the travel expenses of journalists who were respected but understood to have limited finances. Some journalists were even on the official payroll of government programs (Departemen Penerangan 1975: 102). Such occasional gifts later became a norm. Many journalists began to see the envelope as *wajar* (something natural and proper), while sources often viewed it as a 'service fee', tied to solicitations, whether implied or directly stated, for the journalist to write or not write about certain topics.

Bribes, gifts and graft

In an idealised context, the significance of the envelope should lie not in the exchange of money or gifts but in the source's expression of fellowship with the journalistic community. Tulevski (1996: pers. comm.) says that in theory, giving an envelope 'would be like sitting down and having a good chat, understanding each other, and at the end of it, the source saying "Here's something to help your trip home" so that the friendship is preserved'. There are, indeed, benevolent sources who offer gifts as a gesture of respect. Such sources act as patrons because they recognise that journalists, in common with many Indonesian intellectuals and artisans, are often very lowly paid. These sources do not seem to harbour expectations about such gifts directly influencing news coverage. One *Surya* reporter describes the relationship by insisting that he will only take money from sources that 'are like family, close friends. If I don't know them well, I accept nothing.' The intensity of the personal relationship and friendship bonds between journalists and these kinds of sources would appear a greater barrier to objective reporting than the actual transferral of money.

Sources who might be described as benevolent are in the minority. The majority of sources appear to offer envelopes at press conferences and similar events merely because it has become a habit. Such sources do not, on the one hand, generously desire to enhance the journalists' living conditions or, on the other hand, cynically hope to bribe journalists. Such sources assume, usually correctly, that journalists expect money and will ask for it if envelopes are not automatically forthcoming.

For these sources, the journalists' envelope is like the *uang pelicin* (facilitation money) many citizens pay to bureaucrats, who, like journalists, are a class with low income but high social status and important powers within their own domain. Indonesians often hand over their facilitation fees to civil servants with the aim of speeding up the sluggish wheels of bureaucracy rather than to alter the result of bureaucratic processes. Journalists are often offered envelopes as a similar kind of facilitator. Sources see it as a way of encouraging journalists to attend media events, but without attaching any particular strings about whether or how the story should be covered.

Many anti-envelope journalists are uneasy about such behaviour by their colleagues. For example, a *Gatra* magazine reporter expressed concern that the number of journalists who request envelopes 'like beggars' creates 'an image that journalists can be bought'. Public relations specialists from reputable firms, such as Sima, Nama and Indo Pacific, agreed that occasionally clients do think that they can indeed buy journalists and that they can pay for column inches of news coverage. Tulevski further suggests that most of these sources probably fail to perceive any distinction between the value of paid news space compared with space won through the sources' construction of appealing messages that might attract a stronger reader response (1996: pers. comm.).

Only in extreme cases do sources overtly offer envelopes as 'hush money' to smother 'hot' topics or with a conscious intention of substantially slanting news coverage. Attorneys, for example, sometimes offer to pay crime and court reporters not to report on cases that may embarrass clients or that the lawyers do not want their names associated with. Tulevski similarly notes an unhealthy tendency for many businesses to 'feel they can pay off the media so that bad news doesn't get reported' (1996: pers. comm.). They use the envelope as a substitute for developing ongoing relations with the media and wider community. Such sources tend to have an intense push-pull relationship with journalists. Because they place little importance on developing long-term media and community relations in normal conditions, they lack appropriate foundations to build an understanding with journalists when emergencies arise. They ironically swing between being remote and unreachable to paying for media attention.

At the most excessive end of envelope practice are the nefarious *bodrek*, who engage in extortion, blackmail and use of false identities for financial gain. Some *bodrek* are real reporters who turn to exploiting their press identification cards after losing their jobs (*Tempo* 26 Nov. 1983: 32). Most are non-journalists who work in sophisticated gangs often haranguing and blackmailing sources at the five-star hotels and other venues where business launches and press conferences are conducted on a daily basis. *Bodrek* often claim to be from obscure, out-of-town newspapers or impersonate real reporters, often copying the name cards of real journalists in order to make the masquerade more convincing (e.g. *Kompas* 31 Aug. 1995: 8; *Kompas* 20 Sept. 1995: 11; Maryadi 2001; Raharti & Panggabean 1996: 34). There are also 'journalists', real or otherwise, who dig for negative information about vulnerable sources and then blackmail those sources.

Journalists sometimes joke that *bodrek* are *muntaber* (a term which literally means diarrhoea and vomiting) because they *muncul tanpa berita* (emerge without news). Journalists also refer to *bodrek* by using the colloquial term for prostitutes, WTS (an acronym of *wanita tuna susila*, woman without morals), because the *bodrek* is a *wartawan tanpa suratkabar* (journalist without a newspaper). These disparaging terms indicate the hostility that is directed towards those who breach the fine line of acceptable behaviour in relation to envelopes. Most journalists claim that they passively receive envelopes they are offered, acquiescing from politeness rather than personal interest, so that the handover of money is subordinate to the main business of newsgathering. The prime directive of *bodrek*, by contrast, is unequivocally money. The prevalence of *bodrek* demonstrates the ease with which people of low moral integrity can infiltrate the arenas of professional practice and exploit the customs of envelope behaviour.

The wet and the dry

One subeditor from *Suara Pembaruan* insists that 110 per cent of all journalists take money or gifts of one sort or another. Surveys conducted by AJI of 276 journalists across East Java in 2000 found that 70.8 per cent admitted to accepting envelopes (Budiyanto & Mabroer 2000: 51). The figures represent an improvement on those obtained from estimates during the Soeharto era. A survey by *Kelompok Belajar Menulis dan Meneliti* (KBMM) of 82 journalists in six major Javanese cities between 1986 and 1988 found that 82.7 per cent of respondents accepted envelopes (Kartanegara 1989: 4).

Journalists might debate the wetness of particular desks, but few would deny that the business desk is relatively well drenched. Abar's study of envelopes in the early 1990s found that financial institutions, with the exception of banks, provide the most extravagant envelopes (Abar 1994a: 6). Envelopes are so ubiquitous that one reporter I encountered in field research requested to be moved out of the business round because he was embarrassed at the number of envelopes extended. He complained to his editors that he found the stress 'wearying to the point of exhaustion'. The saturation of the business round appears connected to the business sector's culture of relying on payments to officials when personalised contacts fail to obtain requisite permission to invest, gain operating licences or create access to monopoly markets, contracts and concessions. This operating culture has permeated the style of relating with the press and wider community.

While business reporters are stereotyped as the wettest, many dry desks, such as city hall, crime or courts, have considerable potential for reporters who seek personal benefit. Journalists located in the city hall, for example, can profit considerably from their contacts, by offering their services as *calo* (go-betweens) to assist those involved in buying or selling land and other activities. In the crime rounds, police do not usually offer large sums of money to journalists, but some reporters seek commissions for helping people obtain drivers' licenses or assisting lawyers with tip-offs that lead them to new clients.

Regardless of which round a journalist works in, the value of envelopes is usually greater for those who work for prestige news organisations, such as television, up-market magazines (where stories are perceived as both more comprehensive and more credible) and major newspapers that attract a select readership. One PR consultant, who wished not to be named, attributed this to the sources' desire to build connections with prestige media organisations:

With the limited number of pages, the newspapers do need to select stories. Here you really must get into several key publications, because if you don't, the people that you want to read your information are not going to get it. If you don't get in there, you're lost.

Abar's research shows that newspaper and radio journalists generally received envelopes half the value of those given to magazine journalists and one-quarter to one-fifth of those received by television journalists (1994a: 6).

Perpetuating the culture

Envelope culture has often been connected with the fact that, as one *Harian Terbit* reporter described it, most journalists live in a permanent state of 'personal economic recession'. Makarim (1978: 260) noted in the 1970s that the pay of Indonesian journalists was among the poorest in Southeast Asia. A 1996 *Asiaweek* study showed that decades later, despite steady improvements in journalists' incomes, Indonesian reporters' salaries were still poor in relation to those in Malaysia, the Philippines, Thailand and Singapore. Reporters were also the second-lowest paid white-collar workers out of a survey of 46 Indonesian government, corporate and professional jobs, earning 60 per cent of a secretary's wage (*Asiaweek* 29 Nov. 1996: 60–1).

Salaries across the industry were so low in 1996 that 26 per cent of the nation's print-media organisations failed to pay their workers the government-regulated Regional Minimum Wage (Batubara 1997), which is not sufficient to provide the physical needs of a single adult. Many financially unsound organisations were simply unable to pay higher salaries. Even before the advent of the 1997–8 economic crisis, only 30 per cent of Indonesia's 292 news publications were rated as having 'developed' profit levels. The remaining 70 per cent were rated as either 'undeveloped' or 'still developing' (Batubara 1997). Considering the economics of the press industry, Haryanto (1998) describes the envelope problem as structural rather than moral, claiming that those news organisations that 'have surrendered the welfare of their workers to respective "individual creativity" have finally besmirched the name of the journalist corps as well'.

It is believed that envelope acceptance declined slightly in the 1990s, because increases in journalists' salaries reduced dependence on 'outside supplementary payments' (Hill 1995: 70). As in bureaucracy, however, income is an influential but not the only factor involved in 'supplementary payments'. Some journalists and bureaucrats in high-income brackets still accept and even demand envelopes or facilitation money, even though they have no pressing need for such supplementary sources of income.

Envelope acceptance is also rationalised by the stereotype that news sources are offended by journalists who reject their gifts. Makarim (1978: 260) notes that in Indonesian élite society, refusing envelopes, gifts or other favours 'is extremely difficult, if not altogether impossible, if one is committed to remaining within the web of intricate social relationships'. A *Bisnis Indonesia* reporter suggested that his newspaper's no-envelope policy limited the range and depth of journalist–source relationships because the envelope 'is not just money or goods, but the care of that source'. A senior editorial staffer at *Suara Pembaruan* adds that declining envelopes can be complicated, because if the source is offended by the rejection, 'the door will be closed forever'.

The complications of working in an environment that combines the modern technologies, ideologies and practices of the news media with feudalistic political cultures are often intensified by the internal workplace cultures. The senior staff, who act as workplace role models for younger journalists, often naturalise the acceptance of envelopes. Astraatmadja (1996: pers. comm.) says many of his students at the Dr Soetomo Press Institute are 'very defensive' when he teaches that they must not take envelopes. He says that they protest that the lavish dinners, overseas travel and other gifts enjoyed by the senior editorial staff are not mere envelopes but are instead *kalung* (sacks). One *Suara Pembaruan* reporter similarly condemned newspaper managements for being like 'whores' in their acceptance of source 'hospitality'. Rather than acting as a counter-balance against the influence of the envelopes on their journalists, editors are often equally if not more vulnerable to temptation than their subordinates.

There are also recriminations when reporters who refuse envelopes work in the same organisation as those who receive them. One *Suara Pembaruan* reporter says he was once censured by an envelope-receiving office colleague for rejecting an envelope from a particular source, because that source was then made aware that *Pembaruan* had an anti-envelope policy, and from that point in time ceased to offer envelopes. The colleague was upset to lose a supplier of envelopes.

Some reporters further suggest that there is no benefit in declining the envelopes offered at media conferences because the money they reject will be misappropriated by the PR personnel organising the event (Kartanegara 1989: 4; Gintini 1992: 16). One Golkar employee admitted to me that her colleagues, who were assigned to distribute envelopes to journalists, often embezzled up to half the funds. *Tempo* magazine (14 Mar. 1987: 23) has also reported on cases in which PR staff have 'skimmed the top' off envelopes or boldly demanded that journalists sign blank receipts for envelope money. Journalists frequently surmise that part of the money allocated to organising press events is rightfully theirs, and there is no net social gain if they renounce an envelope, because the forgone money will only enrich the PR person's pocket.

Policy responses to the envelope

Organisations with no-envelope policies – such as *Kompas*, *Suara Pembaruan*, *Media Indonesia* and *Jawa Pos*, among many others – have developed procedures for genteel rejection of envelopes. Reporters are required to accept envelopes that are offered personally by a source, but to return them later to the PR personnel or another subordinate. Alternatively the journalists may bring the envelopes to their news organisation's secretary, who may later mail the money back to the source or donate the money to an orphanage or other charity. In the last option, the sources are usually sent a receipt thanking them for the donation so that they know where the money has gone. All these techniques spare the source the embarrassment of having a gift directly or publicly rejected. One *Kompas* subeditor is highly critical of the 'lazy' younger generation of journalists, who 'think it is better we refuse all of them [envelopes] or reject the envelope the first time they meet a person'. He believes that older and more experienced journalists 'have the better approach' by accepting the money and surrendering it later to third party to allow the source to 'save face'. Several newspapers, such as *Bisnis Indonesia* and *Republika*, announce the amount of money received each month so that the procedures might be open to public scrutiny. A few of the newspapers that cannot afford to ban envelopes altogether are reported to pool envelopes, so that individual journalists from wet rounds are no more influenced than those from the dry.

A few organisations, like *Kompas* and *Tempo*, enjoy reputations for low rates of envelope acceptance, because they have clearly articulated anti-envelope policies that are promoted among the staff, procedures to investigate suspected breaches and clearly expressed, serious commitment to dismiss those who breach the policy. They have, furthermore, backed their policies with appropriate remuneration. Most news organisations with no-envelope policies have failed dismally to alter their organisational culture, because they fail to enforce their policies or support their staff with adequate salaries. As a reporter from *Berita Yudha* observed, it is '*omong kosong*' (empty talk or nonsense) to demand idealism of the press and then fail to protect the journalists' welfare.

The PWI's response to the envelope practice has vacillated over time. The first PWI Code of Ethics, drafted at a formal meeting of newspaper editors in 1954, states in Article 5.1 that: 'Acceptance of favours or promises to publish or suppress news, photographs or articles giving advantages or disadvantages to a person, a group or a certain party is strictly prohibited.' Each subsequent revision of the Code has included a passage about gifts. For example, the PWI Code of Ethics which came into effect in January 1995 stated in Article 4 that: 'Indonesian journalists shall not receive recompense for disseminating or not disseminating news, writings, or pictures that can benefit or damage a person or a party.' The elucidation explains that 'recompense' refers to all material goods, money or facilities; that the receipt of such 'recompense' is 'disgraceful'; and that news organisations must clearly declare any news that has involved sponsorship. In the post-Soeharto era, Article 4 has been altered to say: 'Indonesian journalists will refuse any recompense that may influence the objectivity of reportage.'

The Code has never referred to envelopes directly, but has always unequivocally forbidden the acceptance of gifts that may influence news. While the Code appears to outlaw envelopes, the PWI's uppermost echelons have encouraged diverse and sometimes contradictory interpretations of the Code, especially during the New Order period. Comments from Zulharman Said, shortly after he began his five-year term as PWI chairman in 1983, are typical of PWI's long-held flexible stance. Zulharman admitted that the envelope 'fouls the image of journalists'. He also acknowledged that many news organisations cannot provide adequate salaries while others pay no money at all, and declared that envelopes are unimportant if they are truly given as 'transport money' or 'an expression of thanks' only. He enigmatically concluded that: '"A token of thanks" or "transport money" may be considered prohibited, it may also be considered not [prohibited]' (*Tempo* 26 Nov. 1983: 32).

Sofjan Lubis attracted controversy with his 1996 statements that envelopes are '*halal*' (permitted) if '*senang sama senang*' (there is mutual satisfaction) and neither party makes any demand on the other (Setiadi & Firmanto 1996: 5). Lubis himself did not formally forbid journalists at his own *Pos Kota* newspaper from accepting envelopes, saying that policies on envelopes must take into account each publication's state of development and that his newspaper is not as financially strong as other publications with no-envelope policies, like *Kompas* (1998: pers. comm.). His only stipulation was that journalists could not receive envelopes that might influence the news. Lubis's successor, Azzam, takes a similar posture to Lubis for analogous reasons, threatening to expel those who extort money or accept bribes (Azzam 2001: pers. comm.). The PWI's policy is thus to overlook envelope acceptance, as long as those involved desist from overtly corrupt behaviour or forcible expropriation of money.

The PWI only becomes explicit on the issue of *bodrek*, often issuing warnings to sources, journalists and the public in general to be wary of fake journalists (e.g. Badil 1991: 13; Bintang 1995: 4; *Jakarta Post* 16 Sept. 1997: 2; *Jakarta Post* 16 Jan. 1995: 3; PWI Jaya 1996: 1, 5). The organisation's steadfast opposition to *bodrek* does not address the fundamental issues of the envelope culture. While *bodrek* audaciously engage in illegal conduct, their behaviour is only possible because 'real' journalists so regularly engage in similar activities. *Bodrek* only represent the most extreme elements of a widespread culture.

Professional integrity and political context

Chapter 2 discussed how many political ideologues and analysts have argued that patronage, gift-giving and political exchange are not corruption but socially acceptable conduct in non-Western, patrimonial, pre-modern or modernising societies such as Indonesia. Within a journalistic context, Makarim (1978: 260) says that the extension of envelopes and gifts cannot be judged 'from a purely favor-trading viewpoint' because they form a component of 'the prevailing mode of intercourse among the elite'.

> The extension of a gift or a favor is first and foremost a token of kindness, affection, and respect; its acceptance a matter of courtesy and breeding. Only then, almost as an afterthought and a by-product, the relationship forged by a favor transaction is expected to generate a mutual regard for feelings on the part of the parties concerned. This concern for feelings finds

a unique and sometimes very personal expression in newspaper content as well as in the day-to-day relations between the editor and the man of authority. (Makarim 1978: 261)

While many commentators have relied on cultural explanations for corruption (Liddle 1988: 88), reliance on such an approach runs the risk of implying that envelopes or other behaviours involving a patron–client relationship are automatically acceptable in Indonesia. Several studies point to evidence that most pre-modern states have historically developed their own conceptions of public responsibility, attempted to eliminate corruption and opposed bureaucratic decision-making that runs contrary to established guidelines (Alatas 1980: 52–83; Alatas 1990: 90–124; Theobald 1990: 40–5). Most cultures would define corruption as behaviour by public officials that deviates from accepted laws, regulations or norms or involves misuse of public resources with the aim of serving private ends. Such a definition marks clear boundaries between the resources and powers belonging to the general community and those of the private sphere of individual, family or clan interests (Theobald 1990: 2).

The entrenchment of the envelope in Indonesia does not indicate that Indonesians approve of either corruption or the envelope culture, but rather that the participants have found it feasible and expedient to use their public position for private benefit. The envelope cannot be considered a personal relationship affecting only source and journalist, because the money rarely comes from sources' personal funds. The money most commonly comes from public funds held by the state institutions or investors' funds held by businesses. Correspondingly, many journalists, such as Pudjomartono, say that the envelope cannot be considered as a separate issue from the corruption, collusion and nepotism that has plagued Indonesia (*Kompas* 3 Jun. 1998: 10).

Although survey respondents rarely used the word corruption to describe envelope culture, almost half (48.8 per cent) volunteered an opinion on the degrading nature of envelopes. These critical respondents did not vilify individual envelope recipients. They expressed concern that even if envelope recipients wrote exactly as they pleased, without being prejudiced by the money they received, the envelope culture demeaned the authority of journalism as a profession. Key words used to express concern were professionalism, integrity, dignity, respectability, idealism, independence, autonomy and commitment.

While many journalists suggested that the envelope relationship was degrading and exploitative, respondents were divided about whether it was the journalist or the source who suffered degradation and exploitation. On first glance the sources appear the dominant party in the relationship, since their use of financial power can, intentionally or not, manipulate journalists into dependency positions. The resultant obligation for journalists to reciprocate enables sources to increase their influence over news agendas and consequently expand or protect their public authority. One attorney general exemplified this by saying:

Napoleon once said that he was more afraid of the pen than the sword; more afraid of one writer than a battalion of soldiers. But these days I am more afraid of one soldier than a battalion of journalists. If I faced a battalion of journalists I would simply prepare 100 envelopes, without knowing exactly how much was in them, and it would be okay.... (Departemen Penerangan 1975: 94)

The dilemma lies in the nature of patron–client relationships. Once a relationship is established, both parties must maintain certain unspoken expectations or risk losing the connection. The unspoken expectations of many sources become clear when one considers that most envelopes come from sources who contact journalists seeking to gain or avoid publicity; they rarely give envelopes when they are contacted regarding stories generated by the reporters' own initiative. Dissatisfied sources do not demand their money back, but the envelope relationship creates a psychological demand on journalists who do not want to hurt someone who has been generous to them. Anti-envelope journalists often describe emotional tension as a key motivation for rejecting envelopes. One reporter from the tabloid, *Citra*, said: 'Envelopes make our thinking *sungkan*.[1] It is a feudalistic culture perhaps.'

Journalists cannot simplistically be described as subordinates in the relationship, because they control the 'news hole', a resource of financial, political and social value. Borrowing Jackson's terminology, sources may not perceive themselves as the village head; rather the journalist may be the chieftain to whom visitors must bring gifts before they might be granted an audience. Such a position is evident in those sources who have lamented that they must outlay an additional budget before journalists will deign to report on their fields of activity. PR practitioners note that sources who do not provide envelopes must work much harder to obtain journalistic attention. While journalists are vulnerable to dependency relations, they also have considerable leeway to dictate with whom and the terms by which these relationships will be conducted. Both source and journalist have the potential to dominate the other through their control of differing forms of status, economic resources and power. The exploitative elements of the envelope relationship are characterised not so much by an automatic and intrinsic dominance of either the journalist or the financially privileged envelope donor, but rather by an unhealthy symbiosis and mutual manipulation that may be obscured by the gracious gestures of camaraderie involved in gift giving.

Life in the 'reformist' era

With so much media attention being paid in the post-Soeharto era to issues of corruption, collusion and nepotism in government and business, it might be expected that the envelope culture might wither under the heat of journalistic and public opposition to any practice with a potential connection to KKN. However, the envelope culture has been affected more by the economic downturn than it has by the change in the dominant political paradigm. The collapse of the Rupiah in late 1997 caused newsprint prices to rise by as much as 500 per cent, leading to drastic cost-cutting measures in news organisations (Batubara 1998: 2–3; *Kompas* 22 Jun. 1998: 1; Lingga, Nurdiana & Wibawa 1998: 12–13). As many cash-strapped businesses have cut their advertising budgets, the media's advertising revenue has been unsteady. In 2000, for example, the print media lost Rp 1 trillion (US$112 million) in advertising income (*Kompas* 8 Feb. 2001: 6). Paradoxically, some of the changes in the political structure have further exacerbated the problem. In the 15 months after the government lifted strict licensing restrictions for those wishing to establish-ment media organisations, 1,379 new organisations emerged in the print media alone. Many had insubstantial economic foundations, and it is estimated that at least 80 per cent have subsequently collapsed. The diminished advertising pie was being shared among a record number of media organisations.

Most smaller news organisations are in a poor position to provide suitable salaries and stable work prospects to journalists. A few organisations, most notably Antarta, have raised journalists' salaries with the aim of 'increasing professionalism' (Yuni 2000). Salaries for online journalists temporarily skyrocketed between 1998 and 2000 but subsequently nosedived in most cases. The AJI survey of journalists in East Java in 2000 found that 15.9 per cent received a monthly income of below Rp 250,000 (US$28), while 34.1 per cent were paid Rp 250,000 to Rp 500,000 (Budiyanto & Mabroer 2000: 9). The inadequacy of such a salary is highlighted by the comparison to LBH's 1999 estimates that the minimal wage needs of one female, blue-collar worker in the East Javanese capital, Surabaya, was Rp 406,000 (US$45). Reporters have various travel, telecommunications, recording and paging equipment, and other expenses beyond that of blue-collar workers. AJI concludes that it becomes difficult to imagine how the 50.0 per cent in East Java with salaries of less than Rp 500,000 manage to survive (Budiyanto & Mabroer 2000: 12). In North Sumatera, only five out of more than 40 media organisations pay their journalists the Regional Minimum Wage (Meuraxa 2000: 37). AJI has attempted to address the problem by providing news organisations with tables of proposed minimum wages for journalists, but the Alliance has no power to compel media managers to follow the recommendations.

Among the professional journalists' associations, AJI is the most prominent and active opponent of envelopes. The Alliance engages in research on envelopes and conducts anti-envelope promotions, involving posters, postcards, advertisements, workshops and public announcements targeted at journalists, media organisation managements and news sources. The 1998 AJI Code of Ethics states that journalists are not permitted to receive bribes (*sogokan*). Bribes are defined as 'all forms of gifts or offerings in the form of money, goods and/or other facilities that can directly or indirectly influence journalists in the performance of their journalistic work'. The organisation has strict sanctions for those who accept envelopes, even when the source does not attach any strings to their gift.

Most other journalists' organisations are less stringent in their policies relating to envelopes. The PWI, as discussed above, only bans envelopes that influence the journalists' reportage. Even then, Azzam acknowledges that there are major problems in proving that a journalist has been influenced by the envelopes he or she has received (Azzam 1999: pers. comm.). The KEWI was meant to provide agreement on the basic ethical standards that all of Indonesia's journalists' organisations would support, but the problematic issue of envelopes prolonged negotiations before a compromise code was formulated. AJI's efforts to reduce or eliminate envelopes have faced hostility from journalists from other organisations. Such antipathy was expressed in two forums held in April 2000 in Semarang on the topic of media ethics. Observers at the events say non-AJI journalists argued that they needed envelopes because they are paid low wages, and 'accused AJI of forcing them to agree to regulations that ban the acceptance of envelopes' (SEAPA 2000: 6).

Even some AJI members and potential members are averse to the Alliance's strict no-envelope policy. One organiser of AJI workshops, aimed at assisting news organisations to create journalists' unions, faced workshop participants who bluntly rejected appeals to give up the practice (Stanley 2001: pers. comm.). Many journalists, who are receptive to the concept of forming unions to protect workers rights, hesitate to accept AJI's offers of help in establishing unions in their workplaces because they disagree with the Alliance's anti-envelope campaigns. Although unions might eventually improve journalists' wages and conditions, such outcomes are not guaranteed, and would often require many years of exertion. The envelope, on the other hand, offers an instant albeit short-term salve to low wages. The evidence suggests that attempts to move journalists from a patriarchal culture to one of self-sufficiency will be protracted and unsteady.

AJI and SEAPA leaders believe that envelope acceptance by the journalistic fraternity is worse than before. *Bodrek* have also been well placed to take advantage of the liberalisation of the political culture and the subsequent relaxation of state regulation of journalism. On the one hand, the focus on KKN has meant that some hotels are more careful about monitoring the *bodrek* who loiter in their lobbies. On the other hand, with the bewildering myriad of media organisations that have mushroomed in the post-Soeharto era, it has become harder for many sources to check whether the journalists who ask for interviews or attend media events actually belong to a real news organisation. Additionally, there are increasing incidents of small publications selling press identity cards, enabling *bodrek* to easily acquire the full trappings that enable them to appear as journalists (e.g. Soedjiartono & Elbees 2000a: 26; 2000b, 21). Some publications appear to set up solely with the purpose of selling press cards (*Detak* 2000). Unpublished SEAPA research found one such 'newspaper' reportedly offering services such as home delivery of pizza and fried chicken in addition to selling ID cards. With the boom of online news organisations, *bodrek* can also easily claim to be journalists from 'something-or-another-news.com'. Sources have unwittingly handed out envelopes to *bodrek* before checking that these pseudo e-publications actually exist or regularly publish. The elimination of the PWI's status as the 'one and only' journalists' organisation may have compounded the problem, with some evidence that *bodrek* have established their own organisation. Jakarta *bodrek* have reportedly organised the *Gabungan Wartawan Indonesia* (GWI) to help members pool information about press conferences where envelopes will be offered and to work in teams to blackmail sources (*Jakarta Post* 5 Jan 2001: 3).

Although the activities of *bodrek* are illegal, there have been relatively few arrests. This is possibly because police say that the Criminal Code Procedures permit them only to arrest suspects after a victim lays a complaint. Victims of extortion are often loath to draw attention to the issues that they were being blackmailed over.

AJI and other organisations have called on sources to cease providing journalists with envelopes, but such exhortations have had little impact. Many state institutions, provincial-level parliaments and local governments continue the 1960s and 1970s culture of providing regular rounds reporters with *jatah beras* (rice allowances) and payments of money on a monthly basis, partly because it has become 'tradition' (Budiyanto & Mabroer 2000: 57–68). Such allowances have been accepted as legitimate for so long that they are openly included in the formal budget statements of such institutions. Businesses continue to give envelopes to journalists, and many university PR courses continue to teach their students that they should give an envelope to journalists who attend press conferences and other events. The culture has even spread to NGOs. The NGO sector previously stood out as one that did not offer envelopes. With the influx of money from foreign donors immediately before and after Soeharto's resignation to help with activities like election monitoring, many received more financial aid than they were capable of managing (Heryanto & Adi 2001). A minority of these cash-flushed NGOs have started giving envelopes.

Despite the best attempts of individual newsrooms and particular journalists' associations, the final solution to the envelope will most probably rely on a general political will to cleanse the wider political and economic sphere of bribery and graft. Alatas (1990: 75) notes that: 'Extortion spreads to the professions once it is all-pervasive in government.' Envelope journalism is also widespread in other developing and industrialising nations that suffer from entrenched corruption in the political-economic spheres and large, low-paid bureaucracies. Countries with documented envelope cultures include the Philippines (Habito-Cadiz 1996: 104; Shafer 1995: 123–30, 138), China (Chen, Zhu & Wu 1998: 12), South Korea (Auh, Lee & Koo 1998: 62) and Mexico (Garcia 1993: 46). The envelope was also prevalent until the 1970s in Hong Kong (Chan, Lee & Lee 1996: 11, 15–16) and Singapore (Chin 1996: pers. comm.), but the culture has withered with increased wages and the heat of laws and regulations against corruption. The experience of these two nations demonstrates that the envelope can be eradicated when there is sufficient commitment and effort from the parties involved.

12 Journalism in a transitional culture

This book has outlined the key characteristics of Indonesian political culture, illustrating how most elements of journalistic practice or professional self-perception are touched and transformed by that culture. The traits and characteristics evident in journalistic culture have historically exemplified the patterns evident in all other major social, political and economic institutions, because they were all similarly influenced by the state–military apparatus. Megawati's new government was days old at the time that writing of this book was completed. It is not the purpose of this book to predict what changes her leadership may bring to politics, journalism or the wider community. However, the book sets an example of how people may study dominant political trends (described in the Introduction as the macro-culture) to determine the impact such trends will have on journalistic culture (the micro-culture), both at a wider occupational level and at the day-to-day individual organisational level. Readers who wish to understand how journalists will be affected by the political system that will evolve under Megawati's administration – or the administration of any future leader who replaces her – can do so by following the same systems this book has used to study contemporary political culture, the historical forces that have brought Indonesia to its present state and the dominant philosophies among élite groups.

Journalists and the new order

Given the residual influence of New Order philosophies, it is important to understand the long-term impact of the 32 years of Soeharto's rule on political and journalistic cultures. Schwarz has attempted to counts the costs of Soeharto's convictions that 'differences need to be subordinated to the common good' and that 'the common good can best be divined by an authoritarian state unbeholden to the interests of any one social group'. He concludes that obsession with government control led to an economy held back by corruption, the absence of a modern legal framework, the squashing of initiative and the fear of individuals to speak their minds. The New Order's defenders tried to solve all inconsistencies that arose in this system through the 'ideological blanket' of *Pancasila* as if it had 'incantatory powers, able to do away with anything not to their liking' (Schwarz 1994: 47).

The immense, monist New Order state – involving an omnipotent president and a dominant army which controlled the bureaucracy and the main political grouping, Golkar – based its claims to represent authentic Indonesian values and popular sovereignty on the enforcement of the 1945 Constitution, the upholding of *Pancasila* and the protection of development and stability. Such patterns similarly emerged in the news media. The state used all the key tenets of its integralistic ideology in its constant exhortations, backed by an assortment of laws and regulations, for journalists to guard and enhance the *Pancasila* philosophy, the constitutional values, development and order.

Chapter 2 indicates that the New Order executive, which represented itself as the guardian of the nation, allowed competitors to its powers – in the form of political parties, parliament, elections and other institutional signifiers of democracy as well as a small business class in the private sector – but in a highly managed form. In each case, political parties, parliamentary, elections and other institutions mimicked the forms of similar institutions in the West and drew from the legacy of their Western counterparts to claim democratic representativeness. None, however, functioned in the same fashion as their Western equivalents. These institutions operated with the aim of assisting state control rather than popular representation of societal sectors. The New Order pointed to its assiduous attention to the conduct of elections and other legal-democratic institutions as proof of its authority and integrity (Van Langenberg 1990: 130), but none of these rituals or institutions truly functioned to test the government's claim to represent popular sovereignty. The business sector's support for the New Order resulted largely due to its symbiotic dependency on government institutions rather than confidence in the quality or efficiency of state management. The downfall of the New Order following the 1997 economic collapse illustrates how strongly the cult of economic development supported all other elements of the integralistic state.

Journalists, development and social mission

This book has explained that there are at least four principal ways of viewing development and the ideal relationship between the state, the people and the press in developing societies. The New Order state, however, tolerated no significant deviations from its blend of corporatist and modernisation philosophies, which were described as consistent with harmonious and consensus-seeking Asian values and, more specifically, family-oriented *Pancasila* values. In official perspectives, the *Pancasila* press was neither a watchdog nor a loyal opposition, since opposition in any form is contrary to monist, familial values.

The New Order Government argued that Indonesian journalists regarded themselves as different to the Western press and that a watchdog role was culturally alien. Indeed, many survey respondents disparaged the Western press, often perceiving the Western media as ruthlessly antagonistic and pugnaciously critical. Despite this, just over half the survey respondents described watchdog elements as desirable. Although the Western model may be unacceptable if transported wholesale into the Indonesian environment, there appeared to be strong liberal tendencies in the journalists' conception of their role, particularly in the endorsement of the sentinel or watchdog function. The results indicate that the gap between Western and Indonesian journalistic ideals was not as large as the New Order claimed.

Despite the New Order's attempts to inculcate a coherent press model based on what was described as local, integralistic culture, journalists themselves were disinclined to classify themselves as the *Pancasila* or development press when describing their own identity. There were strong expressions of dissatisfaction that the paradigms were artificially imposed upon journalists by power holders to limit rather than develop professional behaviours. Respondents' descriptions of their reasons for joining the profession suggested that they were committed to developing and improving society, so they could be described as pro-development journalism. However, the respondents' answers also referred to aspirations to help the disadvantaged, succour the suffering and enhance democracy – a broader definition of development than the narrow economic modernisation model that dominated New Order policy.

The journalists predominantly wanted a role in which journalistic functions were separate from those of government. Even those respondents who described their role primarily in nation-building terms overwhelmingly rejected the press-as-government-handmaiden perspective. Similar results were found in the 1996 *Paradigma* and Korkom GMNI survey of journalists, with only 4 per cent of that survey's respondents translating a 'free and responsible' press as meaning one that supports or sides with the government. Of the remainder, 26 per cent argued that a free and responsible press meant siding with the people while 70 per cent believed it should be objective, independent and not take sides (*Paradigma* & Korkom GMNI 1996: 5).

The respondents' comments consistently implied that they were frustrated with interference into their activities by their government 'partner' in the name of Indonesian values, *Pancasila*, development, national unity, public order and the common good. This was most evident when 80 per cent claimed to be dissatisfied with the lack of press freedom. Even though the generalisability of the survey results are limited because my survey was not conducted across a random sample of journalists, the consistency of complaints about press freedom indicates the extent to which journalists felt muzzled by the state and the political culture. There were no notable objections to the underlying principle that 'free but responsible' journalists should constrain their freedom of speech when such freedoms threatened development and the common good; instead the journalists' most common complaint was that political authority and the concepts of 'public good' were abused to enable political figures to protect their own good. With the intense frustration regarding lack of press freedom, it was predictable that vocal role models such as Lubis, Mohamad and Anwar who had struggled against the government would hold a far more intense appeal for survey respondents than the 'natural' family-oriented, modern feudalism of

Pancasila which supposedly contains 'values unearthed from the soil of Indonesia itself' (Department of Information 1986: 9).

Examples of obstructions to the watchdog function are hardly unique to Indonesia. Even in countries where the press has an officially acknowledged watchdog role, politicians and other sources of power regularly seek to oppose, subvert or control journalists' watchdog activities. Journalists can withstand these attacks to a large degree not just because of the media's intrinsic power but also because of the support they might normally expect from other socio-political forces. If journalists are overtly threatened by the executive, for example, they may anticipate aid from the law, the legislature, public and citizen lobbies, business and other countervailing groups. There were almost no significant public protests against newspaper shutdowns or other intimidatory measures against journalists during the New Order, with the exception of the widespread demonstrations and gestures of support for journalists affected by the 1994 closures of *Tempo*, *Editor* and *DëTik*. In the New Order pyramid, described in Chapter 2, the press rarely received substantial support from the weak legal or parliamentary system, the small and fragmented consumer or citizens' groups, the new business classes or religious groups.

The demise of the Soeharto presidency was accompanied by journalistic expressions of pleasure at the corresponding increase in press freedom following the abolition of many of the state powers and restrictions that had been enforced in the name of *kekeluargaan* (e.g. *Jakarta Post* 3 Jun. 1998: 2). Press freedom was described as a panacea for many ills, helping to prevent KKN, to ensure responsive governance and to express the will of the people. Although most patriarchal powers wished to portray themselves as supporters of the *reformasi* movement, many still expressed suspicions that an unbridled press would lead to national decay. One of the many quirky debates between the born-again reformists and the old guard occurred in the parliamentary deliberations over the new press law. The ABRI faction expressed concern about removals of restrictions on the press, while Yunus Yosfiah responded by telling his former military colleagues that a free press would not lead to public unrest or enmity between citizens (*Kompas* 26 Aug. 1999: 15).

It was Wahid, once located at the very heart of the *reformasi* push, who most directly attempted to reverse the flow of press liberalisation by trying to instigate various controls. Such efforts failed, as the press was supported by many other socio-political groups who wished to thwart Wahid's attempt to impose his idiosyncratic will over other sectors of the state and civil society. Megawati's position is yet to be tested, but much of her rhetoric matches with the old integralistic philosophies. She supports a more 'traditional', Javanese concept of communications. She says she supports press freedom, but she does not use watchdog-style terminology. Instead, she stresses the developmental elements of the journalist's role such as education, peace making and community building.

Despite the ambivalence of Indonesian leaders' commitment to press freedom, the biggest threat to journalists are no longer laws and regulations that are designed by the executive and parliament. Instead, physical violence is the journalist's greatest risk. There dramatic increase in attacks and threats against journalists and their workplaces corresponds with the frustration of a populace that has long abandoned the hope that disputes might be resolved through the mechanisms laid down in law. Such attacks also often arise out of attempts by political groups, the military and police who marshal the masses to take actions on their behalf, while maintaining the guise that such behaviour is an impulsive, unprompted expression community outrage. This tendency for the élite to mobilise community unrest to advance their political or economic interests is notable not just in journalism but also in most aspects of current Indonesian political life.

Freedom of organisation and association

The New Order's official description of journalists' identity encapsulated the notion that journalists were professionals rather than mere workers. The designation of journalists as professionals did not encompass the common discourses surrounding professionalisation, such as whether journalism was characterised by special education, a service ethic or professional control of a market sector, but instead identified professionalism with journalists' status as *karyawan*. The debate had an integralistic flavour, rejecting the possibility that *karyawan* might simultaneously be considered as *buruh*, because the latter was seen as disruptive to the elements expected of professionals: family-oriented values, non-adversarial collegiality and independence from vested interests. The demand for journalists to contribute as compliant children to their news-organisation families was generally not coupled with commensurate rewards such as a generous salary, allocation of shares, involvement in the *Dewan Komisaris* or significant input into the direction of the organisation-cum-family's activities. Despite the support of high-profile figures, like Sudomo, in efforts to promote unionism, it was impossible to establish the principle that journalists were workers in a socio-political power structure that consistently renounced the same notion.

As professionals, journalists were overwhelmingly dissatisfied with the PWI during the late New Order period. Sofjan Lubis (1998: pers. comm.) admits that on assuming the chairmanship of the PWI in 1993, his main goal was to overcome the journalistic community's disaffection with the professional association. The results of my analysis suggest that despite the efforts of both Lubis and Hadi, who conducted an extensive campaign of promotional visits to news organisations during their terms in office, hostility towards the PWI remained trenchant.

The main source of discontent stemmed from the impression that the corporatised association, although not formally part of Golkar, was primarily a tool of Golkar and the state. After the end of the New Order, Hadi announced that the number one priority of the association was to sever links with Golkar and to replace executives holding Golkar positions (*Jakarta Post* 5 Aug. 1998b: 2). This change was an acknowledgement of journalists' concerns that corporatisation in practice equalled cooption.

The New Order's opposition to the unionisation of journalism and to rival groupings to the PWI had common ideological bases. Both unions and rival professional groupings were regarded as inherently disruptive and divisive forces because of their adversarial and competitive nature. Following the factionalism, disorder and economic decay of the Sukarno era and the chaos subsequent to the 1965 coup, the New Order depicted corporatisation of professions and containment of the unions as two of many mechanisms necessary to maintain harmony, order and development. Unification of journalists into one professional, non-unionised grouping was not only perceived as essential to maintaining collaboration and stability within the news media but also as important for wider socio-political stability. Such a philosophy ignored the evidence of the 1970 Anwar–Diah case, which showed early in the New Order that corporatism provided no guarantee of consensus and unity within the field of journalism let alone within society as a whole.

The revocation of the PWI's corporatised status led to a boom in new journalists' groups, although the majority of these groups have insufficient organisational skills, resources or membership support to remain viable in the long term. In some ways, the escalation in numbers of journalists' groups has the potential to damage journalists' collective power more than it may damage the PWI. With so many groups, no one group can claim to represent all journalists' interests in negotiations with media owners, government, economic interests or community groups. The many associations present a divided rather than united front when issues or threats emerge in relation to journalists.

There may be too many professional associations, but there are comparatively few unions. AJI's position is that journalists need capital if they are to uphold professionalism and morality, and unions can help provide the salaries and working conditions that provide the foundations for good journalism (Nurbaiti 2000: 33). However, in its attempts to set up union-style bodies in the news media, AJI has found that relatively few journalists are interested in germinating new associations to protect their rights as workers. This apathy arises because unions often have relatively little power to prise higher salaries from the hands of poorly financed news managements. Additionally, envelopes are so readily available. Ironically, although unions are designed to serve workers and labourers, union organisers are often seen as elitist, because they commonly hold dogmatic anti-envelope views.

As Chapter 6 discusses, journalists feel that they can easily find new jobs if they are dismissed or unfairly treated at their old ones. This was especially the case in late 1998. When economy was contracting, journalism was one of the few areas where job vacancies had multiplied exponentially. Ultimately, although there are many new jobs for journalists who are sacked or seek new horizons, the conditions offered by new employers are unlikely to provide greater remuneration or professional satisfaction than those offered by their old employers.

Journalists also largely uphold the New Order philosophy that reliance on workers' associations or unions is debasing to journalists' professional status.

This perspective is not supported by the experience of Western countries, where media professionalisation has commonly been advanced when employees across different organisations established connections to defend common interests against employers. Mark Osiel, for example, has studied the pre-1960s U.S. news media, when firms where commonly family-owned businesses led by a founding 'patriarch'. He finds that the relatively personalised, familial style of U.S. news management at that time hampered both union activity and the formation of professional identity (Osiel 1986: 168). Indonesian academics have similarly described family values in business leadership as the country's 'biggest obstacle to professionalism' (*Jakarta Post* 5 Jul. 1995: 2; also *Warta Ekonomi* 17 Jul. 1995: 38–9). The work of these theorists supports Kuhon's contention that the systems of logic and institutional structures which uphold unionism will serve to augment rather than diminish professionalism.

Where are the women?

The intensely patriarchal political culture can also be linked to a scarcity of women in journalism and other arenas of political life. The *peran ganda*, which allowed women to work but prioritised their activities in the family, was perceived as essential to development, stability and order. Women were permitted to work as long as they also acted as faithful backstops to their supposedly more industrious husbands and bore, nourished and socialised new generations of healthy, sound, *Pancasila*-oriented workers. Women experienced difficulties in joining and staying in journalism jobs because of the challenges of combining the idealised mother–homemaker role with that of the professional woman.

The appointment of Indonesia's first female president may enhance prospects for the progression for women in journalism and the three estates of politics. However, Megawati has no history of advancing women's issues. Although she has a mass-support base, she also relies on the backing of historically patriarchal institutions, such as the military.

Liawati Sidarto notes that in the post-Soeharto era, Indonesian women are playing an increasingly important role in the family economy, as they shoulder the burden of making up shortfalls in family incomes during the current period of financial insecurity. Sidarto finds that in addition to this, women are still performing the bulk of the housework (Sidarto 2000). This suggests that the familial pressures that limit women's involvement in journalism and other political activities may have intensified, regardless of the attempts to end the old, patriarchal political structure. In this context, it is unlikely that the percentages of women in journalism or the other arenas of political life will increase in the immediate future.

Straight from the source

Chapter 9 describes how journalists faced constant barriers in their access to political, military and bureaucratic figures during the New Order. Even after obtaining access, they found such sources were usually hesitant to engage in open and comprehensive discussions. The connections that would enable frank, complete, two-way communications were limited because of paternalistic philosophies that implied father-like figures only needed to share information when they deemed it necessary for the public good. The business community was similarly inaccessible, with business leaders often reluctant to share information with journalists, because it was usually of far greater moment for businesses to cultivate connections with political decision-makers than with consumers or the general populace.

When élite sources did communicate, they had inflated and unrealistic expectations about the importance and thus the news value that the media would attach to their communiqués. This indicated the degree to which they viewed their own activities as being essential to the public interest and common good rather than merely representative of their own concerns and needs. They acted as if the media was obliged to publish or broadcast their messages without alteration or abbreviation, and in the terminology of James Carey (1983), the media's 'information' role subsumed that of 'conversation'.

Notably more accessible and reliable were the intellectuals and other expert sources, who often occupied positions outside the New Order's political structures and who have traditionally played oppositional or watchdog roles to the state. These intellectuals and experts frequently represented or agitated on behalf of a variety of social and political constituencies, gathering large quantities of information about events, issues and social trends and packaging that information into formats that were accessible to journalists. Students, academics, activists from NGOs, religious leaders and retired military leaders thus became important sources of counter-hegemonic discourses in the news.

This book shows, however, that integralistic leaders have been more approachable during periods of political transition. During such times, military and political leaders, from the president down, are unable to claim that they have the automatic authority of father figures. In Soeharto's case, it was only as he entrenched his power throughout the bureaucratic and military structure that he progressively withdrew himself from public scrutiny. The relationship of the élite with the press during periods when the New Order was secure in its dominance of political processes was thus markedly different to that during periods of political transition. Integralistic leaders only claimed that they were one with the people and thus not subject to popular scrutiny during times when there were no advantages to be gained from submitting to the media's investigative spotlight. As president, Habibie lacked the strong political support base of his predecessor and was anxious to establish his credentials as a reformer. His accessibility to the media was an important element in his attempts to distance himself from the New Order's sullied reputation.

Megawati is a reticent news source. The early days of her presidency suggest she will rely primarily on stage-managed engagements with the media. Given that she is not reputed to be an original thinker or dynamic presenter, she is unlikely to win much popular acclaim through accessibility to journalists. Her political circle is therefore unlikely to wish to expose her to media attention. However, current attempts to introduce shield and FOI laws are a means by which journalists and other sectors of the community can force leaders to resign themselves to media and other public examination, even when it is not to their direct advantage.

Passing the buck

The historical culture of source opacity is interconnected with the envelope culture. This culture arose in part from the patron-client relations that the New Order fostered to maintain political support. It is also both a symptom of and panacea for sources' failure to build bridges with the media through other mechanisms. Sources who rarely cultivate connections with the news community in normal conditions often attempt to use the envelope as a tool to build instant links when they want publicity or need to address contingencies in the public domain. Although many sources appear to give the envelope with benign rather than manipulative intentions, the practice helps to perpetuate a culture in which paternalistic sources maintain an often advantageous power differential with journalists.

The political corruption that accompanied the New Order period has often been attributed to an essentially feudalistic approach to governance and to the large funds that were entrusted to a poorly supervised and bloated bureaucracy (Antlöv 1994: 90–1; Vatikiotis 1993: 37, 54). The New Order openly used patronage as a system of maintaining authority and bureaucratic stability. Such patronage was the New Order's chief instrument of reward and punishment, requiring extensive outlays of cash and other resources (Liddle 1991: 118, 121–2). Systemic corruption in the New Order was thus not merely cultural, but political, aimed at consolidating the socio-economic positions of groups and interests connected with political stakeholders.

If the New Order's economic patrimonialism had ever been truly culturally appropriate, it becomes difficult to explain why so many Indonesian academics, journalists and public figures devoted so much effort to exposing it or why so many influential figures inevitably reacted negatively to its revelation. The New Order itself displayed an acute understanding of the public's intolerance to corruption during 1966 and 1967 when it attempted to shore up its legitimacy and destroy Sukarno's reputation by publicising details of the former president's corruption and abuses of power for his personal advantage (Anderson 1990: 53). Similarly, the twilight months of the New Order and the years following Soeharto's resignation have been marked by daily newspaper articles and innumerable public demonstrations railing against KKN.

Envelopes influence journalistic behaviour. This may involve altering the tone and content of stories, adding or abandoning stories, changing the balance of sources in existing stories or disrupting the collegial professional behaviours necessary to investigate stories. Alternatively, it may simply involve tempting journalists to a story that they would not otherwise have covered. Because of this, envelopes are inimical to the essence of development and investigative journalism. Those who have engaged in the prolific development-journalism debate have almost without exception failed to note that third world journalists are usually lowly paid but tantalisingly close to the peaks of politico-economic authority. They are, therefore, highly vulnerable to external inducements. Such emotional handicaps thwart the achievement of the development-journalism ideal.

The envelope culture is unlikely to be eradicated from Indonesian journalism without far-reaching efforts to eliminate the systemic corruption in business and political life. Within journalism, attempts to eliminate envelope journalism have focussed on codes of ethics and, less directly, the establishment of union-style associations. Christopher Warren, head of the International Federation of Journalists, told Indonesian news workers at a workshop during the Wahid era that trade unionism would help build professionalism by improving the workplace conditions; this would both reduce the temptation to become involved in corruption and protect against threats to press freedom (*Suara Serikat* 20 Mar. 2000a: 4). To date, his message has not made a significant impact on the numbers of journalists joining unions. However, such attempts to connect professionalism and unionisation in the minds of Indonesian journalists are important if old cultures are to change.

Political, professional and social 'cultures'

Many of the elements of journalism in New Order Indonesia bore a striking resemblance to those observed by Eduardo José Garcia in Mexico. Garcia (1993: 46) gives a standard example of a newspaper reporter being assigned to fill several columns with the details of a ministerial visit, regardless of its newsworthiness.

> After a bumpy bus ride to the provincial centre, the Interior Minister delivers his standard speech and you hurry back to a cramped press room .... Forget making a few telephone calls for background or public reaction. Not only will you not have enough time – since you are inundated with press releases that you will rewrite to fill your quota of stories – but if you call around almost nobody will talk to you ....
>
> Finally at night, after completing your page-filling duties, a fat envelope, full of money, will await you in your hotel room, just to make sure you have enjoyed your visit and to guarantee that you remain good friends with the Interior Secretary.

Garcia's description indicates the adjustment that journalists in a developing country make to accommodate an authoritarian, corrupt political culture. In Indonesia, such patterns were attributed during the New Order to local, village-derived traditions. However, such patterns emerge in many developing countries with paternalistic political systems. Since the social cultures of Mexico and other developing countries are markedly different from that in Indonesia, commonalities with Indonesian journalistic culture appear more directly attributable to similar politico-economic pressures than to social culture alone.

The elements of Indonesian journalistic culture described in this book – including the *Pancasila*-development press model, the lack of representation as workers, the corporatisation of the profession, the predominantly male makeup of the journalistic corps, journalistic deference to sources and the envelope culture – were often described as suited to Indonesia's family-oriented, consensus-driven social culture. However, integralism did not flow purely from Indonesia's many and diverse cultures but rather was kept alive by a privileged class which had been influenced by the *priyayi* worldview and European and Japanese organic philosophies. This is not to suggest that local cultures have not had a dynamic influence on the identity and activities of journalists. However, the alterations in journalistic activities which have followed Soeharto's resignation and the resultant change in the political order have also indicated the degree to which journalistic culture was not purely derived from social culture but was linked to the political hegemony and élite cultures and interests. It is thus unsurprising that journalists' comments indicate that they often felt they were not the state's fraternal colleagues during the New Order but political captives, suffering diminution of professional control and loss of creativity. The *Pancasila* press philosophy was fraught with contradictions and limitations that were unable to be reconciled through the narrowly conceived political culture of the integralistic state.

Indonesian political culture is currently in a state of flux, and expectations are mixed about the type of system that will grow under Indonesia's fifth president. The periods in which Habibie and Wahid governed have been characterised by bold and dynamic reportage and increased freedoms to organise and associate. This trend may be reinforced by Megawati's political regime or it may just as easily be overturned when the relationships of political power and communication mutate under the influence of a new political structure. Those favouring a liberalisation of journalism and the wider political system are using the present transitional period to pass legal and constitutional changes that will prevent the élite from returning to integralistic systems when it is no longer useful or convenient to maintain an image of open dialogue with other sectors of society. Indonesian history has shown, however, that the élite can change or simply ignore laws as alliances between the powerful are created, broken or adapted and as modifications occur in the ways and means by which leaders establish their legitimacy. Journalists often like to think that they help to shape these ever-changing patterns of interaction between state and society, but as this book shows, they are in turn shaped by these relationships and the evolving balance of power in their communities.

Notes

1 The 'authentic' Indonesian character

1 There is no official transcript of the BPUPKI proceedings. The most commonly cited references come from Yamin's (1959) incomplete record of events.
2 Important and influential philosophies of collectivism and *kekeluargaan* were also developed by Ki Hadjar Dewantoro and the Taman Siswa school (Reeve 1985: 9–20; Shiraishi 1997: 93–5), Sukarno (Reeve 1985: 25–36) and Hatta (Reeve 1985: 36–41). This work concentrates on Supomo's contribution both because of limitations of space and because of the New Order's conscious drawing on constitutionalism and integralism as conceived by Supomo.
3 Supomo uses the terms *kawula* and *gusti*, which can be translated as servant and master, as humanity and God almighty or as subject and lord.
4 Yamin's (1959) text shows that these include Yamin himself (pp. 228–30, 232–6, 330, 335) and Mohammad Hatta (pp. 299–300), among others.
5 Prior to 1946, the élite indigenous civil servants who worked under Dutch colonial or Japanese colonial rule were known as the *pangreh pradja* (rulers of the realm).
6 Djokosutono was an important adviser to Sukarno and Nasution, as well as the *Dewan Nasional* (National Council) during this period, promoting corporatist 'functional groups' which represented different sectoral interests and a strong state to coordinate and control the groups in accordance with general interests (Bourchier 1996: 130–9).
7 Nasakom is an abbreviation of *Nasionalisme* (nationalism), *Agama* (religion) and *Komunisme* (communism), the three competing political and ideological interests that Sukarno claimed to unite.

2 The organic New Order state

1 For further on New Order's use of *Pancasila* as a tool of ideological legitimation and control see Pabotinggi 1995: 246–53; Pranowo 1990: 491–4; Ramage 1994, 156–67; Ramage 1995: 24–7; Van Langenberg 1986: 20–1; Van Langenberg 1990: 132–3.
2 One of the most comprehensive histories of the regulatory and cultural systems for the government to control the ownership and operations of Indonesian television is available in Kitley (2000).
3 Useful summaries of the gains that Soeharto's family and closest friends have made from corruption, collusion and nepotism can be found in Aditjondro (1998) and Schwarz (1994, ch. 6).
4 It would be impossible to detail the innumerable articles published on the subject throughout the New Order. General details of the complaints about corruption during the early New Order period are available in Crouch (1988: 235, 294–9), Schwarz (1994: 137–79) and Southwood and Flanagan (1985: 180–1).

5 Professional image in the community of journalists

1 Respondents were allowed to nominate more than one reason for joining. Only reasons that were nominated by a substantial number of journalists, in this case than 10 respondents, were included in the table.
2 Anwar's figures only include the first four most-commonly nominated reasons, so the table does not add to 100 per cent.
3 The remaining 10 per cent did not give a clear indication of how often their news was censored.
4 Examples of the subtle and allusive writing style of journalists are available in Awanohara (1984: 24–5), Aznam (1992: 22), Button (1991: 66), Hill (1990: 16), Hill & Sen (1991: 6), Milne (1989: 448), Murphy (1989: 62) and Razak (1985: 22).
5 The remaining 18 per cent did not give a clear indication of how often they received telephone calls.
6 Journalists were allowed to nominate more than one answer, so the figures add to more than 100 per cent.
7 No other journalist was nominated as a hero or role model by more than 10 per cent of respondents.

7 Professional affiliation: politics and the PWI

1 The government released the two journalists eight months early with no explanation (Berlian 1997).
2 The figures are available in the Department's IPPPN Journalistic Data series (Departemen Penerangan (1996/7–1998/9).
3 One respondent, interviewed in the early phases of the survey, was not asked questions about the PWI.

8 No woman, no cry

1 The five were Universitas Indonesia in Depok, Lembaga Pers Dr Soetomo in Jakarta, Universitas Gajah Mada and LP3Y in Yogyakarta and Universitas Diponegoro in Semarang.
2 PWI records for 1973 show an increase from 2.0 per cent in 1973 to 10.4 per cent in 1998. Department of Information surveys show an increase from 10.1 per cent in 1986, the first year such surveys were conducted, to 13.2 per cent in 1998 (Departemen Penerangan 1986/7–1998/9).

9 News sources in the political labyrinth

1 Many papers and books have published about freedom of the press in Indonesia by institutions such as AJI (the Alliance of Independent Journalists), Amnesty International, Article 19, Freedom Forum, Index on Censorship, ISAI (the Institute for Study of Free Flow of Information), IPI (International Press Institute), Human Rights Watch/Asia and *Reporters Sans Frontières*, among others.
2 The Department of Information similarly reported in 1975 that Soeharto had only ever conducted one background briefing with journalists and noted that the meeting was 'not satisfying' to journalists because it related to 'incorrect reporting' (Departemen Penerangan 1975: 67). Although it does not specify whether the briefing was in relation to the family-tree issue, it seems to be the same meeting referred to by Index on Censorship.
3 The preference of Western politicians for personalised interviews is discussed in Bell and Leeuwen (1994: 1).

4 It is a well-known Indonesian joke that parliamentarians' work comprises of the five Ds. These are *datang, duduk, dengar, diam* and *duit* (arriving, sitting, listening, being silent and collecting money).

10 Information broking in the public sphere

1 I would like to thank Daniel Dhakidae for providing copies of several articles and conference papers that form the basis of this section.

11 The envelope please

1 *Sungkan* is a Javanese term for reluctance to approach or take action against someone of a higher status.

Glossary

AAP Australian Associated Press wire service.
ABC Australian Broadcasting Corporation (formerly Australian Broadcasting Commission).
ABRI *Angkatan Bersenjata Republik Indonesia*, the Armed Forces of the Republic of Indonesia.
Adat Traditional laws and customs.
AFP Agence-France Presse wire service.
Aliran Political, religious or other socio-cultural groups or orientations.
AJI *Aliansi Jurnalis Independen*, Alliance of Independent Journalists.
Amplop Literally an envelope, *amplop* also describes gifts of money which are often concealed in small envelopes.
APEC The Asia Pacific Economic Cooperation forum, which comprises 21 member 'economies' around the Pacific rim.
Asas tunggal The sole-foundation policy, enforced by law in 1985, obliging all social and political organisations and political parties to adopt *Pancasila* as their sole philosophical foundation.
Bakorstansas *Badan Koordinasi Bantuan Pemantapan Stabilitas Nasional*, the Coordinating Agency for Assisting the Consolidation of National Stability. See Kopkamtib.
Bodrek Journalists or pseudo-journalists who harass sources for money.
BP7 *Badan Pembinaan Pendidikan Pelaksanaan Pedoman Penghayatan dan Pengamalan Pancasila*, the Supervisory Body for the Implementation of the Guide to the Realisation and Practice of *Pancasila*, formed in 1979.
BPHPR Body for the Protection of the People's Political Rights Facing the 1992 General Election.
BPS *Badan Pendukung Sukarnoism*, Body for Support of Sukarnoism.
BPUPKI *Badan Penyelidik Usaha Persiapan Kemerdekaan Indonesia*, the Investigating Committee for the Preparation of Indonesian Independence, conducted in 1945 during the final months of Japanese occupation.
Bulog *Badan Urusan Logistik*, the National Logistics Agency.
Buruh A labourer, usually one who works on a farm or in other manual activities.
CESDA Centre for the Study of Democracy and Development.

CPJ Committee to Protect Journalists.

Dewan Karyawan Staff Council.

Dewan Komisaris Board of Commissioners.

Dharma Pertiwi Mother Earth's Duty, a compulsory organisation for wives of male police and military personnel.

Dharma Wanita Women's Duty, a compulsory organisation for wives of male civil servants.

DPR *Dewan Perwakilan Rakyat*, People's Representative Council, Indonesia's 500-seat parliament.

DPRD *Dewan Perwakilan Rakyat Daerah*, Regional People's Representative Council, the provincial parliament.

Dwifungsi The dual-function doctrine in which the Armed Forces have a role in social and political affairs as well as defence and security functions.

ELSAM Institute for Policy Research and Advocacy.

FBSI *Federasi Buruh Seluruh Indonesia*, All Indonesia Workers' Federation, formed in 1973 and superseded by the SPSI in 1985.

FOI Freedom of Information.

G-30-S *Gerakan September Tiga Puluh* or Gestapu, the communist September 30 Movement deemed responsible for the 1965 assassination of five of Indonesia's most senior Army generals and attempted assassination of one other in a coup attempt.

GBHN *Garis-garis Besar Haluan Negara*, Broad Outlines of State Policy, the policy directives which are ratified during the five-yearly session of the MPR.

Gestapu See G-30-S.

Golkar *Golongan Karya*, the Functional Groups, was the dominant New Order political grouping and consists of various sub-groupings representing cross-societal interests including farmers, fishermen, peasants, business, civil servants, professionals, youth and women.

Gotong Royong The principle of mutual cooperation.

HIP *Hubungan Industrial Pancasila*, *Pancasila* Industrial Relations, a term which replaced HPP in the 1970s.

HPP *Hubungan Perburuhan Pancasila*, *Pancasila* Labour Relations, a creed of familial harmony between workers and their employers.

HRW/A Human Rights Watch/Asia.

IBRA Indonesian Bank Restructuring Agency.

IMF International Monetary Fund.

ISAI *Institut Studi Arus Informasi*, Institute for the Study of Free Flow of Information.

Karyawan A functionary or worker.

Kekeluargaan Familialism or family-oriented philosophy, a doctrine which asserts that the interests of the whole group precede those of individuals or sectors.

KEWI *Kode Etik Wartawan Indonesia*, the Indonesian Journalists' Code of Ethics.

KKB   *Kesepakatan Kerja Bersama*, Cooperative Work Agreements.

KKN   *Korupsi, Kolusi dan Nepotisme* (corruption, collusion and nepotism).

KLW   *Karya Latihan Wartawan*, Journalistic Work Exercises, a three-day education program organised by the PWI for new candidates.

KNI   *Kantorberita Nasional Indonesia* (Indonesian National News Bureau).

Kodrat   Intrinsic character and God-given nature.

Komnas HAM   *Komisi Nasional Hak Asasi Manusia*, National Human Rights Commission.

Kontrol Sosial   Social control, the control of the state by the civil society.

Kopkamtib   *Komando Pemulihan Keamanan dan Ketertiban*, Operational Command for the Restoration of Security and Order, a security organisation formed by General Soeharto in October 1965 following the failed coup d'état of September 1965. It was replaced in 1988 by Bakorstansas.

Korkom GMNI   *Koordinator Komisariat Gerakan Mahasiswa Nasional Indonesia*, Coordinating Commissariat of the Indonesian National Students' Movement.

Kyai   An Islamic scholar.

LCHR   Lawyers Committee for Human Rights.

Lekra   *Lembaga Kebudayaan Rakyat*, the People's Cultural Institute.

LP3Y   *Lembaga Penelitian Pendidikan dan Penerbitan Yogyakarta*, the Yogyakarta Institute for the Research, Education and Publication.

Mabes   *Markas besar*, the headquarters.

MPR   *Majelis Permusyawaratan Rakyat*, People's Consultative Assembly – the Indonesian equivalent of a Congress.

Mufakat   Consensus or unanimous acceptance, based on the family principle, resulting from mutual deliberation and consultation.

Musyawarah   Mutual deliberation, negotiation and consultation to achieve consensus.

Nahdlatul Ulama   Indonesia's largest Islamic organisation, with an estimated 35 million members.

Nasakom   An acronym of the *nasionalis* (nationalist), *agama* (religion) and *komunis* (communist) streams that Sukarno supposedly united and represented.

Negara Integralistik   The integralistic state or nation, a concept first outline by *adat* scholar Supomo in 1945 during meetings by a Japanese-created assembly to discuss preparations for national independence and to draft a constitution.

NWICO   New World Information and Communication Order.

P4D   *Panitia Penyelesaian Perselisihan Perburuhan Daerah*, Regional Committee for Resolution of Labour Disputes.

Pamong praja   Literally 'the guardians of the realm', a term referring to the bureaucratic class during the late twentieth century.

PAN   *Partai Amanat Nasional*, National Mandate Party.

Pancasila   The 'five pillars' of the Republic of Indonesia, introduced by Sukarno in a June 1945 speech in order to provide a platform for unifying

Indonesia's multitudinous political forces. The five *Pancasila* principles are belief in one God Almighty, a just and civilised humanity, national unity, democracy guided by the wisdom of consensus through representative deliberation, and social justice for all Indonesians.

PDI *Partai Demokrasi Indonesia*, Indonesian Democratic Party.

PDI-P *Partai Demokrasi Indonesia – Perjuangan*, the Indonesian Democratic Party of Struggle.

Pekerja Worker.

Pemberdayaan Empowerment.

Pemimpin Redaksi Editor in chief.

Peran Ganda Dual function.

Petisi 50 The Petition of 50, comprising 50 prominent citizens who signed the *Pernyataan Keprihatinan* (Statement of Concern) sent to Soeharto in 1980.

PKB *Partai Kebangkitan Bangsa*, the National Awakening Party.

PKI *Partai Komunis Indonesia*, the Indonesian Communist Party, banned in March 1966.

PKK *Pembinaan Kesejahteraan Keluarga*, the Family Welfare Development program.

PPP *Partai Persatuan Pembangunan*, the United Development Party.

Priyayi The petty aristocracy, commonly integrated into the colonial civil service.

PWI *Persatuan Wartawan Indonesia*, the Association of Indonesian Journalists.

Reformasi Reform.

Repelita *Rencana Pembangunan Lima Tahun*, Five Year Development Plan.

Resi An ascetic.

RRI *Radio Republik Indonesia*, Radio of the Republic of Indonesia.

SBSI *Serikat Buruh Indonesia Sejahtera*, Indonesian Prosperous Workers Union, established in 1992 as a rival to the SPSI.

SEAPA South East Asian Press Alliance.

Sekber Golkar *Sekretariat Bersama Golongan Karya*, the Joint Secretariat of Golkar Organisations, established in 1964.

SIT *Surat Izin Terbit*, Licence to Print. Under the 1966 Press Law, all would-be publishers had to apply for an annually renewable SIT permit. The SIT provision was abolished by the 1982 Press Law, which instead required that all publishers obtain a publication business licence, the SIUPP.

SIUPP *Surat Izin Usaha Penerbitan Pers,* Press Publisher's Business Permit. Under the 1982 Press Law, publishers had to obtain a SIUPP for each and every newspaper and magazine they wished to publish. Government withdrawal of the SIUPP effectively revoked the publishers' right to publish that newspapers or magazine. In 1999, the government abolished the requirement for publishers to have a SIUPP.

SOBSI *Sentral Organisasi Buruh Seluruh Indonesia*, Central Federation of Indonesian Labour Organisations, a PKI-affiliated union organisation, formed in 1946.

SOKSI   *Sentral Organisasi Karyawan Sosialis Indonesia*, Central Organisation of Indonesian Socialist Employees, formed in 1961 as an umbrella organisation for anticommunist trade unions and conservative functional groups.

SPS   *Serikat Penerbit Suratkabar*, the Association of Newspaper Publishers.

SPSI   *Serikat Pekerja Seluruh Indonesia*, the government-sponsored All Indonesia Workers' Union.

Tukang   Skilled labourer or craftsman.

UNDP   United Nations Development Program.

Wanita   Woman.

Wartawan   Literally means news man but is commonly used to refer to both male and female journalists.

Wartawati   News woman, ie a female journalist.

Yayasan   Charitable or social foundations.

YLBHI   *Yayasan Lembaga Bantuan Hukum Indonesia*, the Foundation of Indonesian Legal Aid Institutes.

Appendix

The information presented in this book derives from ethnographic research, interviews with more than 100 sources, a small survey of 65 journalists and study of existing literature, such as newspapers, government documents, laws and regulations and so on. The research was preceded by a pilot study in 1994 to 1996, involving interviews with 20 Jakarta-based foreign correspondents from four newspapers, four weekly magazines, six radio and television networks and six wire services. The aim of the interviews was to take advantage of the foreign correspondents' positioning at a nexus point between Western and Indonesian journalistic practice. They worked within Indonesian geographic and ideological domains, but their socialisation, training, audiences and news organisations were predominantly Western. They balanced the demands generated by Indonesia's cultural and material infrastructure against the often oppositional requirements of their Western employers and audiences. Because of this positioning, they were aware of different routines, *modus operandi*, and underlying assumptions that local journalists who had been socialised in the system might take for granted.

The ethnographic research was conducted at five Indonesian news media organisations between February 1996 and April 1998. Observation, participant observation and interview activities totalling three months were conducted at four newspapers, *Suara Merdeka*, *The Jakarta Post*, *Kompas* and *Suara Pembaruan* newspapers and a television station, SCTV. The range of news organisations visited provided opportunities to observe contrasting organisational and professional styles. Although all the newspapers were dailies, each had different political agendas and each was commonly identified as being loosely connected to different religious groupings. The secular, English-language *Jakarta Post* identified its main agenda as encouraging political democratisation, and journalists from other publications regularly described the newspaper as *berani* (brave or bold). The Catholic-oriented, Indonesian-language *Kompas* was conservative but maintained a mission to oppose socio-political injustices. The Islamic-oriented, Indonesian-language *Suara Merdeka* was conservative and pro-government, with a strong commercial focus. The Protestant-oriented *Suara Pembaruan* aimed to provide a 'quality' newspaper, but its journalists often offered me unsolicited expressions about the insecurity that still haunted the organisation following the 1986 closure of its predecessor,

Sinar Harapan, following the government's withdrawal of its license to publish. The routines of the afternoon *Suara Pembaruan* also differed considerably from the other publications, which were all morning newspapers, while *Suara Merdeka* differed in its regional focus compared with the Jakarta-dominated focus of the other national newspapers. SCTV aimed to offer a quality news service. Its news values and activities were shaped by the specificities of the broadcast medium, and also differed from those of the newspapers.

In common with many ethnographic studies, the research was backed by a sampling of opinions on the character, structure and functions of journalistic culture. I sought a general perspective on journalistic views and behaviour through a survey of 65 Indonesian journalists conducted between October 1996 and April 1998. The sample was conducted using a snowballing technique, in which I followed journalists I met during the ethnographic research phase to news events or press conferences, where I met other journalists covering the same event. I interviewed journalists and then arranged to meet colleagues of those journalists, and so on. Each journalist was asked a series of open-ended questions in semi-structured, semi-formal interviews that usually lasted between 30 and 60 minutes.

Of the 65 survey respondents, 63 worked for 25 news organisations:

- the domestic news wire service, Antara,
- the English-language, Jakarta-based, daily newspapers, the *Indonesia Times* and *Jakarta Post*,
- the Jakarta-based, Indonesian-language, daily newspapers, *Berita Buana, Harian Ekonomi Neraca, Harian Terbit, Kompas, Jayakarta, Media Indonesia, Pos Kota, Republika, Suara Pembaruan*,
- the Central Java daily newspaper, *Suara Merdeka*,
- the Yogyakarta daily newspaper, *Bernas*,
- the East Java daily newspaper, *Surya*,
- the North Sumatran weekly newspaper, *Dobrak*,
- the Jakarta-based, weekly tabloid, *Citra*,
- the Jakarta-based, weekly magazines, *Gatra* and *Jakarta-Jakarta*,
- the Jakarta-based, fortnightly magazine, *Info Bank*,
- the Jakarta-based, monthly magazine, *Matra*,
- the Jakarta-based, Golkar magazine, *Media Karya*,
- the government-controlled radio station, Radio Republic Indonesia,
- the Indonesian-language section of the BBC,
- the commercial television station, SCTV.

The two remaining survey respondents had previously been employed by Jakarta daily newspapers but, following their dismissal, had established successful freelance businesses – one writing for local and the other for foreign publications.

The 65 journalists surveyed comprise approximately 1 per cent of the 6414 journalists who worked for print media and wire service organisations in 1996

(Departemen Penerangan 1996/1997a: iii). Because the survey was small and was not conducted across a stratified random sample, the results are qualitative rather than quantitative. The results are by no means absolute barometers of the warmth of journalistic feelings. The research instead aims to identify different trends in journalistic perspectives on development-journalism theory, professional organisation, news source and similar topics. Percentages of how many journalists supported one line of thinking against another have been included throughout the thesis to indicate how strong each of the different trends were; the figures are not intended to represent a definitive, quantitative gauge of journalistic sentiment.

While the survey sample cannot be described as exhaustive, comparisons of the survey sample with the total journalistic population suggest the group was not atypical. Of the survey sample, 60.9 per cent (54) were members of the *Persatuan Wartawan Indonesia* (PWI, Indonesian Journalists' Association) and 16.9 per cent (11) were women. Information Department figures for 1996 show that of all print and wire service journalists, 62.2 per cent were PWI members and 12.8 per cent were women (Departemen Penerangan 1996/1997a: i–iii).

The research also included interviews with a judgemental sampling of specially targeted journalists and other informants who could provide idiosyncratic but strategically significant insights. Several industry representatives, such as 1993–98 PWI chiefs Sofjan Lubis and Parni Hadi, were interviewed to explore the official explanations of journalistic behaviours and ideological perspective. I interviewed journalism educators at universities and colleges and media theorists, such as Ashadi Siregar, Budi Susanto and Ariel Heryanto, to examine the symbolic patterns that local industry analysts employed to explain journalistic beliefs and practices. Nine women, in addition to the 11 included in the survey, were interviewed about their experiences as women working in a patriarchal system. Fetterman (1989: 19) points to the value to ethnographers of selecting vocal and articulate members of a dissatisfied subculture to help identify intracultural diversity and systemic undercurrents and tensions. I also sought the views of vocal and dissatisfied journalists, such as several journalists banned by the PWI and, during the Soeharto era, attended the meetings of rebellious, technically illegal groups such as the *Aliansi Jurnalis Independen* (AJI, Alliance of Independent Journalists) and *Forum Demokrasi Wartawan Yogyakarta* (FDWY, Yogyakarta Journalists' Democracy Forum). Other journalists were targeted because they worked in positions of special interest, such as in the Presidential Palace or armed forces headquarters. Additionally, I talked both formally and informally with a range of public relations personnel and news sources about their perspectives of the journalists they dealt with.

Practical limits on time and budget have meant that the ethnographic study and all survey interviews, except one, were conducted on the island of Java, most often in the national capital, Jakarta. The Jakarta- and Java-centrism are not inappropriate given the distribution of population and the news media throughout Indonesia. Forty-nine per cent of publications are based in Jakarta and 68.5 per cent on the island of Java. The Java-based publications also have significantly larger readerships than those on other islands, with circulations in Jakarta comprising 69.7 per cent and in Java comprising 89.7 per cent of all print media circulations (Batubara 1996: 25).

Department of Information figures also show that in 1996, 3074 (47.9 per cent) of the nation's 6414 print media journalists were employed by Jakarta-based news organisations and 4328 (67.5 per cent) by Java-based news organisations (Departemen Penerangan 1996/1997a: i–iii). The Department of Information results must be regarded with caution because the geographical categories are defined according to the location of the head offices of the news organisations that employ the journalists, rather than the location of the journalists themselves. Most regional publications have at least one reporter to report from the business and political centre of Jakarta, whereas the national and local publications based in Jakarta rely heavily on stringers or wire services to cover many regions outside the capital, especially for the regions outside Java. It thus appears that the data could have underestimated the number of journalists based in Jakarta and Java.

In ethnographic and observation work, there is also the possibility of error or distortion in observing and recording events, or the potential for subjects to change their behaviour because they are aware of being observed (Robson 1993: 192; 1991; Tuchman 1991: 85–6; Yin 1994: 80). Such limitations are exacerbated when researchers try to interpret the significance of actions that occur within a foreign cultural perspective. Several techniques were used to try to reduce the potential for errors that might arise through faulty perception, recording or analysis, through cultural bias or through informants 'performing' rather than acting naturally. Although a white, Western woman will always be relatively conspicuous at gatherings of predominantly male Indonesian journalists, I spent a considerable amount of time working with the journalists in order to encourage respondents to forget their 'company manners'. Many journalists seemed to become complacent about my loitering around police headquarters, local parliamentary offices and other places where foreigners, least of all female foreign researchers, rarely venture. A large amount of time was also spent socialising with journalists. I also regularly visited the newsrooms of journalistic friends at about 8 or 9 p.m. after they were relaxing after finishing work, to join in the banter about their perceived personal highlights and lowlights, the swapping of professional folktales and the deconstruction of the day's news events. Three key confidants, each of whom have worked for seven to 25 years as journalists, have also provided extensive critique of my research.

Bibliography

Abar, Akmad Zaini (1994a) 'Budaya wartawan amplop' (The culture of envelope journalism), *Republika*, 26 Apr., p. 6.

—— (1994b) 'Pers dan publisitas DPR' (The press and publicity of the DPR), 8 Feb., p. 4.

Abrar, Ana Nadhya (1995) *Panduan Buat Pers Indonesia* (A Guide to the Indonesian Press), Yogyakarta: Pustaka Pelajar.

Adamson, Tracey (1996) Account director, IndoPacific public relations firm, interview conducted in Jakarta, 28 Nov.

Aditjondro, George Junus (1998) *Harta Jarahan Harto* ([Soe]Harto's Plundered Wealth), np: Pustaka Demokrasi.

—— (1992) 'Proses rekayasa pemberitaan masalah lingkungan dalam pers Indonesia' (The process of engineering news on environmental problems in the Indonesian press), discussion panel for the 36th anniversary of the Satya Wacana Christian University, Salatiga, Indonesia, 16 Nov.

Ahooja-Patel, Krishna (1996) 'Emerging gender inequalities within Asia', *Asia – Who Pays for Growth? Women, Environment and Popular Movements*, eds Jayant Lele and Wisdom Tettey, Aldershot, England: Dartmouth Publishing, pp. 124–50.

Alatas, Syed Hussein (1990) *Corruption: Its Nature, Causes and Functions*, Aldershot, England: Avebury.

—— (1980) *The Sociology of Corruption*, 2nd edn, Singapore: Times International.

Ali, Owais Aslam (1994) 'Roundtable', *Media Asia*, vol. 21, no. 2, p. 90.

Aliansi Jurnalis Independen (AJI) (2000) *Journalists Harassed by Minister, Expelled from Meeting*, statement issued on 2 Mar., Jakarta

—— (1995) press release, 21 Mar. From apakabar@clark.net.

—— (1994a) *Banning 1994*, Jakarta: AJI.

—— (1994b) Self-titled promotional brochure.

Alfian M., M. Alfan (1999) 'Mencermati fenomena "cendekia–politik"', *Republika*, 3 Mar., p. 6.

Almatsier, Renville (1994) 'Humas dan pers: Dua saudara yang bagai anjing dan kucing' (Public relations and the press: Two siblings who are like cats and dogs), *Kompas*, 21 Sept., p. 4.

Amin, Nuruddin (1998) FDWY presidium member and regional NU secretary, meeting in Yogyakarta, 21 Apr.

Amir Machmud N.S. (1998) 'Rosihan Anwar tidak akurat', *Kompas*, 21 Nov., p. 4.

Amirris, Aris (1993) 'Tak ada lagi pembatalan SIUPP' (There is no more revocation of SIUPP), *Editor*, 9 Dec., p. 51.

Amnesty International (1992) *Amnesty International Report 1992*, London: Amnesty International.

Anderson, Benedict (1994) 'Rewinding "Back to the Future": The left and constitutional democracy', in *Democracy in Indonesia: 1950s and 1990s*, eds David Bourchier and John Legge, Melbourne: Monash University, pp. 128–42.

—— (1990) (1972) 'The idea of power in Javanese culture', in *Language and Power: Exploring Political Culture in Indonesia*, Ithaca, New York: Cornell University, pp. 17–77.

Anderson, Michael H. (1984) *Madison Avenue in Asia: Politics and Transnational Advertising*, Cranbury, New Jersey: Associated University Presses.

—— (1976) 'The guided press in Indonesia: Freedom versus responsibility', in *Guided Press in Southeast Asia: National Development Versus Freedom of Expression*, ed. John A. Lent, New York: State University of New York, pp. 29–65.

Anggraeni, Dewi (1994) Australian correspondent, *Tempo*, telephone interview from Melbourne, 26 Sept.

Angkatan Bersenjata (10 Jun.1996) '"Di tangan" konglomerat idealisme pers makin menurun' ('In the hands' of conglomerates press idealism is progressively declining), p. 1.

—— (10 Feb.1996) 'Presiden pada HPN: Masih terjadi pemurarbalikan fakta' (President on the HPN [National Press Day]: Distortion of facts still occurs), pp. 1, 11.

—— (11 Dec.1987) 'Sekjen DPP SPSI: Wartawan masuk SPSI tidak mengaburkan keanggotaannya di PWI' (DPP SPSI Secretary General: Journalists who enter the SPSI will not forget their membership in the PWI), p. 12.

Antara (22 Mar.1988a) 'Hasnan Habib: Buktikan kemampuan dan terima kritik sehat' (Hasnan Habib: Prove your ability and accept healthy criticism), *Warta Berita*, no. 082A, pp. A24–A25.

—— (22 Mar.1988b) 'Koperasi diberi prioritas dalam usaha pembangunan' (Cooperatives given priority in development efforts), *Warta Berita*, No. 082A, pp. C12–C13.

—— (10 Dec.1987) 'Presiden: Koporasi harus ikut memiliki saham perusahaan' (President: Cooperatives must participate through owning company shares), *Warta Berita*, No. 343B, p. H11.

—— (15 Aug.1985) 'Sudomo tentang serikat pekerja suratkabar' (Sudomo about newspaper unions), *Warta Berita*, no. 226B, p. A15.

—— (22 Nov.1984) 'Kapolres Jakarta Pusat minta maaf kepada wartawan' (The Central Jakarta Police Chief apologises to journalists), *Warta Berita*, no. 326A, p. C4.

—— (21 Nov.1984) 'Harmoko lapor Presiden hasil lawatan ke Tunisia' (Harmoko reports to the President on the results of his expedition to Tunisia), *Warta Berita*, No. 325B, pp. A15–A16.

—— (20 Nov.1984) 'Menaker Sudomo akan buka pertemuan tripartit I ASEAN' (Manpower Minister Sudomo will open the Tripartite ASEAN I meeting), *Warta Berita*, No. 324B, pp. A7–A9.

—— (15 May 1978) 'Wartawan bukan buruh atau anggota serikat buruh' (A journalist is not a labourer or a member of labour union), *Warta Berita*, no. 136B, p. 7.

—— (22 Oct.1975) 'Lokakarya buruh grafika pers dibuka' (Press graphics workers' workshop opened), *Warta Berita*, no. 294A, p. 9.

—— (24 Jun.1969) 'PWI-Djaya opposes decision Nr. 02/1969 by Information Minister', *News Bulletin*, no. B, p. 10.

—— (20 Jun.1969) 'Information Minister says press participation demands honest attitude', *News Bulletin*, pp. 4–5.

Antlöv, Hans (1994) 'Village leaders and the New Order', *Leadership on Java: Gentle Hints, Authoritarian Rule*, eds Hans Antlöv and Sven Cederroth, Richmond, Surrey: Curzon Press, pp. 73–96.

Anto (1995) 'Indonesia Tidak Menganut Paham Integralistik', *Hidup*, 5 Feb., p. 19

Anwar, Dewi Fortuna (1998) 'The Habibie presidency', presentation to Indonesia Update conference, 28 Sept., Canberra: Australian National University.

Anwar, Rosihan (1998a) '"Post mortem" Kongres PWI' ('Post mortem' of the PWI Congress), *Kompas*, 22 Oct., p. 4.

—— (1998b) 'Menghapus citra buruk PWI', *Republika*, 10 Oct. 1998, p. 6.

—— (1993) 'Hanya kewartawanan moderat yang tepat' (Only appropriate moderate journalism), in *Tajuk-Tajuk dalam Terik Matahari: Empat Puluh Tahun Surabaya Post* (Editorials in the Warmth of the Sun: Forty Years of the *Surabaya Post*), eds Hotman M. Siahaan and Tjahjo Purnomo W., Surabaya: Yayasan Keluarga Bhakti, pp. 233–8.

—— (1977) *Profil Wartawan Indonesia* (Profile of Indonesian Journalists), Jakarta: Deppen RI & LP3ES.

—— (1973) 'Newsmen can take heart when they look across the border', *IPI Report*, Nov.–Dec., pp. 4–5.

Arifin, Anwar (1996) 'Eksistensi dan perkembangan pers Pancasila' (The existence and development of the *Pancasila* press), press release, 20 May.

Arismunandar, Satrio (1998) Journalist and AJI activist, interview conducted in Jakarta, 28 Mar.

Arismunander, Satrio (1997) 'The mass media and press freedom in Indonesia', in *Broadcasting in Asia*, ed. Bhimanto Suwastoyo, Jakarta: AJI & ISAI, pp. 121–7.

Ariva, Gadis (1998), 'Logika kekerasan terhadap perempuan' (The logic of violence against women', *Jurnal Perempuan*, no. 8, Aug.–Oct, pp. 4–12.

Asia Watch (1988) *Human Rights in Indonesia and East Timor*, New York: Asia Watch.

Asiaweek (29 Nov.1996) 'The *Asiaweek* salaries survey: Your guide to pay packets across Asia', pp. 60–1.

—— (14 Mar.1995) 'Out you must go, too: Another MP faces expulsion from Parliament', p. 37.

—— (2 Nov.1994) 'Crackdowns: Targeting the intellectuals', p. 52.

Asmarani, Devi M. (1998) 'Don't expect power to sap Hasan's brashness', *Jakarta Post*, 22 Mar., p. 7.

Aspinall, Edward (1998) Opposition and elite conflict in the fall of Soeharto, paper delivered to the Asian Studies Association of Australia conference, Sydney: University of New South Wales, 28 Sept.–1 Oct.

Associated Press (14 Aug.1998) 'Indonesian official says press freedoms inhibiting to some ministers'.

Astaga.com (3 May 2001) 'Dari 240 RUU, DPR baru selesaikan 10 UU' (From 250 draft laws, the DPR has finalised only 10 laws). From http://www.mail-archive.com/indonews@indo-news.com/msg08508.html.

Astraatmadja, Atmakusumah (2001) Head of the Doctor Soetomo Press Institute and the National Press Council, interview conducted in Jakarta, 28 Feb.

—— (2000) 'Dewan Pers Independen' (An Independent Press Council), *Kompas*, 27 June, p. 4.

—— (1998) 'After Suharto, disillusionment among young Indonesian journalists', *Freedom Forum Online*. From http://www.freedomforum.org/international/1998/7/10suharto.asp.

Atmo, Suwito R.S. and Vidarta (1995) 'Membangun rationalitas baru' (Building a new rationality), *Bernas*, 7 Apr., p. 4.

Auh, Taik Sup, Lee, Chang Keun and Kang, Myung Koo (1998) 'Korean Journalists in the 1990s', in *The Global Journalist: News People Around the World*, ed. David H. Weaver, Cresskill, New Jersey: Hampton Press, pp. 55–70.

Awanohara, Susumo (1984) 'The media freedom fighters', *Far Eastern Economic Review*, 1 Mar., pp. 24–6.

Aznam, Suhaini (1992) 'Closure contested', *Far Eastern Economic Review*, 26 Nov., pp. 20–2.

Azzam, Tarman (2001) National chairman of the PWI for the 1998–2003 term, interview conducted in Jakarta, 12 Mar.

Badan Perencanaan Pembangunan (1999) *Konsep Awal: Program Pembangunan Nasional (Propenas) 2000–2004, Konsep IA* (Initial Concept: National Development Program (Propenas) 2000–2004, Concept IA), Jakarta: Badan Perencanaan Pembangunan.

Badan Pusat Statistik (2000a) *Statistik dan Indikator Jender* (Statistics and Indicators on Gender), Jakarta, Badan Pusat Statistik and United Nations Development Fund for Women.

—— (2000b) *Wanita dan Pria di Indonesia 2000* (Women and Men in Indonesia 2000), Jakarta: Badan Pusat Statistik and United Nations Development Fund for Women.

Badil, Rudy (1991) 'Wartawan "pusat-muntaber-obyektif-bodrek"' ('Centre-diarrhoea-objective-bodrek' journalists), *Kompas*, 10 Feb., p. 13.

Badrie, Sofyan (1998) 'Sekitar interaksi pers, masyarakat, pemerintah' (About the interaction of the press, community and government), *Suara Karya*, 10 Feb., p. 5.

Baskoro and Riza (1993) 'Komisi HAM gaya pemerintah', (The government-style human rights commission), *Forum Keadilan*, 23 Dec., p. 94.

Batubara, Leo S. (1998) Prospek harga kertas koran mendatang (Future Prospects for Newsprint Prices), *Suara Pembaruan*, 23 Mar., pp. 2–3.

—— (1997) 'Penyelenggaraan Penerbitan Pers Nasional Dalam Kebersamaan', address to Karya Latihan Wartawan Angkatan II, PWI Cabang Jakarta, 9 Oct.

—— (1996) 'Agenda Pers Nasional Paska 50 Tahun PWI, SPS' (The National Press Agenda after 50 years of the PWI, SPS), *Jurnal Pers Indonesia*, no. 3, Sept., pp. 25–8.

Bayuni, Endy (1996) 'Asian values in journalism: Do they exist?', in *Asian Values in Journalism*, ed. Murray Masterton, Singapore: AMIC, pp. 39–43.

Bektiati, Bina, Fibri, Rommy and Prabandari, Purwani Diayah (2000) 'The president's mouthpiece', *Tempo English Edition*, 16 Oct., p. 30.

Bell, Philip and Leeuwen, Theo van (1994) *The Media Interview: Confession, Contest, Conversation*, Kensington, New South Wales: University of New South Wales Press.

Berita Buana (23 Mar.1988) 'Wartawan ditindak karena berusaha mendirikan serikat pekerja' (Action taken against journalist because he attempted to build a union), p. 6.

—— (3 Dec.1987) 'Menaker minta perusahan pers perhatikan perlindungan kerja' (Manpower Minister asks press companies to pay attention to worker protection), pp. 1, 9.

—— (2 Dec.1987) 'Wawancara "impromptu" dengan Pak Harto, "rejeki" buat wartawan' ("Impromptu" interview with Father Harto, "good fortune" for journalists', p. 12.

—— (10 Oct.1983) 'Dirjen Penum: Kwalitas juru penerangan di bawah standar' (Director General of General Information: Quality of information officers is below standard), p. 3.

—— (22 Oct.1975) 'Boleh memberikan wawancara kepada pers' (Permitted to give interviews to the press), p. 12.

Berlian, Samsudin (1997) 'Release of jailed journalists baffles many', *IPS (InterPress Service)*, 31 Jul.

Bernas (20 Mar.1995) 'Tiga pengelola "*Independen*" resmi dijadikan tersangka', p. 1.

—— (7 Jul.1993) 'Pers terlibat feodalisme politik' (The press is entangled in political feudalism), p. 1.

Berry, Chris, Birch, David, Dermody, Susan, Grant, Jennifer, Hamilton, Annette, Quilty, Mary and Sen, Krishna (1995) *Perceiving 'the Media'*, Australian-Asian Perception Project Working Paper No. 8, Sydney: Academy of Social Sciences and Canberra: the Asia-Australia Institute.

Besar, Abdulkadir (1984) '"Negara Persatuan" citanegara integralistik anutan UUD 1945' (The integralistic 'Unitary State' philosophy as the basis of the 1945 Constitution) in *Guru Pinandita: Sumbangsih untuk Prof Djokosoetono SH* (The Wise Professor: A Contribution for Prof. Djokosoetono SH), Lembaga Penerbit Fakultas Ekonomi, Jakarta: Universitas Indonesia, pp. 87–132.

Beutler, Warwick (1982) 'Comment', in *Australia, Asia and the Media*, ed. Alison Broinowski, Nathan, Queensland: Griffith University, pp. 25–9.

Bintang, Ilham (1995) 'Phony reporter', *Jakarta Post*, 14 Jan., p. 4.

Birch, David (1993) *Singapore Media: Communication Strategies and Practices*, Melbourne: Longman Cheshire.

Bisnis Indonesia (19 Sept. 1998) 'Ketua PWI Jateng diadukan ke Kejakgung dengan tuduhan KKN', (PWI Central Java head faces complaints by the District Attorney regarding KKN), p. 19.

Blackburn, Susan (2001) 'Women and the nation', *Inside Indonesia*, no. 66, Apr.–Jun., pp. 6–8.

—— (1994) 'Gender interests and Indonesian democracy', in *Democracy in Indonesia: 1950s and 1990s*, eds David Bourchier and John Legge, Centre for Southeast Asian Studies, Clayton, Victoria: Monash University, pp. 168–81.

Boileau, Julain M. (1983) *Golkar: Functional Group Politics in Indonesia*, Jakarta: Centre for Strategic and International Studies.

Booth, Anne (2000) 'The impact of the Indonesian crisis on welfare: What do we know two years on?', *Indonesia in Transition: Social Aspects of Reformasi and Crisis*, eds Chris Manning and Peter van Diermen, Singapore: Institute of Southeast Asian Studies, pp. 145–62.

Bourchier, David (1996) 'Lineages of organicist political thought in Indonesia', Ph.D. thesis, Melbourne: Monash University.

—— (1993) 'Totalitarianism and the "national personality": Recent controversy about the philosophical basis of the Indonesian state', revised version of a paper written for the Indonesian Culture: Asking the Right Questions conference, 28 Sept–4 Oct 1991, Adelaide.

Breed, Warren (1955) 'Social control in the newsroom: A functional analysis', *Social Forces*, no. 33, May, pp. 326–35.

Bresnan, John (1993) *Managing Indonesia: The Modern Political Economy*, New York: Columbia University Press.

Brown, David (1994) *The State and Ethnic Politics in Southeast Asia*, New York: Routledge.

Bucher, Rue and Stelling, Joan (1969) 'Characteristics of professional organisations', *Journal of Health and Social Behaviour*, no. 10, Mar., pp. 3–15.

Buchori, Binny and Bianpoen, Carla (1996) *Through Women's Eyes: An Annotated Bibliography*, Jakarta: International Bank for Reconstruction and Development/World Bank.

Budijanto, Rahman (1993) 'PWI dan wadah tunggal organisasi profesi', *Bernas*, 2 Dec., p. 4.
—— and Mabroer M.S., (2000) *Kesejahteraan Jurnalis: Antara Mitos dan Kenyataan: Potret Sosial Ekonomi Jurnalis Jawa Timur* (Journalists' Welfare: Between Myth and Fact: A Socio-Economic Portrait of East Javanese Journalists), Surabaya: Aliansi Jurnalis Independen and Jakarta: The Asia Foundation.
Budiman, Arief (1996) Political scientist and lecturer, Satya Wacana Christian University, interview conducted in Salatiga, 30 Jan.
—— (1978) 'The student movement in Indonesia: A study of the relationship between culture and structure', *Asian Survey*, vol. XVII, no. 6, Jun., pp. 609–25.
—— (1973) 'Portrait of a young Indonesian looking at his surroundings', *Internationales Asienforum*, Jan., pp. 76–88.
Budiyarso, Edy (1997) 'Pers Menempel Kepada Mereka Yang Berkuasa', *Tempo Interaktif: Beringin Lebat Daunnya Bingtang Lebih Terang Sinarnya Tapi Bangeng Kok Loyo*, vol. II, Sept. 1996–Feb. 1997, Jakarta: Pusat Data dan Analisia Tempo, pp. 645–7.
Buku Putih Tempo: Pembredelan Itu (The *Tempo* White Book: That Licence Revocation) (1994) Jakarta: Alumni Majalah Tempo.
Button, James (1991) 'Neighbour's views', *Time Australia*, 18 Nov., pp. 66–7.
Byrnes, Michael (1995) Former Indonesia correspondent, *Australian Financial Review*, telephone interview conducted from Sydney, 4 Aug.
Cahyono, Edi (1997) 'The *unjuk rasa* movement', in *State and Labour in New Order Indonesia*, ed. Rod Lambert, University of Western Australia Press and Asia Research Centre, Western Australia: Murdoch University, pp. 105–22.
Caplen, Brian (1995) 'Coming out of the shadows' *Asian Business*, Apr., pp. 58–9.
Carey, James (1983) 'The press and public discourse', *Center Magazine*, no. 20, pp. 4–16.
Carey, Peter and Houben, Vincent (1992) 'Spirited Srikandhis and sly Sumbadras: The social, political and economic role of women at the Central Javanese courts in the 18th and early 19th centuries', in *Indonesian Women in Focus*, rev. edn, eds Elsbeth Locher-Scholten and Anke Niehof, Leiden: KITLV Press, pp. 12–42.
Case, William (1998) 'Pseudo-democracy in Southeast Asia: Uncovering state leaders and the business connection', paper delivered to the Asia in Global Context conference, Asian Studies Association of Australia, Sydney: University of New South Wales, 28 Sept–1 Oct.
Centre for the Study of Democracy and Development (CESDA-LP3ES) (1994) *Pers and Masyarakat: Laporan Hasil Pengumpulan Pendapat Umum tentang Peranan Pers Indonesia* (Press and the Community: A Report on the Result of a General Survey about the Role of the Indonesian Press), Jakarta: CESDA-LP3ES.
Chan, Joseph Man, Lee, Paul S.N. and Lee, Chin-Chuan (1996) *Hong Kong Journalists in Transition*, Hong Kong: Hong Kong Institute of Asia-Pacific Studies.
Chen, Chongshan, Zhu, Jian-Hua and Wu, Wei (1998) 'The Chinese journalist' in *The Global Journalist: News People Around the World*, ed. David H. Weaver, Cresskill, New Jersey: Hampton Press, 9–30.
Chenery, Ahluwalia, Hollis Montek S., Bell, C.L.G., Duloy, John H. and Jolly, Richard (1974) *Redistribution with Growth*, World Bank, London: London and Oxford University Press.
Chew, Lee Kim (1998) 'Queue to fill "power vacuum" in Indonesia', *Straits Times*, 25 Aug, p. 30.
Chibnall, Steve (1977) *Law-and-Order News: An Analysis of Crime Reporting in the British Press*, London: Tavistock Publications.

Chin, Francis (1996) Subeditor, *The Straits Times*, personal communication in Singapore, 6 Dec.

Chu, Leonard L. (1988) 'Mass communication theory: A Chinese perspective', *Communication Theory: The Asian Perspective*, ed. Wimal Dissanayake, Singapore: AMIC, pp. 126–38.

Clark, L., and Lange, L. (eds) (1979) *The Sexism of Social and Political Theory: Women and Reproduction from Plato to Nietzsche*, Toronto: University of Toronto Press.

The Commission on Freedom of the Press (1947) *A Free and Responsible Press*, Chicago: University of Chicago Press.

Committee to Protect Journalists (1991) *In the Censor's Shadow: Journalism in Suharto's Indonesia*, New York: CPJ.

Cooley, Laura (1992) 'Maintaining Rukun for Javanese Households and for the State', in *Women and Mediation in Indonesia*, rev. edn, eds Sita van Bemmelen, Madelon Djajadiningrat-Niewenhuis, Elsbeth Locher-Scholten and Elly Touwen-Bouwsma, Leiden: KITLV Press, pp. 229–47.

Coté, Joost (trans.) (1992) 'Introduction', *Letters from Kartini: An Indonesian Feminist: 1900–1904*, Monash Asia Institute, Melbourne: Clayton and Hyland House, pp. vii–xxxii.

Crawford, Robert (1971) 'Indonesia', in *The Asian Newspapers' Reluctant Revolution*, ed. John A. Lent, Iowa: Iowa State University Press, pp. 158–78.

Crouch, Harold (1999) 'Wiranto and Habibie: Military-civilian relations since May 1998', *Reformasi: Crisis and Change in Indonesia*, eds Arief Budiman, Barbara Hatley and Damien Kingsbury, Melbourne: Monash Asia Institute.

—— (1994) 'Democratic prospects in Indonesia', in *Democracy in Indonesia: 1950s and 1990s*, eds David Bourchier and John Legge, Centre for Southeast Asian Studies, Clayton, Victoria:, Monash University, pp. 115–27.

—— (1988) *The Army and Politics in Indonesia*, rev. edn, Ithaca, New York: Cornell University Press.

—— (1984) *Domestic Political Structures and Regional Economic Cooperation*, Singapore: Institute of Southeast Asian Studies.

Curry, Jane Leftwich (1990) *Poland's Journalists: Professionalism and Politics*, Cambridge: Cambridge University Press.

Dailami (1999) Director General for Press and Graphics, Department of Information, interview conducted in Jakarta, 18 Jun.

—— (1998) *Himpunan Ceremah Direktur Jenderal Pembinaan Pers dan Grafika Departemen Penerangan Republik Indonesia 1997–1998* (Collection of Speeches by the Director General of Press and Graphics, Department of Information, Republik of Indonesia, 1997–1998), Direktorat Jenderal Pembinaan Pers and Grafika, Proyek Pembinaan dan Pengembangan Pers dan Grafika, Jakarta: Deppen RI.

Daud, Amir (1998), former *Pedoman* journalist, interview conducted in Jakarta, 24 Apr.

Departemen Penerangan (1998/9) *Data Kepemilikan Kolektif Wartawan/Karyawan Pers IPPPN Tahun 1998*, Direktorat Jenderal Pembinaan Pers and Grafika, Proyek Pembinaan dan Pengembangan Pers dan Grafika, Jakarta: Deppen RI.

—— (1997/8) *Data Kepemilikan Kolektif Wartawan/Karyawan Pers IPPPN Tahun 1997*, Direktorat Jenderal Pembinaan Pers and Grafika, Proyek Pembinaan dan Pengembangan Pers dan Grafika, Jakarta: Deppen RI.

—— (1996/7a) *Data Kewartawan Berdasarkan IPPPN Tahun 1996*, Direktorat Jenderal Pembinaan Pers and Grafika, Proyek Pembinaan Pers, Jakarta: Deppen RI.

—— (1996/7b) *Data Pengasuh Penerbitan Pers IPPPN Tahun 1996*, Direktorat Jenderal Pembinaan Pers and Grafika, Proyek Pembinaan Pers, Jakarta: Deppen RI.

—— (1995/6) *Data Kewartawan Berdasarkan IPPPN Tahun 1995*, Direktorat Jenderal Pembinaan Pers and Grafika, Proyek Pembinaan Pers, Jakarta: Deppen RI.
—— (1993/4) *Data Kewartawan Berdasarkan IPPPN Tahun 1993*, Direktorat Jenderal Pembinaan Pers and Grafika, Proyek Pembinaan Pers, Jakarta: Deppen RI.
—— (1992/3) *Data Kewartawan Berdasarkan IPPPN Tahun 1992*, Direktorat Jenderal Pembinaan Pers and Grafika, Proyek Pembinaan Pers, Jakarta: Deppen RI.
—— (1991/2) *Data Kewartawan Berdasarkan IPPPN Tahun 1991*, Direktorat Jenderal Pembinaan Pers and Grafika, Proyek Pembinaan Pers, Jakarta: Deppen RI.
—— (1990/1) *Data Kewartawan Berdasarkan IPPPN Tahun 1990*, Direktorat Jenderal Pembinaan Pers and Grafika, Proyek Pembinaan Pers, Jakarta: Deppen RI.
—— (1989/90) *Data Kewartawan Berdasarkan IPPPN Tahun 1989*, Direktorat Jenderal Pembinaan Pers and Grafika, Proyek Pembinaan Pers, Jakarta: Deppen RI.
—— (1988/9) *Data Kewartawan Berdasarkan IPPPN Tahun 1988*, Direktorat Jenderal Pembinaan Pers and Grafika, Proyek Pembinaan Pers, Jakarta: Deppen RI.
—— (1987/8) *Data Kewartawan Berdasarkan IPPPN Tahun 1987*, Direktorat Jenderal Pembinaan Pers and Grafika, Proyek Pembinaan Pers, Jakarta: Deppen RI.
—— (1986/7) *Data Kewartawan Berdasarkan IPPPN Tahun 1986*, Direktorat Jenderal Pembinaan Pers and Grafika, Proyek Pembinaan Pers, Jakarta: Deppen RI.
—— (1975) *Laporan Penelitian Interaksi Pers dengan Pejabat Pengambil Keputusan* (Research Report on the Interactions of the Press with Decision Makers), Proyek Penelitian dan Pengembangan Penerangan Deppen, Jakarta: Jakarta and P.T. Inscore.
Department of Information (1996/7) *Indonesia 1997: An Official Handbook*, Jakarta: Department of Information.
—— (1986) *The Process and Progress of Pancasila Democracy*, Jakarta: Department of Information RI.
—— (1982) *Indonesia 1981: An Official Handbook*, Jakarta: Department of Information.
Detak (22–28 Aug. 2000), 'Ya kartu pers, ya biro bisnis kartu pers' (Yes press card, yes business office for press cards), p. 21.
Dewan Pers (1974) *Lampiran Keputusan Dewan Pers No. 79/XIV/1974* (Appendix to Press Council Decision No. 79/XIV/1974).
Dhakidae, Daniel (1998) Head of research, *Kompas*, interview conducted in Jakarta, 20 Mar.
—— (1996a) 'Preliminary discussion', Sarasehan Rancangan Undang-Undang Statistik (Discussion on the Draft Law on Statistics) at Hotel Sari Pan Pacific, Jakarta, 15 Oct. 1966, pp. 7–10.
—— (1996b) 'Tantangan jiwa dan badan Rancangan Undang-undang Statistik' (The body and soul challenge of the Draft Law on Statistics), paper delivered to LP3ES's Sarasehan Rancangan Undang-undang Statistik (Discussion on the Draft Law on Statistics) at Hotel Sari Pan Pacific, Jakarta, 15 Oct. 1966, pp. 38–46.
—— (ed.) (1994) 'Perempuan dan profesi jurnalistik dalam perkembangan kelas tengah' (Women and the journalistic profession in the development of the middle class), in *Perempuan, Politik dan Jurnalisme: Tujuhpuluh Tahun Toety Azis* (Women, Politics and Journalism: Seventy Years of Toety Azis), Jakarta: Yayasan Padi dan Kapas, pp. 49–73.
—— (1993a) 'Social will, political demand, and public opinion: Political economy of Indonesian social research', paper presented to the Public Polling and Democracy conference, USIS American Cultural Center, Jakarta, 23 Jun.
—— (1993b) 'Negara dan ekonomi pers Indonesia' (The state and the Indonesian press economy), *Tajuk-Tajuk Dalam Terik Matahari: Empat Puluh Tahun Surabaya Post*,

eds Hotman M. Siahaan and Tjahjo Purnomo W., Surabaya: Yayasan Keluarga Bhakti, pp. 363–82.

—— (1991) 'The state, the rise of capital and the fall of political journalism: Political economy of Indonesian news industry', Ph.D. thesis, New York: Cornell University.

Diah, Herawati (1993) *Kembara Tiada Berakhir* (Wandering Without End), ed. Debra H. Yatim, Yayasan Keluarga, Jakarta.

Diener, Edward and Crandall, Rick (1978) *Ethics in Social and Behavioural Research*, Chicago: University of Chicago Press.

Dingwall, Robert (1983) 'Introduction', in *The Sociology of the Professions*, eds Robert Dingwall and Philip Lewis, New York: St Martin's Press, pp. 1–13.

Dixit, Kunda (1994) 'Global news: A view from the South', *Who's Telling the Story: A Conference on Media and Development in Australia and the Region*, Melbourne: Community Aid Abroad, pp. 20–5.

Djajadiningrat-Nieuwenhuis, Madelon (1992) 'Ibuism and priyayization: Path to power?', in *Indonesian Women in Focus*, eds Elsbeth Locher-Scholten and Anke Niehof, rev. edn, Leiden: KITLV Press, pp. 43–51.

Dodd, Tim (1999) 'Three-way struggle for power', *Indonesian Observer*, 8 Jun., p. 4.

D&R (28 Mar. 1998) 'Siapa sudi mendengar mahasiswa?', (Who will agree to hear the students?), pp. 26–7.

—— (7 Mar. 1998) 'Seorang presiden di tengah krisis' (A president in the midst of crisis), pp. 21–5.

Effendi, Onong Uchjana (1993) *Ilmu, Teori dan Filsafat Komunikasi* (The Science, Theory and Philosophy of Communication), Bandung: Citra Aditya Bakti.

Eldridge, Philip J. (1995) *Non-Government Organizations and Democratic Participation in Indonesia*, Kuala Lumpur: Oxford University Press.

Elison, Eddi (1995) 'Konglomerat dan pers' (Conglomerates and the press), *Tiras*, vol. 1, no. 38, 19 Oct., p. 40.

Elly, B., Novie, Handrini Ardiyanti and Eryoen, (1995) 'PWI dan Korporatisme Orde Baru', *Opini*, vol. 11, no. 18, pp. 45–9.

Elshtain, Jean B. (1981) *Public Man, Private Woman: Women in Social and Political Thought*, Princeton, New Jersey: Princeton University Press.

Emmerson, Donald K. (1978) 'Bureaucracy in political context: Weakness in strength', in *Political Power and Communications in Indonesia*, eds Karl D. Jackson and Lucian W. Pye, Berkeley: University of California Press, pp. 82–136.

Endah, W.S. and Hermien Y. Kleden (22 Jan. 2001) 'Sinta Nuriya Abdurrahman Wahid: "Many religious interpretations discriminate against women"', *Tempo English Edition*, Jan., pp. 68–71.

Ericson, Richard V., Baranek, Patricia M. and Chan, Janet B.L. (1989) *Negotiating Control: A Study of News Sources*, Milton Keynes, England: Open University Press.

Fajar 15 May, (1996) 'Pernyataan Ketua BP7 Pusat dinilai keliru' (The statement of the Central BP7 Chairman is considered wrong), p. 2.

Fehring, Ian and Lindsey, Timothy (1995) *Indonesian Labour Law Under the New Order: The Military and Prospects for Change*, Centre for Employment and Labour Relations Law, Nathan, Brisbane: Griffith University.

Feith, Herbert (1963) 'The dynamics of Guided Democracy', in *Indonesia*, ed. Ruth McVey, New Haven: Yale University, pp. 309–410.

—— (1962) *The Decline of Constitutional Democracy in Indonesia*, Ithaca, New York: Cornell University Press.

Fetterman, David M. (1989) *Ethnography: Step by Step*, Newbury Park, California: Sage.

Firmansyah, Agung, Luthfie, Nukman, Lewa, Arfan Arsyad and Nurhayati, Irma (1991) 'Pijar-Pijar *Pelita*' (*Pelita*'s glow), *Prospek*, 10 Aug., p. 29.

Fishman, Mark (1980) *Manufacturing the News*, Austin: University of Texas Press.

Forum Keadilan (23 Dec.1993) 'Pers Indonesian bukan watchdog' (The Indonesian press is not a watchdog), vol. II, no. 18, p. 28.

Freidson, Eliot (1983) 'The theory of the professions: State of the art', in *The Sociology of the Professions*, eds Robert Dingwall and Philip Lewis, New York: St Martin's Press, pp. 19–37.

—— (1977) 'The futures of professionalisation', in *Health and the Division of Labor*, ed. Margaret Stacey, Margaret Reid, Christian Hath and Robert Dingwall, London: Croom Helm Ltd, pp. 14–40.

Freire, Paulo (1997) *Pedagogy of the Oppressed*, rev. 20th anniversary edn, New York: Continuum Publishing.

—— (1974) 'Conscientisation – unveiling and transforming reality', in *Education for Liberation and Community*, Melbourne: Australian Council of Churches, pp. 3–6.

Friel, Terry (1995) Former Indonesia correspondent, Australian Associated Press, telephone interview from Canberra, 6 Sept.

Gaffar, Afan (1992) *Javanese Voters: A Case Study of Election Under a Hegemonic Party System*, Yogyakarta: Gadjah Mada University Press.

Gall, Peter (1996) 'What really matters – human developpment' in *The Political Economy of Development and Underdevelopment*, 6th edn, eds Charles K. Wilber and Kenneth P. Jameson, Singapore: McGraw-Hill, McGraw-Hill, pp. 530–8.

Galtung, Johan and Vincent, Richard C. (1992) *Toward a New World Information and Communication Order?*, Cresskill, New Jersey: Hampton Press.

Gans, Herbert (1979) *Deciding What's News*, New York: Pantheon.

Garcia, Eduardo José (1993) 'The Mexican Press Today', *Dollars, Development and Human Rights: The New Media Challenge* (eds) Peter Desbarats, Robert Henderson and Madeleine Cote, Graduate School of Journalism, London, Ontario: University of Western Ontaria, pp. 46–50.

Geertz, Clifford (1963) *Agricultural Involution*, Berkeley: University of California Press.

Geertz, Hildred (1961) *The Javanese Family: A Study of Kinship and Socialization*, USA: Free Press of Glencoe.

Gelman Taylor, Jean (1989) 'A new edition of Kartini's letters', *ASAA Review*, vol 13, no 2, Nov., pp. 156–60.

Gintini, Tuti (1992) 'Dilema wartawan, mengejar berita atau uang' (Journalists' dilemma, to chase news or money), *Suara Pembaruan*, 9 Feb., pp. 1, 16.

Goenawan, Andrew (1987) 'The Indonesian press, Indonesian journalism and guided democracy', in *The Indonesian Press: Its Past, Its People, Its Problems*, ed. Paul Tickell, Glen Waverley, Victoria: Aristoc Press, pp. 15–19.

Goh, Angela (1998) 'Suharto on how press could have helped the people cope with crunch', *Straits Times*, 18 Jan., p. 4.

Gojek Joko Santosa (1996) 'Makna politis kelahiran PWI' (The political purpose of the PWI's birth), *Suara Merdeka*, 8 Feb., p. 2.

Goulet, Denis (1996) (1971) '"Development" ... or liberation?' in *The Political Economy of Development and Underdevelopment*, 6th edn, eds Charles K. Wilber and Kenneth P. Jameson, Singapore: McGraw-Hill, pp. 543–50.

Greenlees, Don (2000) 'Big brother hands over the power to little sister', *The Weekend Australian*, 12–13 Aug., p. 10.

—— (1998) 'Habibie feels lash of unshackled press', *The Australian*, 8 June, p. 7.

Griffin, Keith and Knight, John (1996) (1989) 'Human development: The case for renewed emphasis', in *The Political Economy of Development and Underdevelopment*, 6th edn, eds Charles K. Wilber and Kenneth P. Jameson, Singapore: McGraw-Hill, pp. 610–39.

Habito-Cadiz, Maria Celeste (1996) 'The changing media environment', in *Asian Values in Journalism*, ed. Murray Masterton, Singapore: AMIC, pp. 102–8.

Hachten, William A. (1987) *The Third World News Prism: Changing Media, Clashing Ideologies*, 2nd edn, Ames: Iowa State University Press.

Hadi, Parni (1998) Secretary-general, PWI, interviews conducted in Jakarta, 30 Mar. and 27 Apr.

Hadiz, Vedi R. (1997) 'State and labour in the early New Order', in *State and Labour in New Order Indonesia*, ed. Rod Lambert, University of Western Australia Press and Asia Research Centre, Western Australia: Murdoch University, pp. 23–55.

—— (1993) 'Workers and working class politics in the 1990s', in *Indonesia Assessment 1993: Labour: Sharing the Benefits of Growth*, eds Chris Manning and Joan Hardjono, Department of Political and Social Change, Canberra: Australian National University, pp. 186–200.

Hafidz, Wardah (1992) 'Gerakan perempuan dulu, sekarang, dan sumbangannya kepada transformasi bangsa' (The women's movement then, [and] now and its contributions to transformation of the nation), in *Dinamika Gerakan Perempuan di Indonesia* (The Dynamics of the Women's Movement in Indonesia), ed. Fauzie Ridjal, Lusi Margiyani and Agus Fahri Husein 1993, Perpustakaan Yayasan Hata, Yogyakarta, Lembaga Studi and Pembangunan Perempuan and Anak, Jakarta: Yogyakarta and Friedrich Ebert Stiftung.

Hagen, Everett E. (1962) *On the Theory of Social Change*, Homewood, Illinois: Dorsey Press.

Hall, Stuart, Critcher, Chas, Jefferson, Tony, Clarke, John and Roberts, Brian (1978) *Policing the Crisis: Mugging, the State, and Law and Order*, Houndmills, Hampshire: Macmillan Education Ltd.

Haq, Mahbub ul (1995) *Reflections on Human Development*, New York: Oxford University Press.

Harian Kami (22 Jan.1970) 'Menpen bilang: Pers Indonesia belum dewasa' (The Information Minister says: The Indonesian press is not yet mature), 22 Jan., p.2.

—— (7 Jul.1969) 'Wartawan-2 daerah pahami sikap PWI-Djaya', (Regional journalists understand the attitude of the PWI-Greater Jakarta), p. 1.

—— (5 Jul.1969) 'Tentang "wartawan" amplop' (About envelope 'journalists'), 5 Jul., p.1.

—— (7 Jun.1969) 'Menpen mengenai keanggotaan PWI', (Information Minister on PWI membership), p. 1.

Harian Umum AB (1 Aug.1985) 'Penerangan kepada masyarakat perlu diberikan secara cepat dan tepat' (Information to the community needs to be given quickly and precisely'), pp. 1, 7.

—— (3 Mar.1982) 'Kurangnya penerangan bisa menyebabkan masyarakat menjadi apatis'" (Lack of information can cause the community to become apathetic), p. 8.

—— (15 Mar.1979) 'Sekitar pernyataan Pangkopkamtib tentang status wartawan' (About the statement of the Kompkamtib head on the status of journalists), pp. 1, 2.

—— (8 Mar.1979) 'Wartawan supaya bentuk serikat buruh' (Journalists aim to form journalists' union), pp. 1, 8.

Hariyati, M.T., (1995) 'Pandangan faham integralistik Indonesia' (An observation on Indonesia's integralistic concept), paper delivered at a meeting of Coordinators of *Pancasila* lecturers, Semarang, 4 Dec.

Harmoko, (1997) press conference, Jakarta, 13 Feb.

Hartowardojo, Harijadi S. (1969) 'Bravo, PWI Djaya' (Bravo, PWI Greater Jakarta branch), *Sinar Harapan*, 26 Jun., p. 3.

Haryanto, Ignatius (1998) 'Ketenagakerjaan dalam industri pers' (The workforce in the press industry), unedited draft of an article subsequently published, in abbreviated version in *Kompas*, 9 Feb., pp. 4–5.

Haryanto and Toha (1993) 'Kongres tanpa jago ABRI' (Congress without ABRI sponsorship), *Forum Keadilan*, vol. 2, no. 17, 9 Dec., p. 70.

Hasbullah, Jousairi (1999) 'Dominasi "Intelektual Musiman"' (The Domination of 'Seasonal Intellectuals'), *Republika*, 6 Jul., p. 6.

Hasibuan, Adaham (1957) 'Genesis of a press: Economic aspects of the national press in Indonesia', *Gazette*, no. 3, pp. 29–46.

Hasjim, Jusuf (1979) 'Duduknya ABRI dalam Golkar menimbulkan keraguan' (ABRI's position in Golkar creates reservations), *Prisma*, vol. 8, no. 8, pp. 63–6.

Hasnain, Imtiaz (1988) 'Communication: An Islamic approach', in *Communication Theory: The Asian Perspective*, ed. Wimal Dissanayake, Singapore: AMIC, pp. 183–9.

Hassan, Asnawi (1987) *Legal Bases for Cooperative Development in Indonesia*, Department of Cooperatives, Jakarta: Jakarta and Friedrich Ebert Stiftung.

Hastuti, Rita Sri, Gantra, Maman and Almayan, Reno (1988a) 'Serikat (baru) dalam pers?' ((New) union in the press?), *Editor*, vol. 1, no. 26, pp. 67–8.

—— (1988b) 'Wartawan menggugat' (Journalist makes claim), *Editor*, vol. 1, no. 26, p. 68.

Hawkins, Everett D. (1963) 'Labor in transition' in *Indonesia*, ed. Ruth McVey, New Haven: Yale University, pp. 248–71.

Head, Sydney W. (1963) 'Can a journalist be a "professional" in a developing country?' *Journalism Quarterly*, vol. 40, no. 4, pp. 594–8.

Hedebro, Göran (1982) *Communication and Social Change in Developing Nations: A Critical View*, Ames, Iowa: Iowa State University Press.

Hegel, Georg W.F. (1977) (1807) *Phenomenology of Spirit*, trans. A.V. Miller, Oxford: Oxford University Press.

—— (1942) (1821) *Philosophy of Right*, trans. T.M. Knox, Oxford: Oxford University Press.

Henningham, John (1996) 'Australian journalists' professional and ethical values', *Journalism and Mass Communication Quarterly*, vol. 73, no. 1, Spring, pp. 206–18.

Herman, Edward S. (1986) 'Gatekeeper versus propaganda models: A critical American perspective', in *Communicating Politics: Mass Communications and the Political Process*, eds P. Golding, G. Murdock and P. Schlesinger, New York: Holmes and Meier, pp. 171–95.

—— and Chomsky, Noam (1988) *Manufacturing Consent: A Political Economy of the Mass Media*, New York: Random House.

Heryanto, Ariel (1996) Columnist and lecturer, Satya Wacana Christian University, interview conducted in Salatiga, 6 Apr.

—— (1990) 'State ideology and civil discourse', in *State and Civil Society in Indonesia*, ed. Arief Budiman, Centre for Southeast Asian Studies, Clayton, Victoria: Monash University, pp. 289–300.

Hester, Albert L. (1987) 'The role of the Third World journalist', in *Handbook for Third World Journalists*, eds Albert L. Hester and Wai Lan J. To, Athens, Georgia: University of Georgia, pp. 5–12.

Hidayat, Komaruddin (1993) 'Sosok Kartini tanpa publikasi' (Kartini's frame without publication), in *Kembara Tiada Berakhir* (Wandering Without End), ed. Debra H. Yatim, Jakarta: Yayasan Keluarga, pp. xv–xix.

Higgott, Richard and Robison, Richard (eds) (1985) 'Theories of development and underdevelopment: Implications for the study of Southeast Asia', in *Southeast Asia: Essays in the Political Economy of Structural Change*, London: Routledge and Kegan Paul, pp. 16–61.

Hill, David T. (1995) *The Press in New Order Indonesia*, rev. edn, Jakarta: PT Pustaka Sinar Harapan.

—— (1990) 'Publishing within political parameters', *Inside Indonesia*, no. 23, Jun., pp. 16–17.

—— (1987) 'Press challenges, government responses', in *The Indonesian Press: Its Past, Its People, Its Problems*, ed. Paul Tickell, Glen Waverley, Victoria: Aristoc Press, pp. 21–38.

—— and Krisna Sen, (1991) 'How Jakarta saw the massacre', *Inside Indonesia*, no. 29, Dec., pp. 6–8.

Hoyle, Eric and John, Peter D. (1995) *Professional Knowledge and Professional Practice*, London: Cassell.

Hughes, Everett C. (1958) *Men and Their Work*, Glencoe, Illinois: Free Press.

Hull, Valerie J. (1996) 'Women in Java's rural middle class: Progress or regress', in *Women of Southeast Asia*, rev. edn, ed. Penny van Esterik, Centre for Southeast Asian Studies, Illinois: North Illinois University, pp. 78–95.

Human Rights Watch/Academic Freedom Committee (1998) 'HRW urges Indonesian government to dismantle barriers to academic freedom', 28 May. From http://www.hrw.org/hrw/press98/may/indo0528.htm.

Human Rights Watch/Asia (1995) 'Soeharto retaliates against critics: Official reactions to demonstrations in Germany', public statement released 10 May.

—— (1994) *The Limits of Openness: Human Rights in Indonesia and East Timor*, New York: Human Rights Watch.

Huntington, Samuel P. (1968) *Political Order in Changing Societies*, New Haven: Yale University Press.

Hutabarat, Saur (1993) 'Kemandirian pers dalam era industry dan kebudayaan birokrasi' (Autonomy of the press in the era of industry and bureaucratic culture), *Tajuk-Tajuk Dalam Terik Matahari: Empat Puluh Tahun Surabaya Post*, eds Hotman M. Siahaan and Tjahjo Purnomo W., Surabaya: Yayasan Keluarga Bhakti, pp. 455–66.

Hyland, Tom (1995) Former Indonesia correspondent, Australian Associated Press, telephone interview conducted from Melbourne, 7 Aug.

Idid, Syed Arabi and Pawanteh, Latiffah (1989) 'Media, ethnicity and national unity: A Malaysian report', *Media Asia*, vol.16, no. 2, pp. 78–85.

Ikki, Kita (1958) 'Plan for the reorganization of Japan', in *Japan 1931-1945: Militarism, Fascism, Japanism?*, ed. Ivan Morris 1963, Boston: D.C. Heath and Co., pp. 20–5.

Index on Censorship (1994) 'Indonesia', vol. 23, no. 4-5, p. 241.

—— (1975) 'Indonesia', vol. 3, no. 3, pp. 82–3.

Indoc (1986) *Indonesian Workers and Their Right to Organise: May 1986 Update*, Leiden: Indoc.

—— (1984) *Indonesian Workers and Their Right to Organise: March 1984 Update*, Leiden: Indoc.

—— (1981) *Indonesian Workers and Their Right to Organise*, Leiden: Indoc.

Indonesian Observer (15 Jul. 1998) 'Journalist licensing plan under fire', p. 2.

Inside Indonesia Jul.–Sept. (1996) 'Feminism is a choice of life', no 47, p. 12.

Institut Studi Arus Informasi (1996) *ABRI Punya Golkar?* (ABRI owns Golkar?), eds Santoso, Togi Simanjuntak and Ponco S. Widodo, Jakarta: ISAI.

International Commission of Jurists (1987) *Indonesia and the Rule of Law: Twenty Years of the 'New Order' Government*, ed. Hans Thoolen, London: Frances Pinter.

Isham, Jonathon, Kaufmann, Daniel and Pritchett, Lant H. (1997) 'Civil liberties, democracy, and the performance of government projects', *The World Bank Economic Review*, vol. 11, no. 2, pp. 219–42.

Iskan, Dahlan (1999) 'Serikat pekerja dan pers Indonesia lima tahun mendatang', *Tetap Independen*, Jakarta: Aliansi Jurnalis Independen, pp. 51–60.

Ismail, Abdul Samad (1994) 'Defining the issues', in *Asian Values in Journalism*, ed. Murray Masterton, Singapore: AMIC, pp. 10–14.

Ismail, Suwiryo (1998) 'Marginalisasi pers: Kebebasan berkomunikasi yang macet' (Marginalisation of the press: Blocked freedom of communication), *Kompas*, 21 Jan., p. 5.

Jackson, Karl D. (1978a) 'Implications of structure and culture in Indonesia', *Political Power and Communications in Indonesia*', eds Karl D. Jakson and Lucian W. Pye, Berkeley: University of California Press, pp. 23–42.

—— (1978b) 'Urbanization and patron-client relationships', in *Political Power and Communications in Indonesia*', eds Karl D. Jackson and Lucian W. Pye, Berkeley: University of California Press, pp. 374–5.

Jakarta Jakarta, (24 Jul.1987a) 'Negosiasi Jakarta-London' (Jakarta-London negotiations), pp. 4–5.

—— (24 Jul.1987b) 'Kecil Itu Besar' (Small is Big), p. 13.

Jakarta Post, (10 Feb. 2001) 'Megawati calls on media to create calm', p. 2.

—— (5 Jan. 2001) 'Beware of frauds posing as journalists, warn police', p. 3.

—— (14 Feb. 2000) 'Gus Dur told to be more thorough in building democracy', p. 2.

—— (8 Feb. 2000) 'President asked to curtail his controversial statements', p. 2.

—— (6 Feb. 1999) 'Yunus unafraid of abuse of press freedom', p. 2.

—— (6 Jan.1999a) 'President worried about press freedom', p. 1.

—— (6 Jan.1999b) 'Golkar wants to maintain ABRI's support', p. 1.

—— (5 Jan.1999) 'Golkar sticks to guns on civil servants in politics', p. 2.

—— (5 Aug.1998a) 'ABRI "must trim political role", says Yudhoyono', p. 2.

—— (5 Aug.1998b) 'Journalists' union vows to uphold independent stance', p. 2.

—— (24 Jul.1998) 'Habibie failing to win over the hearts of the people', p. 2.

—— (3 Jun.1998) 'Journalists welcome advent of press freedom', p. 2.

—— (20 Apr.1998) 'Reporters angry with regent', p. 2.

—— (17 Mar.1998) 'Call her "Ibu" Tutut now: Subiakto warns', p. 1.

—— (16 Sept.1997) 'PWI condemns individual "journalists" for extortion', p. 2.

—— (13 Feb.1997) 'Media told to use own spectacles', p. 1.

—— (5 Oct.1995) 'Journalists continue with plan to sue mayor', p. 2.

—— (29 Sept.1995) 'Harmoko warns of latent communist danger', p. 2.

—— (5 Jul.1995) 'Cultural norms slow growth of professionalism', p. 2.

—— (16 Jan.1995) 'Beware of phony journalists', p. 3.

Japan Ministry of Education (1937) 'The unique national polity (Kokutai no Hongi)', in *Japan 1931–1945: Militarism, Fascism, Japanism?*, ed. Ivan Morris, Boston: 1963, D.C. Heath and Co., pp. 46–52.

Jenkins, David (1994) former Indonesia correspondent, *Far Eastern Economic Review* and foreign editor, *Sydney Morning Herald*, telephone interview conducted from Sydney, 26 Oct.

—— (1986) 'Indonesia: Government attitudes towards the domestic and foreign media', *Australian Outlook*, vol. 40, no.3, pp. 155–61.

—— (1984) *Suharto and His Generals: Indonesian Military Politics, 1975–1983*, Ithaca, New York: Cornell Modern Indonesia Project.

Jhamtani, Hira (1991) 'Redefining feminism as the women's movement', *Asian Studies Review*, vol. 15, no. 1, Jul., pp. 96–100.

Johanson, Vanessa (2001) 'Out in front', *Inside Indonesia*, no. 66, Apr.–Jun., pp. 4–5.

Johnson, Terence J. (1972) *Professions and Power*, London: Macmillan.

Kabar dari Pijar (1995) 'Soeharto a king? TASS demurrer rejected, trial to be continued', Jul., no. 7. From apakabar@clark.net.

Kahin, George McTurnan (1952) *Nationalism and Revolution in Indonesia*, Ithaca, New York: Cornell University Press.

Kakiailatu, Toeti (1997) *B.M. Diah: Wartawan Serba Bisa* (B.M.Diah: The Versatile Journalist), Jakarta: Pustaka Sinar Harapan.

Kakiailatu, Toeti (1994) 'Berubah pandang setelah APEC' (A change of opinion after APEC), *Gatra*, 26 Nov., p. 71.

Kartanegara, E.H. (1989) 'Amplop, obat untuk wartawan' (Envelopes, the cure for journalists), *Kompas*, 9 Feb., pp. 4–5.

Kartowijono, Sujatin (1976) 'The awakening of the women's movement in Indonesia', in *Indonesian Women: Some Past and Current Perspectives*, ed. B.B. Hering, Brussels: Centre d'Etude du Sud Est Asiatique et de l'Extreme Orient, pp. 3–19.

Kaufman, Daniel, Kraay, Aart and Zoido-Lobatón, Pablo (1999) *Governance Matters: World Bank Policy Research Working Paper No. 2196*, Washington: World Bank.

Kausikan, Bilahari (1994) 'Human rights: Asia's different stand', *Media Asia*, vol. 21, no. 1, pp. 45–51.

Kelly, Paul (1998) 'B.J. in a bind', *The Weekend Australian*, 8–9 Aug., p. 23.

Khaiyath, Nuim (1996) 'Red is nice but blue's better', paper presented to Communications With-In Asia, 20th Anniversary Conference of the Asian Studies Association of Australia, LaTrobe University, Melbourne, 4–6 Jul. Records lodged in the National Library of Australia, Canberra.

Khamami 2000, 'Ironi demokrasi bagi perempuan' (The irony of democracy for women'), *Media Indonesia*, 25 Nov., p. 4.

King, Seth S. (1966) 'Indonesian press becomes more daring as curbs are eased', *New York Times*, 12 Apr., p. 12.

Kingsbury, Damien (1992) 'Agendas in Indonesian responses to Australian journalism: Some journalists' perspectives', *Australian Journalism Review*, vol. 14, no. 2, pp. 58–67.

Kitley, Philip (2000) *Television, Nationa, and Culture in Indonesia*, Athens, Ohio: Ohio University Press.

Knach, Steven and Keefer, Philip (1995) 'Institutions and economic performance: Cross country tests using alternative institutional measures', *Economics and Policies*, vol. 7, no. 3, pp. 220–7.

KNI (22 Oct.1975) 'Serikat2 buruh sekarang tidak dapat di asosiasikan dengan jaman dulu' (Present workers' unions cannot associate with the past era), *Kantorberita Nasional Indonesia*, no. 295A, pp. 10–11.

—— (21 Oct.1975) 'Wartawan dan buruh percetakan adalah saudara kembar' (Journalists and print workers are twins), *Kantorberita Nasional Indonesia*, no. 294B, pp. 8–9.

Koentjaraningrat (1980) 'Javanese terms for God and the idea of power', in *Man, Meaning and History: Essays in Honour of H.G. Schulte Nordholt*, ed. R. Scheford, J.W. Schoorl and J. Tennekes, The Hague: Martinus Nijhoff, pp. 127–39.

Koesworo, F.X., Margantoro, J.B. and Viko, Ronnie S. (1994) *Di Balik Tugas Kuli Tinta* (Behind the Journalist's Duties), Solo: Sebelas Maret University Press, and Yogyakarta: Yaysan Pustaka Nusatama.

Kompas (8 Feb. 2001) 'Akibat kehilangan kredibilitas tiras media cetak turun' (As result of the loss of credibility, print media circulations decline), p. 6.

—— (14 Sept. 1999) 'RUU Pers disepakati DPR: Pasal perlindungan wartawan dinilai tidak terlalu jelas', p. 11.

—— (7 Sept. 1999) 'Kepemilikan saham kolektif perlu diatur dalam undang-undang pers' (Ownership of collective shares needs to be administered in the press law), p. 6.

—— (2 Sept. 1999) 'RUU Pers atur pembagian saham dan laba perusahaan pers', p. 15.

—— (26 Aug. 1999) 'Pemasungan pers dalam RUU Keselamatan Negara: DPR harus beri perhatian' (Firing at the press in the Draft National Security Law: The DPR must give it attention), p. 15.

—— (11 Jun. 1999) 'Ghalib minta maaf' (Ghalib apologises), p. 3.

—— (9 Feb. 1999) 'Organisasi wartawan: Mau sejahtera atau profesional?' (Journalists' organisations: Do you want welfare or professionalism?), p. 1.

—— (27 Oct. 1998) 'AJI kritik Akbar Tandjung', p. 6.

—— (23 Oct. 1998a) 'PWI di mata mereka', p. 7.

—— (23 Oct. 1998b) 'PWI jangan ulangi kesalahan', p. 7.

—— (22 Jun. 1998) 'Industri pers terancam bangkrut' (Press industry threatened with bankruptcy), p. 1.

—— (18 Jun. 1998) '113 Juta penduduk miskin Indonesia' (113 million poor Indonesian citizens), p. 8.

—— (15 Jun. 1998) 'MA berniat pisahkan diri dari eksekutif' (Supreme Court aims to separate itself from the executive), p. 7.

—— (7 Jun. 1998) 'Habibie: Saya tidak perlu berbicara banyak' (Habibie: I don't need to talk much), p. 1.

—— (3 Jun. 1998) 'Reformasi media massa perlu diikuti professionalisme pers' (Mass media reform needs to be accompanied by press professionalism), p. 10.

—— (1 Jun. 1998) 'Gubernur diboikot wartawan' (Govenor boycotted by journalists), p. 11.

—— (26 May 1998) 'Mennaker: Serikat buruh boleh berdiri' (Manpower Minister: Labour unions permitted to form), p. 6.

—— (21 Apr. 1998) 'Statistik pengangguran membingungkan' (Unemployment statistics are confusing), p. 2.

—— (9 Apr. 1998) 'Wartawan masih dianggap hantu menakutkan' (Journalists are still considered frightening evil spirits), p. 3.

—— (20 Jan. 1997) 'Mengembangkan jurnalisme presisi lewat "polling"' (Developing precision journalism through 'polling'), p. 20.

—— (20 Sept. 1995) 'Wartawan "Kompas" gadungan berkeliaran di Riau' (Bogus '*Kompas*' journalist engages in illegal activities in Riau), p. 11.

—— (31 Aug. 1995) 'Tiga wartawan gadungan coba memeras' (Three bogus journalists try to blackmail), p. 8.

—— (16 Dec. 1994) 'Pers harus mampu mengimbangi tuntutan, dinamika masyarakat' (The press must be able to match the demands, dyamics of the community), p. 13.

—— (18 Nov. 1994) 'DPRD minta bupati tinjau kembali larangan memberi keterangan pers' (The DPRD requests the regent to review the ban on giving information to the press), p. 17.

—— (27 Sept. 1994) 'Budaya amplop sudah kronis' (The envelope culture is already chronic), p. 16.

—— (15 Oct. 1992) 'Gaya bahasa siaran pers, gaya bahasa pejabat' (The language of press releases is the language of officials), p. 12.

—— (2 May 1991) 'Wakil Kepala BPS: Distribusi pendapatan belum bisa dideteksi' (Deputy Chief of the BPS: Income distribution cannot yet be detected), p. 1.

—— (1 May 1991) 'Perbaikan terjada pada pemerataan absolut' (Improvement comes from absolutely even distribution), p. 1.

—— (29 Apr. 1991) 'Saiful Sulun: Pers tak bantu suarakan rakyat' (Saiful Sulun: The press does not help to express the voice of the people', p. 1.

—— (1990) 'Young professionals of Jakarta: Millions in salary, lack of hard work', in *The Politics of Middle Class Indonesia*, eds Richard Tanter and Kenneth Young, Centre for Southeast Asian Studies, Monash University, Clayton, Victoria, pp. 167–74.

Kompas Media Nusantara (2000) *Wajah Dewan Perwakilan Rakyat Republik Indonesia: Pemilihan Umum 1999* (The Face of the Republic of Indonesia People's Representative Council: 1999 General Elections), Jakarta: Kompas Media Nusantara.

Kompas Online (3 Jun. 1998) 'RI ready to ratify ILO Convention 87: Govt recognize SBSI'. From http://www.kompas.com/9806/03/ENGLISH/rire.htm.

Konsorsium Lembaga Pengumpul Pendapat Umum (2000), *Suara Raykat untuk Wakil Rakyat: Laporan Terakhir Survai Nasional Tentang Masalah Politik* (The Voice of the People for the People's Representatives: The Final Report of the National Survey on Political Problems), Jakarta: Konsorsium Lembaga Pengumpul Pendapat Umum, Sekretariat MPR RI, Sekretariat DPR RI and CSSP.

Kristanto, Tri Agung (2000) 'Atmakusumah Astraatmadja: "Jembatan" pers dan Masyarakat' (Atmakusumah Astraatmadja: A "bridge" between the press and the community), *Kompas*, 27 Jun., p. 12.

Kuhon, Albert (2001) Former *Kompas* journalist, former editor of *Jayakara*, former foreign correspondent with *Suara Pembaruan*, editor with SCTV, interview conducted in Jakarta, 12 Mar.

—— (1998) 'Upaya pemberayaan pekerja pers Indonesia' (Attempts at empowerment of Indonesian press workers), discussion panel paper at *Mencari Format Organisasi Insan Pers yang Ideal*, Jakarta Design Centre, Jakarta, 2 Jun.

Kunczcik, Michael (1988) *Concepts of Journalism: North and South*, Bonn: Friedrich-Ebert-Stiftun.

Kusnadi (1996) 'Wartawan dan sikap transparansi birokrat' (Journalists and bureaucratic transparency), *Angkatan Bersenjata*, 31 May, p. 4.

Kvale, Steiner (1996) *InterViews: An Introduction to Qualitative Research Interviewing*, Thousand Oaks, California: Sage.

Laksmana.net (21 Jun. 2001) 'Character assassination and criticism in the Indonesian media'. From http://www.laksamana.net/vnews.cfm?news_id=966

Lambert, Robert (ed.) (1997) 'Authoritarian state unionism in New Order Indonesia', in *State and Labour in New Order Indonesia*, University of Western Australia Press and Asia Research Centre, Western Australia: Murdoch University, pp. 56–82.

Lane, Max (1991) *'Openness', Political Discontent and Succession in Indonesia: Political Developments in Indonesia, 1989–91*, Australia Asia Papers, Nathan, Brisbane: Griffith University.

Larson, Magali Sarfatti (1977) *The Rise of Professionalism: A Sociological Analysis*, Berkeley: University of California Press.

Latief, A. (1980) *Pers di Indonesia di Zaman Pendudukan Jepang* (The Press in Indonesian in the Japanese-Occupation Era), Surabaya: Usana Offset.

Lawyers Committee for Human Rights (LCHR) and Institute for Policy Research and Advocacy (ELSAM) (1995) *In the Name of Development: Human Rights and the World Bank in Indonesia*, New York: LCHR.

Leclerc, Jacques (1972) 'An ideological problem of Indonesian trade unionism in the sixties: "Karyawan" versus "buruh"', *RIMA: Review of Indonesian and Malayan Studies*, vol 6, no. 1, pp. 76–91.

Legge, John D. (1988) *Intellectuals and Nationalism in Indonesia: A Study of the Following Recruited by Sutan Sjahrir in Occupation Jakarta*, Ithaca, New York: Cornell Modern University Project.

Leksono-Supelli, Karlina (1998), 'Pemerintah yang berdiri di atas darah perempuan' (Government based on the blood of women), *Jurnal Perempuan*, no. 8, Aug.–Oct, pp. 24–29.

Lele, Jayant and Tettey, Wisdom (1996) *Asia – Who Pays for Growth? Women, Environment and Popular Movements*, Aldershot: Dartmouth Publishing.

Lembaga Penelitian Pendidikan Penerbitan Yogyakarta (LP3Y) (1999), *Media dan Gender* (Media and Gender), Yogyakarta: LP3Y and Jakarta: Ford Foundation.

Lent, John A. (1979) *Topics in Third World Mass Communication: Rural and Development Journalism, Cultural Imperialism, Research and Development*, Hong Kong: Asian Research Service.

—— (1977) 'A Third World news deal? Part one: The guiding light', *Index on Censorship*, vol. 6, no. 5, Sept.–Oct., pp. 17–26.

Lerner, Daniel (1958) *The Passing of Traditional Society*, New York: Free Press.

Levine, Marvin J. (1997) *Worker Rights and Labor Standards in Asia's Four New Tigers: A Comparative Perspective*, New York: Plenum Press.

Liddle, R. William (1991) 'The relative autonomy of a Third World politician: Suharto and Indonesian economic development in comparative perspective', in *Leadership and Culture in Indonesian Politics*, 1996, Sydney: Allen and Unwin, pp. 107–40.

—— (1988) 'Politics and culture in Indonesia', in *Leadership and Culture in Indonesian Politics*, 1996, Sydney: Allen and Unwin, pp. 63–106.

—— (1985) 'Suharto's Indonesia: Personal rule and political institutions', in *Leadership and Culture in Indonesian Politics*, 1996, Sydney: Allen & Unwin, pp. 15–36.

Lim, Ivan (1985) 'The Singapore Press and the fourth estate', in Abdul Razak, *Press Laws and Systems in ASEAN States*, Jakarta: Garuda Metropolitan Press, pp. 101–18.

Lindsey, Tim (2001) 'State loses control over "preman"', *The Jakarta Post*, 19 Mar., p. 4.

Lingga, Heriyanto, Nurdiana, Titis and Wibawa, Satrija Budi (1998) 'Krisis ini membunuh pers sendiri' (This crisis is killing the press itself), *WartaEkonomi*, 16 Feb., pp. 12–13.

Lloyd, Genevieve (1984) *The Man of Reason: 'Male' and 'Female' in Western Philosophy*, London: Methuen.

Locher-Scholten, Elsbeth (1992) 'Female labour in twentieth century Java: European notions – Indonesian practice', in eds Elsbeth Locher-Scholten and Anke Niehof, *Indonesian Women in Focus*, rev. edn, Leiden: KITLV Press, pp. 77–103.

Loo, Eric (1996) 'Value formation in journalism education in Asia', in *Asian Values in Journalism*, ed. Murray Masterton, Singapore: AMIC, pp. 114–23.

—— (1995) 'Teaching community service reporting values as an identifiable component of Asian-centred journalism', Asian Values in Journalism Conference, Kuala Lumpur: AMIC, 24–25 Aug.

Loveard, Keith (1997) 'Playing the cheating game? Critics say Golkar employed overkill to win big', *Asiaweek*, 27 Jun., p. 24.

Lubis, Mochtar (1998) Former editor of *Indonesia Raya*, artist, author, historian and government critic, interview conducted in Jakarta, 10 Apr.

—— (1993) 'Berbagai persoalan pers Indonesia' (Various problems with the Indonesian press), *Jawa Pos*, 10 Feb., p. 111.

—— (1992) 'Etos pers Indonesia' (Indonesian press ethos), in *Visi Wartawan 45* (Vision of the '45 Journalists), Jakarta: Media Sejahtera, pp. 1–20.

—— (1989) 'Media massa dan bahasa yang terus terang' (The mass media and straightforward language), *Prisma*, vol. 23, no. 1, pp. 47–51.

—— (1980) *Catatan Subversif* (Subversive Notes), Jakarta: Sinar Harapan.

Lubis, Sofyan (2000) 'Benarkah UU Pers tidak melindungi pers?' (Is it true that the Press Law does not protect the press?), *Kompas*, 15 Feb., p. 4.

—— (1998) National chairman of the PWI for the 1993–8 term, interview conducted in Jakarta, 27 Mar.

Luwarso, Lukas (1999) 'AJI dalam transisi', *Tetap Independen*, Jakarta: Aliansi Jurnalis Independen, pp. 19–32.

McBeth, John (1995) Indonesia bureau chief, *Far Eastern Economic Review*, interview conducted in Jakarta, 4 Aug.

MacBride, Sean et al. (1980) *Many Voices, One World*, Report by the International Commission for the Study of Communications Problems, Unesco, London: Paris & Kogan Page.

MacDougall, John A. (1982) 'Patterns of military control in the Indonesian higher central bureaucracy', *Indonesia*, no. 33, Apr., pp. 89–121.

MacIntyre, Andrew (1994) 'Indonesia in 1993: Increasing political movement?', *Asian Survey*, vol. 34, no. 2, Feb., pp. 111–18.

McNair, Brian (1998) *The Sociology of Journalism*, London: Arnold.

McQuail, Denis (1987) *Mass Communication Theory: An Introduction*, 2nd edition, London: Sage Publications.

Mackie, Jamie (1993) 'Indonesia: Economic growth and depoliticization', in *Driven by Growth: Political Change in the Asia–Pacific Region*, ed. James W. Morely, New York: M.E. Sharpe, pp. 69–96.

Mohamad, Mahathir (1985) 'A prescription for a socially responsible press', *Media Asia*, vol. 12, no. 4, pp. 212–15.

Mahfud, Moh. (1993) *Demokrasi dan Konstitusi di Indonesia* (Democracy and Constitution in Indonesia), Liberty: Liberty.

Makarim, Nono Anwar (1978) 'The Indonesian press: An editor's perspective', in *Political Power and Communications in Indonesia*, eds Karl D. Jackson and Lucian W. Pye, Berkeley: University of California Press, pp. 259–81.

Malik, Adam (1974) 'State guide-lines journalists are duty-bound to follow', *IPI Report*, Aug., p. 11.

Manderson, Lenore (ed.) (1983) 'Introduction', in *Women's Work and Women's Roles: Economics and Everyday Life in Indonesia, Malaysia and Singapore*, Development Studies Centre, Canberra: Australian National University, pp. 1–14.

Mangunwijaya, Y.B. (1994) 'The Indonesia Raya dream and its impact on the concept of democracy', in *Democracy in Indonesia: 1950s and 1990s*, eds David Bourchier and John Legge, Centre of Southeast Asian Studies, Clayton, Victoria: Monash University, pp. 79–87.

Mann, Oliver (1998) Asia Officer, National Library of Australia, interview conducted in Jakarta, 3 Mar.

Manning, Chris (1998) *Indonesian Labour in Transition: An East Asian Success Story?*, Cambridge: Cambridge University Press.

Magno, Marcellino Ximenes (1998) Forum Demokrasi Wartawan Yogyakarta presidium chairman, Yogyakarta, 21 Apr.

Marpaung, August (1983) 'Antara – between Indonesia and the World', *Media Asia*, vol 10, no 1, pp. 27–30.

Maryadi 2001 'Minta uang ke jenderal, wartawan 'bodrex' ditangkap di DPR', (Asking for money from the generals, a 'bodrex' journalist is caught in the DPR'), *detik.com*, 9 May. From: www.detik.com/peristiwa/2001/05/09/200159-140416.shtml.

Masduki, Teten (1998) Head of Labour Division, YLBHI, interview conducted in Jakarta, 2 Apr.

Mascab, Mashuri (1999) 'Retorika untuk meraih simpati Islam', *Republika*, *Bidik* supplement, 4 Aug., p. 3.

Mas'oed, Mohtar (1994) *Negara, Kapital dan Demokrasi* (Nation, Capital and Democracy), Yogyakarta: Pustaka Pelajar.

Mattelart, Armand (1979) *Multinational Corporations and the Control of Culture*, Brighton: Harvester Press.

Mauro, Paolo (1995) 'Corruption and growth', *Quarterly Journal of Economics*, Aug., pp. 861–712.

Media Indonesia (4 Mar. 2001) 'Mega diingatkan agar waspada' (Mega is warned to be on her guard'), p. 1.

—— (5 Jan. 2001) 'Sedikit perempuan di eksekutif dan legislative' (Few women in the executive and legislature). From http://www.mediaindo.co.id/cetak/news.asp?id=2001010501115733.

Mehra, Achal (ed.) (1989) 'Introduction', *Press Systems in Asean States*, Singapore: AMIC, pp. 1–11.

Melkote, S.R. (1991) *Communication for Development in the Third World: Theory and Practice*, New Delhi: Sage.

Merdeka (12 Apr. 1999) 'Gubernur Jatim pukul wartawan hingga jatuh' (The East Timor Governor punches journalist to the ground), pp. 1, 8.

Merton, Robert (1982) *Social Research and the Practicing Professions*, Lanham: University Press of America.

Meuraxa, Ahmadi (2000) 'Mulai tuduhan ekslusif hingga konflik kepengurusan' (From accusations of being exclusive to being organisers of conflict), *6 Tahun AJI: Laporan Untuk Public* (6 Years of AJI: A Report for the Public), ed. Willy Pramudya, Jakarta: Aliansi Jurnalis Independen, pp. 36–9.

Mietzner, Marcus (2000) 'The 1999 General Session: Wahid, Megawati and the fight for the presidency', in *Indonesia in Transition: Social Aspects of Reformasi and Crisis*, eds Chris Manning and Peter van Diermen, Singapore: Institute of Southeast Asian Studies, pp. 39–57.

Milne, John (1989) 'Different views of press freedom', *Australian Foreign Affairs Record*, Aug., no. 57, pp. 446–49.

Muhaimin, Yahya (1980) 'Beberapa segi birokrasi di Indonesia' (Several facets of the bureaucracy in Indonesia), *Prisma*, vol 9, no. 10, pp. 21–7.

Muis, Abdul (1996) *Kontroversi Sekitar Kebebasan Pers: Bunga Rampai Masalah Komunikasi, Jurnalistik, Etika dan Hukum Press* (The Controversy Surrounding Press Freedom: An Anthology on the Problems of Communications, Journalism, Ethics and the Press Laws), East Jakarta: Mario Grafika.

Mulder, Niels (1989) *Individual and Society in Java: A Cultural Analysis*, Yogyakarta: Gadjah Mada University Press.

Mulya Lubis, Todung (1996) 'RUU statistik dalam perspektif politics of regularization',

Sarasehan Rancangan Undang-Undang Statistik (Discussion on the Draft Law on Statistics), transcript of LP3ES seminar at Hotel Sari Pan Pasific, Jakarta, 15 Oct. 1966, pp. 34–37.

—— (1993) *In Search of Human Rights: Legal–Political Dilemmas of Indonesia's New Order*, Jakarta: Gramedia.

Munir, Lily Zakiyah (ed.) (1999) *Memposisikan Kodrat: Perempuan dan Perubahan dalam Perspektif Islam* (Positioning God's Will: Women and Change in the Islamic Perspective), Bandung: Mizan.

Muntohar (1996) 'RUU Statistik: Sebuah pandangan praktis' (The Draft Statistics Law: A practical perspective), Sarasehan Rancangan Undang-Undang Statistik (Discussion on the Draft Law on Statistics), transcript of LP3ES seminar at Hotel Sari Pan Pasific, Jakarta, 15 Oct. 1966, pp. 50–3.

Murphy, Kevin (1989) 'This is the enemy?', *The Bulletin*, 28 Nov., pp. 58–64.

Murray, Eileen and Shohen, Saundra (1992) 'Lessons from the Tylenol tragedy on surviving a corporate crisis', *Medical Marketing and Media*, vol. 27, no. 2, Feb., pp. 14–15, 18–19.

Mydans, Seth (1998) 'Quietly, Indonesian says he's taken the reins', *New York Times*, 3 Jun., pp. 1, A6.

Nasution, Adnan Buyung (1993) 'Adakah hak asasi manusia di dalam UUD 1945?' (Are there human rights in the 1945 Constitution?), *Forum Keadilan*, no. 2, p. 67.

—— (1992) *The Aspiration for Constitutional Government in Indonesia: A Scoio-legal Study of the Indonesian Konstituante 1956–1959*, Jakarta: Sinar Harapan.

New Journalist Aug. (1982) 'Indonesia's unfree press', no. 39, pp. 21–3.

Ng'weno, Hilary (1978) 'All freedom is at stake', in *The Third World and Press Freedom*, ed. Philip C. Horton, New York: Praeger Publishers, pp. 127–34.

Ngurah Putra, Gusti (1997) Communications lecturer, Faculty of Social and Political Sciences, Gajah Mada University, interview conducted in Yogyakarta, 4 Apr.

Noerhadi, Toeti Heraty (1982) 'Women and self-image', *Prisma: The Indonesian Indicator*, no. 24, Mar., pp. 30–40.

Nordenstreng, Kaarle (1986) 'The rise and life of the concept', in *New International Information and Communication Order*, eds Kaarle Nordenstreng, Enrique Gonzales Manet and Wolfgang Keinwächter, Prague: International Organisation of Journalists, pp. 9–60.

Notosusanto, Nugroho, Tambunan, A.S.S., Soebijono and Mukmin, Hidayat (1985) *Pejuang dan Prajurit*, ed. Nugroho Notosusanto, Jakarta: Sinar Harapan.

Nurbaiti, Ati (2000) 'Laporan perkembangan wilayah Jawa Barat, Jakarta' (Report on developments in East Java, Jakarta), *6 Tahun AJI: Laporan Untuk Public* (6 Years of AJI: A Report for the Public), ed. Willy Pramudya, Jakarta: Aliansi Jurnalis Independen, pp. 32–5.

Nurdi, Herry (8 Mar. 2001) 'Justice Party only upholds the Constitution', *The Jakarta Post*, p. 8.

Oetama, Jakob (1989) 'The press and society', in *Press Systems in ASEAN States*, ed. Achal Mehra, Singapore: AMIC, pp. 135–44.

Oey Hong Lee (1971) *Indonesian Government and Press During Guided Democracy*, Switzerland: Inter Documentation Company AG Zug.

Okin, Susan M. (1979) *Women in Western Political Thought*, Princeton: Princeton University Press.

Orentlicher, Diane F. (1988) *Human Rights in Indonesia and East Timor*, New York: Asia Watch Committee.

Ortner, Sherry (1974) 'Is male to female as nature is to culture?', *Women, Culture and Society*, eds Michelle Zimbalist Rosaldo and Louise Lamphere, New Haven: Yale University Press, pp. 67–87.

Osiel, Mark J. (1986) 'The professionalization of journalism: Impetus or impediment to a "watchdog" press', *Sociological Inquiry*, no. 56, Spring, pp. 163–89.

Pabotinggi, Mochtar (1995) 'Indonesia', in *Political Legitimacy in Southeast Asia: The Quest for Moral Authority*, ed. Muthiah Alagappa, Stanford: Stanford University Press, pp. 224–56.

Pangaribuan, Luhut (1996) 'Kata pengantar' (Foreword), in *Jurnalis Independen Diadili: Pledoi Tiga Terpidana* (Independent Journalists Brought to Trial: The Defence of the Three Accused), Jakarta: Lembaga Bantuan Hukum Jakarta and AJI, pp. xi–xiii.

Pantau (2000) 'Sensor: Laskar Jihad menolak wartawan perempuan' (Censor: Holy War Soldiers refuse female journalists), no. 9, p. 79.

Paradigma and Koordinator Komisariat Gerakan Mahasiswa Nasional Indonesia (1996) *Hasil Polling Pendapat Karakteristik dan Sikap Politik Wartawan di Daerah Istemewah Yogyakarta* (Results of Opinion Polling on the Characteristics and Political Opinions of Journalists in the Special District of Yogyakarta), Yogyakarta: Paradigma.

Pedoman Rakyat 15 May (1996) 'Pers Pancasila merupakan paradigma baru' (The *Pancasila* press forms a new paradigm), p. 2.

Pelita 21 Sept. (1984) 'Menpen tentang pelaksanaan SIUPP: Perusahaan pers harus berasaskan kekeluargaan dan kebersamaan' (Information Minister about the implementation of SIUPP: Press companies must be based on family orientation and togetherness), p. 1.

Penders, C.L.M. and Sundhaussen, Ulf (1985) *Abdul Haris Nasution: A Political Biography*, St. Lucia, Queensland: University of Queensland Press.

Perkin, Harold (1989) *The Rise of Professional Society*, London: Routlege.

Philliber, Susan G., Schwab, Mary R. and Sloss, G. Sam (1980) *Social Research*, Itasca, Illinois: Peacock.

Platzdasch, Bernhard (2000) 'Islamic reaction to a female president', in *Indonesia in Transition: Social Aspects of Reformasi and Crisis*, eds Chris Manning and Peter van Diermen, Singapore: Institute of Southeast Asian Studies, pp. 336–49.

Political and Economic Risk Consultancy (PERC) (1998) 'Shortcomings of the media in Asia'. From http://www.asiarisk.com/library9.htm.

Polglaze, Karen (1998) 'Military admits blame for activists' disappearance', Australian Associated Press, 29 Jun.

Ponteñila, Roberto (1990) 'Development communication and total human development', in *Monograph on Development Communication*, ed. Fely Imperial-Soledad, Manila: Communication Foundation for Asia Media Group, pp. 19–33.

Pool, Ithiel de Sola (1963) 'The mass media and politics in the modernization process', in *Communications and Political Development*, ed. Lucian W. Pye, Princeton: Princeton University Press, pp. 234–53.

Pranowo, M. Bambang (1990) 'Which Islam and which *Pancasila*? Islam and the state in Indonesia: A comment', in *State and Civil Society in Indonesia*, ed. Arief Budiman, Centre of Southeast Asian Studies, Melbourne: Monash University, pp. 479–502.

Price, Matt (1998) 'Talks the talk, walks the walk but ...', *The Australian*, 27 May, p. 9.

Prisma: The Indonesian Indicator Sept. (1985) 'On the multiple effects', no 37, p. 2.

Pudjomartono, Susanto (1998) 'Indonesia', in *Walking the Tightrope: Press Freedom and Professional Standards in Asia*, ed. Asad Latif, Singapore: AMIC, pp. 102–7.

—— (1996) Editor in Chief, *The Jakarta Post*, interview conducted in Jakarta, 25 Nov.

Purba, Kornelius (2001) 'Managing the military goes beyond maintaining loyalty', *The Jakarta Post*, 20 Mar., p. 4.

PWI Jaya, (1996) 'PWI Jaya imbau aparat dan masyarakat: Waspadai wartawan gudungan' (The PWI Greater Jakarta branch appeals to government apparatus and community: Be on guard for fake journalists), *Buletin PWI Jaya*, vol. 4, no. 37, pp. 1, 5.

PWI (1995) *Peraturan Dasar, Peraturan Rumah Tangga dan Kode Etik Jurnalistik Persatuan Wartawan Indonesia* (The Charter, Bylaws and Journalism Code of Ethics of the Indonesian Journalists' Association), Jakarta: Gatra & PWI Pusat.

—— (ed.) (1955a) 'Code of ethics of "Persatuan Wartawan Indonesia"', in *Code dan Ethiek Djurnalistik* (The Code and Ethics of Journalism), Jakarta: Pengurus Pusat PWI, pp. 55–8.

—— (ed.) (1955b) 'Constitution of "Persatuan Wartawan Indonesia"', in *Code dan Ethiek Djurnalistik* (The Code and Ethics of Journalism), Jakarta: Pengurus Pusat PWI, pp. 73–7.

Pye, Lucian W. (ed.) (1963) *Communications and Political Development*, Princeton: Princeton University Press.

Quebral, Nora C. (1975) 'Development communication: Where does it stand today?', *Media Asia*, vol. 2, no. 4, pp. 197–202.

Radek, Karl (1934) 'Can the reactionary-chauvinist movement in Japan be called fascist?', in *Japan 1931–1945: Militarism, Fascism, Japanism?*, ed. Ivan Morris 1963, Boston: D.C. Heath & Co., pp. 26–35.

Raffles, Thomas Stamford (1978) (1817) *The History of Java*, vol. I, Kuala Lumpur: Oxford University Press.

Raharti, Sri and Panggabean, Wahyudi El (1996) 'Setuhun buat wartawan palsu' (The year of fake journalists), *Forum Keadilan*, vol. 5, no. 2, p. 34.

Rahayu, Ruth Indah (1999), 'Pola kekerasan berbasis gender di Indonesia' (Patterns of violence based on gender in Indonesia), *Jurnal Perempuan*, no. 9, Nov. 1998–Jan. 1999, pp. 10–17.

Rahmanto, Wahid, Pareanom, Yusi A., Rusli, Arif and Luwarso, Lukas (1998) 'Negara kesatuan, federal atau bubar?' (Unified nation, federal or broken up?), *Forum Keadilan*, 19 Aug. From http://www.forum.co.id/forum/redaksi/EK9808/forum_10.htm.

Raillon, François (1994) 'Can the Javanese do business? The awakening of indigenous capitalists in Indonesia', in *Leadership on Java: Gentle Hints, Authoritarian Rule*, eds Hans Antlöv and Sven Cederroth, Richmond, Surrey: Curzon Press, pp. 163–87.

Ramage, Douglas E. (1995) *Politics in Indonesia: Democracy, Islam and the Ideology of Tolerance*, London: Routledge.

—— (1994) 'Pancasila discourse in Suharto's late New Order', in *Democracy in Indonesia: 1950s and 1990s*, eds David Bourchier and John Legge, Centre of Southeast Asian Studies, Clayton, Victoria: Monash University, pp. 156–67.

Razak, Abdul (1999) 'Media set the reporting agenda', paper delivered to the First ACJA–CAJ China–ASEAN Press Seminar on the Media, Beijing and Shenzhen, 4–12 Apr.

—— (ed.) (1985) 'The general characteristics of the Indonesian press', *Press Laws and Systems in Asean States*, Jakarta: Garuda Metropolitan Press, pp. 11–29.

Reeve, David (1990) 'The corporatist state: The case of Golkar', in *State and Civil Society in Indonesia*, ed. Arief Budiman, Centre of Southeast Asian Studies, Clayton, Victoria: Monash University, pp. 151–76.

—— (1985) *Golkar of Indonesia: An Alternative to the Party System*, Singapore: Oxford University Press.

—— (1978) 'Sukarnoism and Indonesia's "functional group" state: Part I: Developing "Indonesian Democracy"', *RIMA: Review of Indonesian and Malayan Affairs*, vo. 12, no. 2, pp. 43–94.

Republika (27 Nov. 1998), 'Ketika kepemimpinan perempuan diperdebatkan', (When women's leadership is debated), *Republika Dialog Jumat*, p. 8.

—— (6 Oct.1995) 'PWI Jatim masih menunggu pernyataan maaf Soenarto, (The East Java PWI branch still waits for apology from Soenarto), p. 11.

—— (31Aug.1995) 'Pers dan konglomerat perlu saling bantu' (The press and conglomerates need to mutually help each other), p. 11.

Reuters (7 Jul.1998) 'Indonesia ruling party to abolish Suharto-led body'.

Richburg, Keith (1998) 'Habibie pushes for visit to U.S.', *Washington Post Foreign Service*, 19 Jul., p. A23.

Ricklefs, M.C. (1981) *A History of Modern Indonesia: c. 1300 to the Present*, London: Macmillan.

Righter, Rosemary (1978) *Whose News? Politics, the Press and the Third World*, London: André Deutsch.

Ritonga, M.J. (1998) 'Mengoptimalkan pengawasan pers' (Optimalising press surveillance), *Merdeka*, 9 Feb.

Robinson, Kathryn (1983) 'Women and work in an Indonesian mining town', in *Women's Work and Women's Roles: Economics and Everyday Life in Indonesia, Malaysia and Singapore*, ed. Lenore Manderson, Development Studies Centre, Canberra: Australian National University, pp. 111–28.

—— (1985) 'Modernisation and mothering', *Prisma: The Indonesian Indicator*, no. 37, Sept., pp. 47–56.

Robison, Richard (1993) 'Indonesia: Tensions in state and regime', in *Southeast Asia in the 1990s: Authoritarianism, Democracy and Capitalism*, eds Kevin Hewison, Richard Robison and Garry Rodan, Sydney: Allen & Unwin, pp. 39–74.

—— (1987) 'After the gold rush: The politics of economic restructuring in Indonesia in the 1980s', *Southeast Asia in the 1980s: The Politics of Economic Crisis*, eds Richard Robison, Kevin Hewison and Richard Higgott, Sydney: Allen & Unwin, pp. 16–51.

—— (1986) 'Explaining Indonesia's response to the Jenkins' article: Implications for Australian–Indonesian relations', *Australian Outlook*, vol. 40, no. 3, pp. 132–8.

—— (1985) 'Class, capital and the state in New Order Indonesia', in *Southeast Asia: Essays in the Political Economy of Structural Change*, eds R. Higgott and R. Robison, London: Routledge & Kegan Paul, pp. 295–335.

—— (1981) 'Culture, politics, and economy in the political history of the New Order', *Indonesia*, no. 31, pp. 1–30.

Robson, Colin (1993) *Real World Research: A Resource for Social Scientists and Practitioner Researchers*, Oxford: Blackwell.

Rodgers, Peter (1982) *The Domestic and Foreign Press in Indonesia: Free but Responsible?*, CSAAR Research Paper No 18, Nathan, Brisbane: Griffith University.

Roem, Mohamad (1982) 'Dia sendiri berkepala granit' (He himself has a head of stone), in *Mochtar Lubis: Wartawan Jihad* (Mochtar Lubis: The Holy War Journalist), 1992, Jakarta: Gramedia, pp. 115–16.

Rogers, Everett M. and Shoemaker, Floyd F. (1971) *Communication of Innovations: A Cross-Cultural Approach*, New York: Free Press.

Rogers, Everett M. (1976) 'Communication and development: The passing of a dominant paradigm', *Communication Research*, vol. 3, no. 2, pp. 213–40.

Romano, Angela (1996) 'The open wound: *Keterbukaan* and press freedom in Indonesia', *Australian Journal of International Affairs*, vol. 50, no. 2, pp. 157–69.

Rostow, W.W. (1960) *The Stages of Economic Growth*, Cambridge: Cambridge University Press.

Rustam, Kardinah Soepardjo (1986) 'Grass-root development with the PKK', *Prisma: The Indonesian Indicator*, Jun., no. 40, pp. 77–84.

Sadli, Mohammad (1967) 'Commemorating the economic policies of 3 Oct. 1966', in *The Politics of Economic Development in Indonesia: Contending Perspectives*, eds Ian Chalmers and Vedi R. Hadiz, 1997, London: Routledge, pp. 50–3.

Said, Tribuana (1988) *Sejarah Pers Nasional dan Pembangunan Pers Pancasila* (The History of the National Press and the Development of the Pancasila Press), Jakarta: Haji Masagung.

—— and Moelijanto, D.S. (1983) *Perlawanan Pers Indonesia (BPS) Terhadap Gerakan PKI* (Opposition of the Indonesian Press (BPS) to the PKI Movement), Jakarta: Sinar Harapan.

Sanit, Arbi (1989) *Mahasiswa, Kekuasaan dan Bangsa* (Students, State and Nation), Jakarta: Linkungan Studi Indonesia & Yayasan LBH.

Santoso, Amir (1997) 'Democratization: The case of Indonesia's New Order', in *Democratization in Southeast and East Asia*, ed. Anek Laothamatas, Singapore: Institute of Southeast Asian Studies, pp. 21–45.

Sapardjaja, Komariah and Padmadinata, Rochaenah (1999) *Pasal-Pasal 'Delik Pers' dalam RUU KUHP Draft 1998* (Articles on 'Press Offences' in the 1998 Draft of the Proposed Criminal Code), Jakarta: Masyarakat Pers & Penyiaran Indonesia.

Schiller, Herbert (1969) *Mass Communication and the American Empire*, New York: A.M. Kelly.

Schramm, Wilbur (1964) *Mass Media and National Development*, Stanford: Stanford University Press.

Schwarz, Adam (1995) Former Indonesia correspondent, *Far Eastern Economic Review*, telephone interview conducted from Hanoi, 1 Sept.

—— (1994) *A Nation in Waiting: Indonesia in the 1990s*, Sydney: Allen & Unwin.

Sen, Amartya (1999), *Development as Freedom*, New York, Random House.

—— (1990) *Public Action to Remedy Hunger*, Arturo Tanco Memorial Lecture, London, 2 Aug. Transcript from http://www.thp.org/reports/sen/sen890.htm.

Sen, Krishna (1998) 'Indonesian women at work', eds Krishna Sen and Maila Stivens, *Gender and Power in Affluent Asia*, London: Routledge, pp. 35–62.

Setiadi, Hilmar Farid (1997) 'Covering strikes: Indonesian workers and "their" media', in *State and Labour in New Order Indonesia*, ed. Rod Lambert, University of Western Australia Press and Asia Research Centre, Western Australia: Murdoch University, pp. 123–45.

Setiadi, Budi Arie and Firmanto, Adhi (1996) '"Amplop" dan integritas wartawan' (The envelope and the journalist's integrity), *Media Indonesia Minggu*, 5 May, p. 5.

Shafer, Richard (1992) 'Constraints on practising ethical journalism in developing nations: A Philippine case study', *Media Asia*, vol 19, no, 3, pp. 123–30, 138.

Shah, Hemant (1996) 'Modernization, marginalization and emancipation: Toward a normative model of journalism and national development', *Communication Theory*, vol. 6, no. 2, 143–66.

Shamdasani, Shanti (1996) Account manager/consultant, Sima Public Relations and Marketing Services, interview conducted in Jakarta, 3 Dec.

Shiraishi, Saya S. (1997) *Young Heroes: The Indonesian Family in Politics*, Ithaca, New York: Cornell University.

Sidarto, Liawati (2000) 'Women bear heaviest burden', *Jakarta Post*, 29 Dec., p. 4.

Siebert, Fred S., Peterson, Theodore and Schramm, Wilbur (1956) *Four Theories of the Press*, Urbana: University of Illinois Press.

Sigal, Leon (1973) *Reporters and Officials: The Organisation and Politics of Newsmaking*, Lexington, Mass: Heath.

Silalahi, Harry Tjan (1993) 'Adakah hak asasi manusia di dalam UUD 1945?' (Are there human rights in the 1945 Constitution?), *Forum Keadilan*, no. 20, 21 Jan., p. 66.

Simanjuntak, Marsillam (1994) *Pandangan Negara Integralistik* (The Philosophy of the Intergralistic Nation), Jakarta: Pustaka Utama Grafiti.

Sinaga, Edward Janner (1989) 'Indonesia', in *Press Systems in Asean States*, ed. Achal Mehra, Singapore: AMIC, pp. 27–41.

—— (1987a) The *Pancasila* Press System, paper presented at the Third ASEAN Editors Conference, Denpasar, Bali, 27 Oct.

—— (1987b) The dilemma of the Western press and its fundamental difference from the national press, attachment to paper presented at the Third ASEAN Editors Conference, Denpasar, Bali, 27 Oct.

Sinar Harapan (1978) 'Menteri Penerangan Ali Murtopo: Penting utk memperbesar wibawa pers di mata bangsa dan negara' (Information Minister Ali Murtopo: Important to increase the authority of the press in the eyes of people and nation), 15 May, pp. 1, 16.

—— (26 Jun.1974) 'Gema seminar pers wanita' (Echoes from the seminar on press women), pp. 3–4.

—— (24 Jun.1969) 'PWI Djaya tolak keputusan Konker Kinilow dan menjerukan agar: Peraturan Wartawan ditangguhkan' (The PWI Greater Jakarta branch rejects Kinilow Working Congress decision and proclaims: The Journalists' Regulation [should be] delayed), p. 1.

—— (10 Jun.1969) 'Seruan kepada Menpen: Tjabut Peraturan Wartawan' (Appeal to the Information Minister: Revoke the Journalists' Regulation), p. 1.

—— (6 Jun.1969) 'Menurut Adam Malik: Hanja dinegara totaliter wartawan diikat pemerintah' (According to Adam Malik: Only in totalitarian countries are journalists tied by the government), p. 1.

Sirait, Midian (1997) *Paham Kebangsaan Indonesia* (An Understanding of Indonesian Nationalism), Jakarta: Pustaka Sinar Harapan.

Siregar, Ashadi (1997) Communications lecturer, Faculty of Social and Political Sciences, Gajah Mada University and director, LP3Y, interview conducted in Yogyakarta, 1 Feb.

—— (1995a) 'Pers Pancasila: Dari kepancasilaan sistem social' (The *Pancasila* press: From the *Pancasila*ism of the social system), *Kedaulatan Rakyat*, 28 Sept., p. 4.

—— (1995b) 'Jagat wartawan Indonesia era Orde Baru: Melalui sosok Threes Nio' (The world of Indonesian journalists in the New Order era: Through the eye of Threes Nio), in R.B. Sugiantoro and Daniel Daniel (eds), *Threes Nio: Laporan dari Lapangan* (Threes Nio: Reports from the Field), Jakarta: Kompas, pp. xvii–xliii.

—— (1993) pp. 'Membangun institusi, mengangun jiwa bebas' (Building institutions, building free spirits), in *Tajuk-Tajuk dalam Terik Matahari: Empat Puluh Tahun Surabaya Post* (Editorials in the Warmth of the Sun: Forty Years of the *Surabaya Post*), eds Hotman M. Siahaan and Tjahjo Purnomo W., Surabaya: Yayasan Keluarga Bhakti, pp. 383–403.

Sjahrir, Kartini (1994) 'Para perempuan Indonesia di media massa' (Indonesian women in the mass media), in *Perempuan, Politik dan Jurnalisme: Tujuhpuluh Tahun Toety Azis*

(Women, Politics and Journalism: Seventy Years of Toety Azis), ed. Daniel Dhakidae, Jakarta: Yayasan Padi dan Kapas, pp. 49–73.

—— (1985) 'Women: Some anthropological notes', *Prisma: The Indonesian Indicator*, no. 37, Sept., pp. 3–17.

Snijders, M.L. (1994) 'Communication ethics in a changing Asia', *Media Asia*, vol. 21, no. 3, pp. 167–9.

Soebagijo I.N., Surjomihardjo, Abdurrachman and Swantoro, P. (1977) *Lintasan Sejarah PWI* (The Course of History of the PWI), Jakarta: PWI Pusat & Deppen.

Soeharto (1995) 'Presiden Soeharto tentang pers nasional' (President Soeharto about the national press), in *Almanak Pers Indonesia 1995* (Indonesian Press Almanack 1995), Jakarta: Matra Multi Media.

—— (1989a) *Soeharto: Pikiran, Ucapan dan Tindakan Saya: Otobiografi seperti dipaparkan kepada G. Dwipayana and Kamadhan K.H.* (Soeharto: My Thoughts, Words, and Deeds: Autobiography as told to G. Dwipayana and Kamadhan K.H.), Jakarta: Citra Lamtoro Gung Persada.

—— (1989b) 'Role of the press in national development', in *Press Systems in Asean States*, ed. Achal Mehra, Singapore: AMIC, pp. 131–4.

Soemandoyo, Priyo (1999) *Wacana Gender and Layar Televisi: Studi Perempuan dalam Pemberitaan Televisi Swasta* (Gender Discourse and the Television Screen: A Study of Women in Commercial Television News), Yogjakarta: LP3Y &ll Ford Foundation.

Soetopo, Eddy J. (1998) 'Tindak kekerasan terhadap wartawan media cetak di Indonesia selama kurun waktu 1946–1996' (Violent actions involving print media journalists in the period of 1946–1996), research proposal to YLBHI & ISAI, Jakarta.

Soetrisno, Loekman (1997) *Kemiskinan, Perempuan dan Pemberdayaan* (Poverty, Women and Empowerment), Yogyakarta: Kanisius.

Soloski, John (1989) 'News reporting and professionalism: Some constraints on the reporting of the news', *Media, Culture and Society*, vol. 11, pp. 207–28.

Sommerland, E. Lloyd (1966) *The Press in Developing Countries*, Sydney: Sydney University Press.

South East Asian Press Alliance (2000) 'Hanya satu kata: Tolak amplop!' (Only one word: Refuse envelopes!), *Alert*, vol. 1, no. 4, Aug.–Sept., pp. 6–7.

Southwood, Julie and Flanagan, Patrick (1983) *Indonesia: Law, Propaganda and Terror*, London: Zed Press.

Spencer, Geoff (1998) 'Indonesian President apologises', Associated Press, 15 Aug.

Spradley, James P. (1980) *Participant Observation*, New York: Holt Rinehart & Winston.

SPS Pusat (ed.) (1971) *Garis Besar Perkembangan Pers Indonesia* (A Broad Outline of the Development of the Indonesian Press), Jakarta: SPS Pusat.

Stanley (2001) Former *Jakarta Jakarta* journalist, interview conducted in Jakarta, 1 Mar. 2001.

—— (2000) 'Soeharta sakit, akses media macet' (Soeharto sick, media access blocked), *Pantau*, no. 8, Mar.–Apr., pp. 42–56.

Stapenhurst, Rick (2000) *The Media's Role in Curbing Corruption*, Washington: World Bank Institute.

Stevenson, Robert L. (1994) *Global Communication in the Twenty-First Century*, New York: Longman.

Stoler, A. (1976) 'Class structure and female autonomy in rural Java', *Indonesian Women: Some Past and Current Perspectives*, ed. B.B. Hering, Brussels: Centre d'Etude du Sud Est Asiatique et de l'Extreme Orient, pp. 124–50.

Straits Times (14 Aug.1998) 'Tough for another strongman to surface'. From http://
www.uni-stuttgart.de/indonesia/news/95/9832/Friday/12418.html.

Suara Karya (17 May 1999) 'Kebebasan pers bukan ancaman bagi suatu bangsa', p. 8.

—— (10 Feb. 1999) 'Pers jangan jadi media agitasi', (Press, don't become a media of
agitation), pp. 1, 7.

—— (30 May 1998) 'PWI tak ingin jadi wadah tunggal' (The PWI does not wish to be
the sole umbrella organisation), p. 3.

—— (15 Jan.1982) 'Wapres Adam Malik: Petugas penerangan dan humas harus
membuang sifat "ambtenarisme"' (Vice President Adam Malik: Information and
public relations officials must discard the characteristic of 'antenna-ism'), pp. 1, 2.

Suara Merdeka (18 Mar.1995) 'PWI Jaya pecat Goenawan, Fikri, Eros Jarot, dan 10
anggota lain' (The PWI Greater Jakarta branch expels Goenawan, Fikri, Eros Jarot,
and 10 other members), p. 1.

Suara Pembaruan (20 Oct. 2000) 'Perempuan Indonesia semakin mundur' (Indonesian
women are increasingly declining), p. 17.

—— (15 May 1999) 'Militer dan birokrat jangan alegi terhadap kebebasan pers' (Military
and bureaucrats, don't be allergic to press freedom), pp. 1, 15.

—— (25 Apr. 1999) 'Eks Ketua PWI Jateng "diadili"', (Ex-PWI head 'judged'), p. 3.

—— (27 Oct. 1998) 'Keputusan Kongres XX PWI sudah demokratis dan sah' (The
decision of the 20th PWI Congress is democratic and valid), p. 5.

—— (25 Apr.1998) 'Wali Kota Denpasar minta maaf kepada wartawan' (Denpasar Mayor
says sorry to journalists), p. 5.

—— (22 Apr.1998) 'Bupati Cilacap tak bermaksud sulitkan tugas wartawan' (Cilacap
Regent did not intend to make journalists' tasks more difficult), p. 5.

—— (17 Sept.1997) 'Wanita dan politik' (Women and politics), p. 5

Suara Serikat (20 Mar. 2000a) 'Saatnya berserikat, Bung!' (This is the moment to
organise, brother!), p. 4.

—— (20 Mar. 2000b) 'Transkrip pemeriksaan "Yayasan Kesejahteraan Fiktif", (1)'
(Transcript of the examination of the 'Fictitious Welfare Foundation' (Part 1)), pp. 8–9.

Sudharmono (1986) 'Wawasan masa depan kita dan peranan ilmu-ilmu sosial' (Insights
into our future and the role of social sciences), *Pelita*, 16 Dec., pp. 1, 5.

Sudradjat, Djadjat (1999) 'Strategi diam' (Strategy of Silence), *Media Indonesia*, 20 Jun., p. 1.

Sukarno (1965) *PWI Benar-Benar Menjadi Alat Revolusi: Amanat Presiden Sukarno
pada Rapat Umum Peringatan Ulang-Tahun Ke-19 P.W.I.* (The PWI is Truly a Tool of
the Revolution: President Sukarno's Speech to the Commemorative General Meeting
for the 19th Anniversary of the PWI), Deppen, Jakarta.

Sukidi (1998) 'Kekerasan perempuan dan hegemoni patriarki' (Violence against women
and the patriarchal hegemony), *Republika*, 16 Dec., p. 6.

Sulasmono, Bambang S. (1991) 'Dewan Perwakilan Rakyat dalam negara birokratik
otoriter' (The People's Representative Council in a bureaucratic authoritarian state),
Bina Darma, no. 34, Sept., pp. 71–82.

Sullivan, Norma (1994) *Masters and Managers: A Study of Gender Relations in Urban
Java*, St. Leonards, Sydney.

—— (1991) 'Gender and politics in Indonesia', *Why Gender Matters in Southeast Asian
Politics*, Monash Papers on Southeast Asia No. 23, ed. Maila Stivens, Glen Waverley,
Melbourne: Aristoc Press, pp. 61–86.

Sundhaussen, Ulf (1978) 'The military: Structure, procedures, and effects on Indonesian
society', in *Political Power and Communications in Indonesia*, eds Karl D. Jackson
and Lucian W. Pye, Berkeley: University of California Press, pp. 45–81.

Supomo (1945) 'Pidato pada tanggal 31-5-1945 dalam rapat Badan Penjelidikan untuk Persiapan Indonesia Merdeka, digedung Chuuoo Sangi-In di Jakarta' (The speech of 31-5-1945 in the Inquiry Body for Preparations for Indonesian Independence meeting, in the Chuuoo Sangi-In building in Jakarta), in *Naskah Persiapan Undang-Undang Dasar 1945* (Minutes of the Preparations for the 1945 Constitution), ed. Muhammad Yamin, 1959, vol I, Jakarta: Jajasan Prapantja, pp. 109–21.

Supono, Joko, Rismansah, Denny and Junaedi, Nanang (1995) 'Trend baru mencekal tokoh kritis' (New trend to squeeze prominent critical figures), *Tiras*, 22 Jun., p. 64.

Supriyanto, Didik (2001) Secretary General of AJI for the 1999–2001 term, interview conducted in Jakarta, 23 Feb.

Suranto, Hanif, Setiawan, Hawe and Ginanjar, Ging (1999) *Pers Indonesia Pasca Soeharto* (The post-Soeharto Indonesian press), Lembaga Studi Pers dan Pembangunan & Aliansi Jurnalis Independen, Jakarta.

Surjomiharjo, Abdurrachman and Suryadinata, Leo (1980) 'Pers Indonesia' (The Indonesian press), in *Beberapa Segi Perkembangan Sejarah Pers di Indonesia* (Several Perspectives on the Historical Development of the Press in Indonesia), ed. Abudrrachman Surjomiharjo, Jakarta: Proyek Penelitian Pembanguan Penerangan Deppen RI & Leknas-LIPI, pp. 65–86.

Suroso (1998) 'Kebebasan pers prasyarat kebangkitan demokrasi' (Freedom of the press is a condition for the resurgence of democracy), *Suara Karya*, 26 May, p. 5.

Suryadinata, Leo (1989) *Military Ascendancy and Political Culture: A Study of Indonesia's Golkar*, Centre for International Studies, Ohio: Ohio University.

Suryakusuma, Julia I. (1997), journalist, feminist and social commentator, personal communication in Brisbane, 19 Dec.

—— (1996) 'The state and sexuality in New Order Indonesia', in *Fantasizing the Feminine in Indonesia*, ed. Laurie J. Sears, Durham & London: Duke University Press, pp. 93–119.

—— (1982) 'Women in myth, reality and emancipation', *Prisma: The Indonesian Indicator*, no 24, Mar., pp. 3–16.

Suryochondro, Sukanti (1984) *Potret Pergerakan Wanita di Indonesia* (Portait of the Indonesian Women's Movement), Jakarta: CV. Rajawali.

Sussman, Leonard R. (1978) 'Development journalism: The ideological factor', in *The Third World and Press Freedom*, ed. Philip C. Horton, New York: Praeger Publishers, pp. 74–92.

Suyono, A.G., Muchtar, Irsyad, Suparto, T. Iman, Sukmawati, Sri, Syafrida, Erizul, Maryetta, A., Wahyu S., Bambang and Astono, Banu (1995) *Koperasi dalam Sorotan Pers: Agenda yang Tertinggal* (Cooperatives in the Press Spotlight: The Remaining Agenda), Jakarta: Pustaka Sinar Harapan.

Swantoro, P. and Atmakusumah (1980) 'Kasus *Indonesia Raya*' (The *Indonesia Raya* case), in *Beberapa Segi Perkembangan Sejarah Pers di Indonesia*, ed. Abdurrachman Surjomihardjo, Jakarta: Deppen RI & Leknas LIPI, pp. 181–245.

Syukur, John A. (1975) 'Catatan dari lokakarya SB Perpen 20–26 Oktober di Puncak: Wartawan tergolong buruh atau tidak?' (Notes from the SB Perpen workshop of 20–26 Oct. in Puncak: Journalists are classified as labourers or not?' *Suara Karya*, 19 Nov., p. 3.

Szende, Andrew (1986) *From Torrent to Trickle: Managing the Flow of News in Southeast Asia*, Singapore: Institute of Southeast Asian Studies.

Tanin, O. and Yohan, E. (1934) *Militarism and Fascism in Japan*, New York: International Publishers.

Tanter, Richard (1990)'The totalitarian ambition: Intelligence and security agencies in Indonesia', in *State and Civil Society in Indonesia*, ed. Arief Budiman, Centre of Southeast Asian Studies, Clayton, Victoria: Monash University, pp. 215–88.

Tartarian, Roger (1978) 'News flow in the Third World', in *The Third World and Press Freedom*, ed. Philip C. Horton, New York: Praeger Publishers, pp. 1–54.

Tasrif, Suardi (1955) 'Code dan ethiek djurnalistik', in *Code dan Ethiek Djurnalistik* (The Code and Ethics of Journalism), Jakarta: Pengurus Pusat PWI, pp. 18–32.

Tempo (11 Dec.1993) 'Duet baru selepas magrib' (New duo after sunset), p. 81.

—— (14 Mar.1987) 'Mengapa (tak semua) wartawan suka amplop' (Why (not all) journalists like envelopes), p. 23.

—— (26 Nov.1983) 'WTS, No. Amplop Yes?', p. 32.

Tempo and Grifitipers (1986) *Apa dan Siapa: Sejumlah Orang Indonesia 1985–1986*, Jakarta: Tempo & Grafitipers.

Tempo Interaktif (1997) 'Ini saatnya tiarap, bung' (This is the moment to lie face down, brother), 5 Jun. From http://www.tempo.co.id/min/14/nas4.htm.

Theobald, Robin (1990) *Corruption, Development and Underdevelopment*, Houndmills, Hampshire: Macmillan.

Tiffen, Rodney (1989) *News and Power*, St. Leonards, Sydney: Allen and Unwin.

—— (1978) *The News From Southeast Asia: The Sociology of Newsmaking*, Singapore: Institute of Southeast Asian Studies.

Tirtosudarmo, Riwanto (1992) 'Indonesia 1991: Quest for democracy in a turbulent year', *Southeast Asian Affairs*, pp. 123–39.

Tiwon, Sylvia (1996) 'Models and maniacs: Articulating the feminine in Indonesia', in *Fantasizing the Feminine in Indonesia*, ed. Laurie J. Sears, Durham & London: Duke University Press, pp. 47–70.

Tjondronegoro, Sediono (1996) 'Komentar atas RUU tentang statistik' (Commentary on the Draft Law about statistics), Sarasehan Rancangan Undang-Undang Statistik (Discussion on the Draft Law on Statistics), transcript of LP3ES seminar at Hotel Sari Pan Pasific, Jakarta, 15 Oct. 1966, pp. 47–9.

Thomson, Andrea (1996) Indonesia correspondent, Australia's Nine Television Network, interview conducted in Jakarta, 27 Oct.

Tuchman, Gaye (1991) 'Media institutions: Qualitative methods in the study of news', in *A Handbook of Qualitative Methodologies for Mass Communication Research*, eds K.B. Jensen and N.W. Jankowski, London: Routledge, pp. 79–92.

—— (1978) *Making News: A Study in the Construction of Reality*, New York: The Free Press.

Tulevski, Miriam (1996) Account director, Nama Network Communications, interview conducted in Jakarta, 4 Dec.

Uhlin, Anders (1995) *Democracy and Diffusion: Transnational Lesson-Drawing among Indonesian Pro-Democracy Actors*, Lund Political Studies 87, Lund, Sweden: Lund University.

United Nations Development Program (UNDP) (1998a) *Human Development Report 1998*, Paris: UNDP.

—— (1998b) *Integrating Human Rights with Sustainable Human Development: A UNDP Policy Document*, New York: UNDP. From http://magnet.undp.org/Docs/policy5.-html#Annex 3.

—— (1997) *Governance for Sustainable Human Development: A UNDP Policy Document*, Chapter 1. From http://magnet.undp.org/policy/chapter1.htm.

van Dijk, Cees (1978) 'Survey of major political developments in Indonesia in the first half of 1978', *RIMA: Review of Indonesian and Malayan Affairs*, Dec., vol.12, pp. 123–56.

van Langenberg, Michael (1990) 'The New Order State: Language, ideology, hegemony', in *State and Civil Society in Indonesia*, ed. Arief Budiman, Centre of Southeast Asian Studies, Melbourne: Monash University, pp. 121–50.

—— (1986) 'Analysing Indonesia's New Order state: a keywords approach', *RIMA: Review of Indonesian and Malaysian Affairs*, Summer, pp. 1–47.

Vatikiotis, Michael R.J. (1994) 'Party and parliamentary politics 1987–1993', in *Democracy in Indonesia: 1950s and 1990s*, eds David Bourchier and John Legge, Centre for Southeast Asian Studies, Clayton, Victoria: Monash University, pp. 236–42.

—— (1993) *Indonesian Politics Under Suharto: Order, Development and Pressure for Change*, rev. edn, London: Routledge.

—— (1990a) 'Muffling the Monitor', *Far Eastern Economic Review*, 15 Nov., pp. 23–4.

—— (1990b) 'Masses of media', *Far Eastern Economic Review*, 26 Jul., pp. 46–7.

—— (1988) 'Jungle-greening of Golkar shows military's concern', *Far Eastern Economic Review*, 10 Nov., pp. 28–9.

Vidich, Arthur J. and Bensman, Joseph (1968) *Small Town in Mass Society: Class, Power and Religion in a Rural Community*, rev. edn., Princeton, New Jersey: Princeton University Press.

Vreede-de Stuers, Cora (1960) *The Indonesian Woman: Struggles and Achievements*, The Hague: Mouton & Co.

Wahid, Abdurrahman (1999) 'Islam dan hak asasi manusia' (Islam and human rights), *Memposisikan Kodrat: Perempuan dan Perubahan dalam Perspektif Islam* (Positioning God's Will: Women and Change in the Islamic Perspective), ed. Lily Zakiyah Munir, Bandung: Mizan, pp. 35–49.

Wahyono, Padmo (1988) 'Pengembangan hak dan kewajiban asasi warga negara dalam mengamalkan Pancasila dan UUD '45' (Development of citizens' rights and duties in applying *Pancasila* and the 1945 Constitution), *Media Karya*, Dec., pp. 58–64.

Walters, Patrick (1994) Indonesia correspondent, *The Australian*, interview conducted in Jakarta, 26 Oct.

Wardani, Sri Budi Eko (1999) 'Aspirasi perempuan anggota parlemen terhadap pemberdayaan politik perempuan' (Aspirations of women parliamentary members regarding the political empowerment of women), *Aspirasi Perempuan Anggota Parlemen terhadap Pemberdayaan Politik Perempuan*, Jakarta: Yayasan Jurnal Perempuan and International Institute for Democracy and Electoral Assistance, pp. 13–40.

Warta Ekonomi (17 Jul. 1995) 'Sulitnya tumbuhkan jiwa profesional' (The difficulty of increasing professional spirit), vol. 7, no. 8, pp. 38–9.

Weaver, David H. (ed.) (1998) *The Global Journalist: News People Around the World*, Cresskill, New Jersey: Hampton Press.

—— and Wilhoit, G. Cleveland (1996) *The American Journalist in the 1990s: U.S. News People at the End of an Era*, Mahwah, New Jersey: Lawrence Erlbaum Associates.

Wertheim, W.F. (1956) *Indonesian Society in Transition: A Study of Social Change*, The Hague: Van Hoeve.

'White Book' on the 1992 General Election in Indonesia (1994), trans. Dwight Y. King, New York: Cornell University.

Wibisono, Christiano (1994) 'Media massa dari politik ke bisnis', *Tempo*, 11 Jun., p. 102.

—— (1993) 'Pers Indonesia, antara industri dan profesi' (The Indonesian press, between industry and profession), *Tajuk-Tajuk Dalam Terik Matahari: Empat Puluh Tahun*

Surabaya Post, eds Hotman M. Siahaan and Tjahjo Purnomo W., Surabaya: Yayasan Keluarga Bhakti, pp. 441–54.

Wieringa, Saskia E. (1993) 'Two Indonesian women's organizations: Gerwani and the PKK', *Bulletin of Concerned Asian Scholars*, vol 25, no 2, pp. 17–30.

Williams, Louise (1998) 'How Yosfiah became a reborn liberal', *Sydney Morning Herald*, 24 Oct., p. 20.

—— (1996) Indonesia correspondent, *Sydney Morning Herald*, interview conducted in Jakarta, 1 Nov.

Williams, Raymond (1966) *Communications*, 2nd edition, London: Chatto & Windus.

Willner, A.R. (1976) 'Expanding women's horizons in Indonesia', in *Indonesian Women: Some Past and Current Perspectives*, ed. B.B. Hering, Brussels: Centre d'Etude du Sud Est Asiatique et de l'Extreme Orient, pp. 115–23.

Wiradja, S. and Bhaskara, Harry (1993) 'Poor reading habit is bane of publisher', *Jakarta Post*, 21 May, p. 6.

Wirosardjono, Soetjipto (1993) 'Peta kemiskinan' (Poverty map), *Tempo*, 15 May, pp. 36–7.

Wisudo, Bambang (2001a) AJI labour division head, interview conducted in Jakarta, 5 Mar.

—— (ed.) (2001b) *Membangun Organisasi Pekerja di Perusahaan Pers* (Building Workers' Organisations in Press Companies), Jakarta: Aliansi Jurnalis Independen.

—— (2000) 'Bulan madu pers telah berakhir' (The press honeymoon is already over), *Kompas*, 9 Feb., p. 7.

Wonohito, Madikin (1977) *Teknik Jurnalistik: Sistim Pers Pancasila* (Journalistic Technique: The *Pancasila* Press System), Jakarta: PT Garda.

Woodcroft-Lee, Carlien Patricia (1983) 'Separate but equal: Indonesian Muslim perceptions of the roles of women', in *Women's Work and Women's Roles: Economics and Everyday Life in Indonesia, Malaysia and Singapore*, ed. Lenore Manderson, Development Studies Centre, Canberra: Australian National University, pp. 173–92.

Yamin, Muhammad (ed.) (1959) *Naskah Persiapan Undang-Undang Dasar 1945* (Minutes of the Preparations for the 1945 Constitution), vol I, Jajasan Prapantja, Jakarta.

Yayasan Lembaga Bantuan Hukum Indonesia (1995) 'Pemecatan keanggotaan 13 orang wartawan oleh PWI' (The membership suspension of 13 journalists by the PWI), Press Release no. 005/SP/YLBHI/III/1995, 20 Mar.

Yayasan Lembaga Bantuan Hukum Indonesia (ed.) (1991) *Demokrasi Masih Terbenam: Catatan Keadaan Hak-Hak Asasi Manusia Di Indonesia 1991* (Democracy Still Out of Sight: Notes on Conditions on Human Rights in Indonesia 1991), Jakarta: YLBHI.

Yin, Robert K. (1994) *Case Study Research – Design and Methods*, 2nd edn, Thousand Oaks, California: Sage.

Young, Kenneth (1990) 'Middle bureaucrats, middle peasants, middle class?: The extra-urban dimension', in *The Politics of Middle Class Indonesia*, eds Richard Tanter and Kenneth Young, Centre for Southeast Asian Studies, Clayton, Victoria: Monash University, pp. 147–66.

Yuni (2000) 'Bonus (lagi) dan struktur gaji baru' ((Another) bonus and the new salary structure), *Kontak: Majalah Keluarga Besar LKBN Antara*, May–Jun., pp. 16–18.

Zelizer, Barbie (1993) 'Journalists as interpretive communities', *Critical Studies in Mass Communications*, no. 10, pp. 219–37.

—— (1992) *Covering the Body: The Kennedy Assasination, the Media and the Shaping of Collective Memory*, Chicago: University of Chicago Press.

Zuldarnis (1999) 'Indonesia baru: Era kepemimpinan guru besar?' (The new Indonesia: The era of leadership by professors?), *Republika*, 1 Mar., p. 6.

Zulharman S. (1969a) 'Pemandangan umum PWI Tjabang Djakarta ttg Peraturan Menpen No. 02/1969 (II–Habis)' (General opinion of PWI Jakarta Branch about the Information Minister's Regulation No. 02/1969 (II–End)), *Harian Kami*, 28 Jun., p. 3.

—— (1969b) 'Mengapa PWI Djaya tolak Per. Menpen ttg wartawan' (Why the PWI Greater Jakarta branch rejected the Information Minister's Regulation on journalists), *Sinar Harapan*, 26 Jun., p. 5.

Index

ABRI *see* military

amplop *see* journalists: envelope culture

AJI (Alliance of Independent Journalists) 67, 81–5, 90–5, 98, 100, 103, 116, 161–3, 169, 185 *see also* journalists: professional organisations *and* PWI

Anwar, Rosihan 63–4, 93, 96, 100, 120, 131, 151, 166, 169

Aziz, Toety 105–106, 110

Azzam, Tarman 81, 100–101, 131–2, 158, 162

BPS (Body for Support of Sukarnoism) 8–9, 77–8, 88, 91

Budiman, Arief 139, 142

bureaucracy *see* civil service

civil service 7–8, 10, 15–17, 19, 21, 24–5, 27, 30, 112, 114, 123, 125–7, 130, 138–40, 144, 151–3, 155, 163, 165, 172, 175

communism/socialism 3, 8, 22, 44–5, 77–8, 87–8, 119–20, 142, 175

Constitution:
  1945 1–4, 6, 8, 13, 44, 49, 88, 91, 113, 120, 131, 175
  1949 6
  1950 6–8
  amendments 49, 174
  and the presidency 28, 32

cooperatives 19, 71, 73–5, 82

corruption 21–2, 26, 29–30, 34, 43, 48, 51–2, 59, 64, 100–101, 138, 147, 151–4, 158–160, 162–3, 167, 172–3, 175 *see also* journalists: bodrek *and* journalists: envelope culture

courts and judiciary 18, 27, 30, 68, 104, 132, 153, 164

Dailami 48, 50, 81

democratisation *see* reform

Department of Information 35–6, 43–4, 47, 50–2, 68, 75, 80–1, 84, 92, 110, 116, 118

development xiv, 13–15, 17, 19–25, 47, 77, 113–14, 137–8, 151–2, 163, 165–6, 168 *see also* media: development journalism

Diah, B.M. 8, 87, 93, 96, 110, 169

Diah, Herwati 106, 110

Djoksutono 7, 9, 14, 18, 175

DPR 16–18, 27–31, 34, 76, 100, 104, 117, 124, 132, 137, 165, 167, 177

dwi fungsi 14–16, 27–8, 35 *see also* military

economy xiv, 12, 19, 26, 29–30, 36, 41, 48, 113, 146–8, 150–1, 161, 165, 170

elections 16, 18, 28, 117, 137, 165

floating mass 17

FOI (Freedom of Information) 51, 131–2, 147, 172

Gestapu 12, 45, 78, 88, 119, 142

Golkar 7, 9, 16, 17, 20, 27–8, 30–1, 33, 91, 96–7, 100, 102, 123, 145, 156, 165, 168

Guided Democracy 7, 87

Habibie, B.J. xiv, 26, 28–9, 32, 35, 49, 51, 81, 96–9, 116, 128–31, 147, 171, 174

Hadi, Parni 70–5, 82, 91–2, 96–7, 151, 168, 185

Harmoko 71, 76, 78, 89–91, 96–7, 100

Hasan, Mohamad (Bob) 30, 137

Hegel, Georg 1, 3–5, 10–11, 15, 23, 112

IMF 40, 42–3, 48, 50–1

For Product Safety Concerns and Information please contact our EU
representative GPSR@taylorandfrancis.com
Taylor & Francis Verlag GmbH, Kaufingerstraße 24, 80331 München, Germany

www.ingramcontent.com/pod-product-compliance
Lightning Source LLC
Chambersburg PA
CBHW050425280326
41932CB00013BA/1999